TEXTUAL
SHAKESPEARE

Writing and the Word

For Tim

with best wishes

Graham

1/10/03

TEXTUAL SHAKESPEARE

Writing and the Word

GRAHAM HOLDERNESS

UNIVERSITY OF HERTFORDSHIRE PRESS

First published in Great Britain in 2003 by
University of Hertfordshire Press
Learning and Information Services
University of Hertfordshire
College Lane
Hatfield
Hertfordshire AL10 9AB

ISBN 1 902806 21 2 paperback
ISBN 1 902806 20 4 case bound

Cover: with apologies to Leonardo de Vinci for our
misuse of his portrait of *Mona Lisa*
Title page: the disputed Sanders portrait of Shakespeare (1603)

Design by Geoff Green, Cambridge CB4 5RA.
Cover design by John Robertshaw, Harpenden AL5 2TB
Printed in Great Britain by Antony Rowe Ltd., Chippenham, SN14 6LH

For Bryan Loughrey

γαρ προεγραφη
εις την
ημετεραν διδασκαλιαν

Contents

৯৹

Preface and Acknowledgements

❧

T HIS IS A NEW BOOK. Where older material is used (see
below), it is redeployed: textually revised, theoretically re-
positioned and philosophically re-oriented. In many cases the
older work was collaborative. I have tried to tease out from it my
own written contributions (conscious of the irony in a book that
insists on the inescapably collaborative nature of all writing), but
the participation of my colleagues is not so easily effaced. The
material is reworked with their kind and generous permission, as
indicated below. We have all moved on from the Text Wars of the
early 1990s, and my erstwhile collaborators are in no way responsible for the directions my work is now taking. The book itself has
benefited enormously from detailed and supportive commentary
from Andrew Murphy and John D. Cox. I am grateful for their
guidance, and any remaining errors are my own.

The other two books in this series, *Cultural Shakespeare* and
Visual Shakespeare, map out and explore relatively new areas of
study, the cultural sociology of Shakespeare, and Shakespeare in
the modern media of film and television, where previous critical
models hardly existed, and where new methodologies had to be
devised to demarcate and establish the terrain of inquiry. *Textual
Shakespeare* addresses the much more venerable field of biblio-

graphical scholarship, which is not only considerably older than Shakespeare himself, but in terms of editorial practice can be said to precede the very texts which mediate 'Shakespeare' to the reader or theatre audience. Yet it is in this field of textual scholarship that Shakespeare studies have experienced their most radical transformation. It is appropriate therefore that while the other two books in the series dwell on critical formations of the 1980s and 1990s, *Textual Shakespeare* follows through on a process of change that has perhaps more than any other visibly altered the landscape of Shakespeare criticism.

Textual Shakespeare reassesses the Bard as a writer in the light of the late twentieth century 'revolution' in bibliography and textual studies. Reviewing recent debates in textual theory and practice, I conclude that 'Shakespeare' is not a writer but a collection of documents, none of which can with any certainty be linked to whatever it was the author wanted to say. But this has nothing to do with any 'Battle of Wills', or the rival claims of Francis Bacon and the Earl of Oxford. Lady Viola de Lessops has it right when in the film *Shakespeare in Love* she asks the writer 'are you the author of the plays of William Shakespeare?' According to modern literary studies the author is secondary to the text, and all texts are in any case copies, always already changed: there are no 'originals'. Editors are translators; and scholars and critics rewrite the writing they study[1].

These lines of argument take us beyond both New Bibliography and 'materialist' textual criticism to show that texts are both physical media, made and remade by a series of craftspeople; and rich repositories of changeable meaning. At the same time we need to acknowledge the presence, or perhaps the constitutive absence, of what much materialist criticism leaves out: so we will still have recourse to notions of origin, source, making. Although grown out of a long history of materialist theory and practice, *Textual Shakespeare* finds itself advocating a recovery of ancient concepts such as creativity and imagination, together with a recognition of the technical and essentially collaborative nature of all writing.

Shakespeare is then situated within this theoretical context, via a brief history of the plays' textual reproduction (Chapter 2). Here I attempt to show that modern Shakespeare editions are radical rewritings, and that contemporary textual theory, in partnership with modern pedagogic practice, opens the way to yet more inventive textual activities of reconstruction and translation[2].

In the second, 'practical' part of the book, a series of chapters on individual plays provides illustrative examples of such textual activities in practice. The two texts of *King Lear* are studied as discrepant reworkings of a traditional narrative that belong to a much larger cultural network of variable and iterable King Lear stories, where radical revisions, such as those of the Restoration stage, appear as natural developments, and not perversions of an authoritative original vision. The poetic and dramatic language of the early Quarto text is addressed directly in its own right, as well as intertextually in terms of its relations with other cognate textualisations. The single text of *Macbeth* is compared to a text that has never come to light in printed form – the version seen by eyewitness Simon Forman in 1611 – and the lost text is partially reconstructed from that evidence. Exploring further the creative potentialities of modern reconstruction, a chapter on *Hamlet* concentrates on twentieth century rewritings of the plays in fiction and drama. The two texts of *Henry V* are then examined as elements in a broader and more diverse continuum, and as possible evidence of a substantial gap between theatrical writing and theatrical practice in the theatre of Shakespeare's day.

The book concludes that all Shakespeare scholarship, editing and criticism are devoted to a quest for something missing: not the lost manuscript (which even if recovered would not in any case answer all our questions)[3], but rather the absence that writing always invokes. It is that absence, that empty space that we continually keep trying to fill with our own activities of cultural production. Where – or rather whither – this insight takes us, is the subject of my Conclusion.

Part of the book's argument is that some of the most interesting examples of critical writing and scholarship are not independent analyses of, but quasi-creative engagements with, the writing of the past. Throughout this book I will be stressing the creativity involved not only in the act of writing, but in the many processes of rewriting that make up any historical culture. By way of extending this argument *Textual Shakespeare* includes a number of short 'creative' works, mostly verse translations of Latin and Old English poems. These are previously unpublished, with the exception of the extracts from *The Ruin* and *The Seafarer* that close Chapter 8 and the Conclusion, and which first appeared in *The Use of English* (49:1, Autumn 1997, pp. 62–3) and *Literature and Theology* (11:4, Autumn 1997, pp. 347–75) respectively. Both poems are translated in full in my *Craeft: poems from the Anglo-Saxon* (Nottingham: Shoestring Press, 2001). Chapter 6 ends with a reconstruction of the Folio text of *Macbeth*, and Chapter 7 with a brief extract from my Shakespearean novel *The Prince of Denmark* (Hatfield: University of Hertfordshire Press, 2002). The book thus attempts to build bridges between writing and criticism, creation and reproduction, 'text' and 'technology'.

Chapter 3 is based on ' "What's the Matter?": Shakespeare and Textual Theory' (with Bryan Loughrey and Andrew Murphy), *Textual Practice* 9:1 (1995); Chapter 4 on 'Shakespeare Misconstrued: The True Chronicle Historie of *Shakespearean Originals*' (with Bryan Loughrey), *Textus* 9 (1996); Chapters 5 and 8 on the 'Introductions' to *M. William Shake-speare: his True Chronicle Historie of the Life and Death of King Lear and his Three Daughters* (Hemel Hempstead: Prentice-Hall, 1995); and *The Cronicle History of Henry the fift (1600)* (with Bryan Loughrey) (Hemel Hempstead: Harvester Wheatsheaf, 1993) respectively. The final paragraphs of Chapter 8 are adapted from a passage in my

Shakespeare: the Histories (London: Macmillan, 2000). Some of the newer work has also already appeared, or is about to appear, elsewhere: part of Chapter One features in *Shakespeare in the Media: From the Globe Theatre to the World Wide Web*, edited by Stefani Brusberg-Kiermeier and Jörg Helbig (Berlin and New York: Peter Lang, 2003); parts of Chapter 2 and some passages of Chapter 6 are published as 'Text and Tragedy', in *A Companion to Shakespeare*, vol. I: *The Tragedies*, edited by Richard Dutton and Jean E. Howard (Oxford: Blackwell, 2003); other parts of Chapter 6 are published as 'Cue One *Macbeth*', in *Re-Visions of Shakespeare: essays in honor of Robert Ornstein*, edited by Evelyn J. Gajowski (Newark: Delaware University Press, 2003). Although even this more recent work has already undergone revision, I am grateful to the editors and publishers mentioned for their kindness in permitting reproduction.

Although flattering myself, as writers like to do, with the illusion that readers will work through this book from beginning to end, I have constructed the Endnotes one chapter at a time. Each work referenced is given in full bibliographical detail on first citation, and thereafter, both in the notes and in-text, is given in a shortened form. In subsequent chapters however an initial citation is again referenced in full.

PART ONE

Textual Theory

CHAPTER ONE

Text

ॐ

I N T H E B E G I N N I N G was the word[1], and written words related together form 'text' (Oxford English Dictionary [*OED*], 'the wording of anything written or printed'). 'Text' derives from Greek τεκτων, (*tektou*), 'to engender, produce, bring into the world', and the complex histories of the word's derivation map the entire terminology of modern textual theory, criticism and practice. More immediately 'text' emerges from Latin '*texere*', 'to weave, plait, braid, join together'; and from there, 'to construct, fabricate, build, compose'. Here it gravitates close to the Greek analogue τεχνη *(techne)*, 'art, skill, craft, method or set of rules, or system of making or doing'[2].

In this semantic interaction of interrelated tongues, this 'polyglossia', we find the key concepts from which the modern term 'text' is variously fashioned. First, the act of making; second, the process by means of which all that is made, is made; then the 'craft or sullen art'[3] the *praxis* that shapes and finishes; and finally the product, the text. *Facio; facere; factum.* I make; to make; made.

From '*texere*' we get both 'textile' and 'text', and τεχνη gives us both 'technology' and 'technique'. It is of interest to this study that these terms have severally parted company down a great historical bifurcation, the division between art and science. 'Technology' now invokes mechanistic construction and practical skill, while 'technique' is more usually reserved for the finer methodologies of dance and music. History has put asunder what was once indissolubly joined. Yet it remains open to us to re-enter, at least at the level of reading and through the semantics of 'text', the possibility of an as-yet-undissociated sensibility.

Everywhere in the various vocabularies of making, construction, composition, shaping, we find these four inter-related elements of a single process frequently ordered into a common sequentiality.

2   And the Spirit of God moved upon the face of the waters.
3   And God said, Let there be light: and there was light.
4   And God saw the light, that it *was* good[4].

First a creative urge, spirit, *in potentia*; then the act of creation, the *fiat* of making ('And God said …'); then the means by which what is made is made ('Let there be light'); and behold, the thing made, light, that now exists in its own right, and is there to be valued and admired ('And God saw the light, that it *was* good'). τεκτων; *texere;* τεχνη; text. The idea; the creation; the fashioning; the finished product.

James Joyce observed a similar sequence, this time tripartite, in his account of artistic creativity in *A Portrait of the Artist as a Young Man.*

[A]rt necessarily divides itself into three forms progressing from one to the next. These forms are: the lyrical form, the form wherein the artist presents his image in immediate relation to himself; the epical form, the form wherein he presents his image in mediate relation to himself and others; the dramatic form, the form wherein he presents his image in immediate relation to others[5].

Joyce's three stages enact for the artefact a trajectory of extrapolation, from idea through process to product, initially linked to the author as self-expression, lyric; then embodied in the narrative form of epic, which lies between writer and reader; and finally the fully-realised independent work of art, the dramatic, which relates immediately to the reader and spectator, no longer to the author at all. These stages or states clearly correspond to the sequence of idea, conception, technology, text, as we find it more explicitly formulated later in the novel:

> The personality of the artist, at first a cry or a cadence or a mood and then a fluid and lambent narrative, finally refines itself out of existence, impersonalises itself, so to speak. The aesthetic image in the dramatic form is life purified in and reprojected from the human imagination (Joyce, *Portrait*, p. 221)

Taking his terms from Aristotle's *Poetics*, Joyce divides these moments – lyric, epic, dramatic; the cadence, the narrative, the consummation – from one another. Yet each moment partakes of the whole continuum[6]. Just as, in Blake's words, 'Eternity is in love with the productions of Time'[7], so the word desires to become flesh, and conception pushes inexorably towards birth. The imagination is essentially practical, it seeks ways of realising its creativity, means of making [8]. And the process of making, whether finished or unfinished, produces, brings something here, complete or incomplete, seeking its own realisation.

In the same way everything to do with 'text' spills over into a contingent or adjoining phase of textualisation or textuality. Romantic ideas of authorship, and many other attempts to describe the imagination at work, often figure the creative process as one of giving birth, engendering, bringing into the world. Readers and critics in their turn frequently find themselves seeking the 'midnight moment's forest', that 'dark hole of the head'[9] where the making took place; and indeed may well be required, by certain kinds of fiction and poetry and drama, to undertake such speculation.

In the act of reading, criticism makes us conscious of the ways in which a text is woven and plaited of sensations and ideas. Similarly bibliography makes us aware of the means by which text is braided, 'joined together', of words and sentences and paragraphs and pages, just as '*letteratura*', literature, is the linking of individual letters. We become aware of the book as a kind of textile, conscious of its material 'texture'. We know it as fashioned from an art of interrelationship and a craft of inter-connection. Writers and critics frequently borrow from the plastic arts metaphors capable of carrying this association, as in Henry James's 'figure in the carpet', or the fragile and finespun web of Tennyson's 'Lady of Shallott'. Textual studies enable us to acknowledge, in addition to the figurative warp and weft of nar-rative and drama, those physical properties of the book that bibliophiles have always, overtly or furtively, relished: typeface, paper, design and layout, covers and jackets[10]. The study of printing technology has as much importance in modern Shake-speare scholarship as the traditional critical analysis of text as artefact or signifier, 'dramatic poem' or semiotic bearer of meaning.

Inevitably as we contemplate the practical formulation of text out of mundane technologies, there is a gravitation back towards the idea that can be held to have preceded the making. We look for a meaning that is not entirely held within the book's physical properties: for an authorial intention that can be envis-aged as prior to the execution; for the manuscript that can be imagined as containing the author's immediate expression; or for that ineffable predecessor, inspiration, 'the fine delight that fathers thought'[11]. Thus 'text' becomes rarefied to a book within a book, like the scholarly 'text' that can easily be isolated from its contextual bricolage of introduction, explanatory notes, com-mentary, appendices (*OED*, 'that portion of the contents of a manuscript or printed book, or of a page, which constitutes the original matter, as distinct from the notes'). And in a further stage of refinement the 'text' can slide off the surface of the printed page and become an abstracted meaning or argument, as in 'my text for today', which is not merely (for instance) John 3.16, the printed Greek, Latin or English words – 'For God so loved the world, that he gave his only begotten Son' (*The Bible*, eds. Carroll and Prickett, NT p. 117) – but an idea, the macro-text of God's forgiving and redeeming love for the world (*OED*, 'a short passage from the scriptures, especially one quoted as authoritative'; 'a short passage from some book or writer considered as authoritative'). Here 'text' is seeking to approximate its own originating idea rather than reflecting the idea's multiple and plural manifestations. At the same time it serves as an opening to discourse, to further textualisation (*OED*, 'the starting-point of a discussion').

These various nuances and definitions revolve around the practices of writing and reading because of their centrality to human social life, and because the problem they adumbrate remains perennially unresolved. Whether we term bibliography a science or an art, we employ it to analyse and understand manifestations of concrete phenomena: books, manuscripts and other artefacts containing writing. One of the most striking changes in bibliographical language over the last twenty years is the increased incidence of terms such as 'materialism', society, culture, and the deployment of interpretative contexts derived from philosophical, sociological and anthropological studies. Yet although methods have been devised to capture all the particularities of cultural activities such as writing and reading, somehow the essence of them continually evades capture.

Editing a work to produce an authoritative text paradoxically entails producing an entirely new textualisation, as in the *OED* definition 'the wording adopted by an editor as (in his opinion) most nearly representing the author's original work'. The mission of editors to ascertain an author's intentions, discussed in more detail below, has been revised and to some extend discredited. But where this is the case, it has been replaced only by an agnosticism that declares such intentions unknowable, or a cautious pragmatism that admits their centrality, but is sceptical about the extent to which they can be recovered. Whether we think of the misplaced confidence of the New Bibliographers in their capacity to restore original conception, or of the efforts of subsequent textual theorists to shift intentionality away from the author and towards an overdetermined social and cultural agency, the moment of composition, of imagining, of making, which is indisputably a precondition of artistic production, is both tantalisingly there, and yet impossible to grasp. An abiding preoccupation of the pages that follow will be this obdurate and insistent question as to whether it is possible to trace a text to any kind of originating space or moment.

But if this is true of writing, it is also true of reading. We can physically handle books and manuscripts, subjecting them to intensive scientific analysis, but we cannot get at the actual cerebral and psychological process that made them in a writer's mind. If the writer tries to tell us what that process is like, as many writers have, he or she merely produces another different kind of text, from a different moment of making. But by the same token, we cannot see or hear or touch an act of reading that entails interpretation, reflection, criticism; that too is locked in the mind of the reader. You can hear a reader read aloud, but what you hear is another text, a performance, already incommensurate with the written text, and not his/her 'reading' of the text, which remains invisible and inscrutable. No doubt an electrocardiogram could display the motion of a reader's brainwaves, and other scientific instruments could detect and record the physiological effects of reading – eye movements, pulse, skin temperature. But this data is all derivative and descriptive, measuring secondary effects. You still cannot get at another's reading, in the same way as you can physically make eye-contact with the print of a book, or the letters of a manuscript.

> Prior to any generalisation about literature, literary texts have to be read, and the possibility of reading can never be taken for granted. It is an act of understanding that can never be observed, nor in any way prescribed or verified. A literary text is not a

phenomenal event that can be granted any form of positive existence, whether as a fact of nature or an act of the mind[12].

Jerome McGann objects against Paul de Man's metaphysic of
reading by arguing that

> Reading appears always and only as text, in one or another physi-
> cally determinate and socially determined form. This is not to
> deny either the reality or the importance of silent and individual
> reading. It is merely to say that textuality cannot be understood
> except as a phenomenal event, and that reading itself can only be
> understood when it has assumed specific material constitutions.
> Silence before a text is neither our best nor our oldest model of
> textuality (*Textual Condition*, pp. 4-5).[13]

This clear, pragmatic insistence on the need to identify and
address only those aspects of reading that 'appear' and can be
'understood' – articulation, critical language, spoken and written
commentary – does nothing to dislodge the inaccessible moment
of communion between reader and text. What it does do is to
acknowledge that from the outset, the processes of reading entail
inevitable and irreversible textual change. After reading, the text
'on the page' remains physically unaltered (unless the reader
annotates …), but as 'understood' text it is already alienated from
itself in a ceaseless process of textual replication. As Derrida puts
it, 'iteration alters'[14]. This is even more self-evident where a dramatic text is treated as a pretext for performance. The medium of
performance is, in David Scott Kastan's words, 'dissimilar and dis-
continuous' (Kastan, *Book,* p. 7) from the written text, and yet is
still further refined in the inaccessible mental perception of the
'auditor' or 'spectator'. Each spectator perceives something different from, as well as something in common with, the rest of
the audience, as any interval conversation will confirm (McGann
makes the same point about any two readers, *Textual Condition*,
p. 10). And though the performance can be retextualised by
audio or video recording, transliteration, notation, no one

would expect such post-performance texts to be identical with a pre-performance textual 'script', or for any of them precisely to reproduce or imitate the hidden moment of 'spectation'.

৯৹

Bibliography, textual criticism, textual theory, in all their manifestations throughout the centuries, have been concerned with similar basic questions about ' text'. For the purposes of this analysis 'text' is largely confined to writing, although modern bibliography is disposed to give a much broader definition of what can be considered 'textual', as when McKenzie defines 'texts' to include 'verbal, visual, oral, and numeric data, in the form of maps, prints, and music, of archives of recorded sound, of films, videos, and any computer-stored information, everything in fact from epigraphy to the latest forms of discography' (McKenzie, *Bibliography*, p. 5).

The first question is likely to be, what does this text mean? This question would certainly come first if the object of scrutiny were an inscription on a Mesopotamian tablet of the third millennium BC or the Rosetta Stone. But it might well be skipped if a scholar or editor were dealing with a text whose 'meaning' has been much more generally explicated, and could therefore be regarded as already in common currency. Bibliography was once considered the poor relation of literary criticism that provided, often invisibly and unacknowledged, the raw materials upon which criticism worked its interpretative operations. This view of bibliography, where textual scholarship is cast as a Cinderella discipline, ancillary to critical interpretation, is today very much at the forefront of the debate. D.F. McKenzie questions the traditional notion of 'a border between bibliography and textual criticism on the one hand and literary criticism and literary history on the other'.

My own view is that no such border exists. In the pursuit of historical meanings, we move from the most minute features of the material form of the book to questions of authorial, literary and social context. These all bear in turn on the ways in which texts are then re-read, re-designed, re-printed and re-published. If a history of readings is made possible only by a comparative history of books, it is equally true that a history of books will have no point if it fails to account for the meanings they later come to make (McKenzie, *Bibliography*, p. 14).

The second question addressed towards a text is likely to be, who wrote it? This is an ancient and fundamental question that is only now theoretically problematised. The identification of authorship is as old as writing. The earliest named author in history is Princess Enheduanna, born c. 2300 BC, and author of some religious hymns to be found on inscribed tablets, signed with her name[15]. The notion of writing as purely, or even primarily, the product of individual authorship is today the subject of intensive debate. But it is only recently that such a sufficiently substantial body of scholars and critics has agreed to analyse the processes of textual production differently. For centuries 'who wrote this?' has been a relatively simple question, or at least one deemed susceptible of a definitive answer.

What is the status of this text? This question is traditionally asked in relation primarily to the author. If a printed text, what was the author's control over it? Is it a first or a subsequent, revised edition? Did the author correct proofs? If revised, was the revision done in a very different context from the production of the first printing? Did anyone else have a hand in it, as for instance Ezra Pound had in the writing of T.S. Eliot's *The Waste Land*? Is it a printing that saw no authorial intervention in the publishing process? If a manuscript, was it the author's autograph or holograph, or a copy? If so, copied by whom and in what context? Is it 'authorised', bearing at least metaphorically the signature of the creator, or 'unauthorised'? As we shall see, this question is now asked differently. It has always been, and remains, a critical question in relation to Shakespeare, especially *vis-à-vis* the various Quarto and Folio texts published in the later sixteenth and early seventeenth centuries, the lack of manuscript and proof sources, the abundant evidence of the author's absence from the production of what remains to us as 'text'.

What are the physical characteristics of this text? This question is intimately related to the previous one, and has again relatively recently fanned out to encompass the multiple influences that impact on the shape and form of a text. If it is a book, when was it printed, by whom and how? What is the relation between the authorial 'text' and those features that are added by decision of the printer or publisher, the designer or the copyeditor? This is an area where bibliographers have traditionally reigned supreme, as critics have tended not to take an interest in such aspects of the text. But all that has changed.

> The specific forms and contexts in which we encounter literature, its modes and mechanisms of transmission, are intrinsic aspects of what it is, not considerations wholly external to it; and no less than its semantic and syntactic organisation, these exert influence over our judgements and interpretations (Kastan, *Book,* p. 3).

This concern with 'the book as a physical object' ushers in more practical questions. What were the technical, cultural and social processes that went into the making of this text? These would include such matters as printing technology, practices of textual design, custom and practice in a printing house or scriptorium. For instance, a 'house style' can supervene between the authorial execution and the printed product, standardising and altering what was initially proposed. Norms of spelling, grammar, page layout are in evidence in the manuscripts produced by twelfth century monastic houses as much as they are in the products of twentieth century publishers[16]. These account for 'non-authorial' contributions to the finished product.

This brings us to the problem of interpretation. How is this text read, interpreted, used, subjected to commentary, given a place in cultural traditions such as literary canons? Bibliography would naturally be interested in details about the circulation of a text and the identification of a readership, for example, the great social extensions of readership by the invention of printing in the fifteenth century, or by the development of mass market paperbacks. What was the print run for a particular book? What sort of people bought and read it? Was it acquired by libraries? In the case of dramatic texts like the plays of Shakespeare, the relations between theatrical practice and the production of dramatic writing will inevitably be in the foreground. How do the early printed texts of Shakespeare, virtually the only source of our knowledge of them, relate to the theatrical productions they both record and then subsequently enable?

On the other hand, this takes us straight into interpretation, the domain of criticism where scholars have only recently decided 'to boldly go'. Formerly the critical reading of texts might or might not pay attention to the concerns of bibliography, depending on the method being employed. Attention to the act, or 'scene', of reading came into play with hermeneutics, the self-conscious and self-reflexive study of reading processes. And here bibliography has perceived a significant opportunity of being able to demonstrate convincingly the extent to which bibliographical issues impact on the scene of reading.

Lastly, what is the role of the editor? This may be considered the point where bibliography itself becomes self-reflexive and starts to theorise its own practice. It is the editor's job to process and present a text to readers. In undertaking this task, the editor will concern him or herself with all the above questions. But what is his/her role? To present the text as a historical document, for example in facsimile (which is still an editorial function, since the product is not the 'original' but *factum simile*, something *made to look like* it)? To modernise the text in order to make it more accessible to contemporary readers? To correct the text, purging it of errors and non-authorial accretions added by the processes of publication? To 'emend' the text where there is strong argument for believing that its historical form does not adequately or accurately represent what the author said, or wanted to say? To interpret between the text and the reader in the sense of providing explanatory notes, critical apparatus, introduction and commentary that mediate an old and possibly unfamiliar cultural form to a modern readership? Is the editor a technician or 'demonstrator' who cleans up a text for exhibition; a translator who mediates the text to a new audience; or a creative collaborator in, or even co-author of, the text?

The ultimate question, brought decisively into play with the new rapprochement of criticism and bibliography, concerns the relations between these various activities that go on with, and around, literary texts – reading, textual scholarship, editorial processing, critical interpretation, textual theory. Are these quite different activities that need to be understood in terms of their interaction with one another, or are they are all aspects of a common search for understanding through writing? Do they represent different ways of interpreting the process of reading; or are they all rather extensions of the single fundamental act of reading – reading, as it were, at a more advanced level? If the latter, then we move from a model in which reading is the primary activity, and all other critical and scholarly functions become secondary, ancillary to the originating act of decoding; to one in which the processes of remaking the text are shared in common between textual study, editing, critical interpretation, indeed all our various 'reading' practices; where 'a real reader is a writer' (Cixous, *Three Steps*, p. 21).

To encounter writing at its most technical, approximating as closely as possible to the physical labour of the writer in putting pen to paper, quill to vellum, keystroke to screen, we can go back to mediaeval literature and find there a rich source of paradigms for modern textual studies. Creative works recorded in mediaeval manuscripts are heavily invested with what McGann calls 'bibliographic' as distinct from 'linguistic' codes (McGann, *Textual Condition*, p. 13). In an oral and manuscript culture, writing changes with every copy, so the illusion of fixity and permanence that we associate with print culture never arises. A 'text' of a poem on a mediaeval manuscript page is part of a larger 'text' that frames or accompanies it with illumination, explanatory glosses, ornamental capitals. Graham Caie observes that a mediaeval text can often be found off-centre on a manuscript page, shifted to 'make space for marginal illustrations and glosses that parody or interpret text, and lemmata that guide the reader who attempts to assimilate and synthesise what can only be called a multidimensional visual experience'[17]. On a single page of the Lindisfarne Gospels, at the opening of St John's Gospel, a few words of Latin text follow a massive architectural capital I – '*In principio erat verbum et verbum erat apud deum*'. The words are framed by elaborate and highly-coloured illuminated images of birds, animals and abstract patterns. Interlineated among the Latin is a translation of the Gospel into Northumbrian English: '*in prima wor word and word wor mid god fader*'. Which is the 'paratext', which the 'text'?[18]

The Lindisfarne Gospels is perhaps an extreme example, and no one would attempt to convey its particular textuality by abstracting the words of the Latin Gospel alone; though this is what happens, in an example given by Jerome McGann, when William Blake's illuminated poems are routinely edited and printed as naked text[19]. Blake composed both together, but a similar effect occurs when 'editorial' supplementations to the text are subsequently purged from it. An example would be when the *Canterbury Tales* is printed as an isolated poetic text, and without the extensive glosses that in the Ellesmere manuscript loom as large, and take up as much space, as the poem itself. Here the role of the scribe is not simply that of a 'copyist' but rather that of an editor, or even co-author, whose commentary and explication become part of the complete text. Such additions, though at first sight merely elaborations of an 'original', can in due course gain recognition as important writing, like patristic commentaries on editions of Christian scripture. An older bibliographical model would wish to detach the 'poem' from its context in order to emulate the authorial 'original'. In the same way older critical methods would wish to discriminate hierarchically between poem and commentary. Current bibliographical thinking, with its insistence that 'forms effect meaning' (McKenzie, *Bibliography*, p. 4) would be more interested in seeing the context as well as the text; and contemporary criticism might well be more interested in the interaction of text and paratext, less confident in distinguishing absolutely between the 'literary ' and the 'non-literary', or between 'great' and 'minor' writing.

The character of the writer that belongs to these forms of literary practice is more that of an artisan, a technician, than the later but more familiar individualistic conception of the singular author. Mediaeval religious writers inevitably saw their work as a commentary on the only writing that had real permanence, the word of God[20]. Similarly there was no notion of 'originality' to inhibit the extensive adaptation and recuperation of traditional materials. In Anglo-Saxon culture the poet was a *'scop'*, a shaper, an oral performer whose technical skill lay in the versification and musical rendering of ancient and new material. In *Beowulf* the *scop* is shown composing, as oral poets do, by taking well-known stories or other narratives (the heroic tales of the Germanic past and the grand narratives of the Bible), applying them to contemporary circumstances, and giving them new expression within a free verse form. The verse was evidently performed as a kind of rhythmical chanting to percussive or musical accompaniment, and therefore had to be free enough to allow for improvisation within a continuous movement. On the other hand, the phrases used by the poets were to a large extent stock formulae drawn from an established and familiar reservoir of such phrases (the Old English coinage 'word-hord' ['word-stock'] exactly describes such a body of linguistic materials):

> Whereas a lettered poet of any time and place, composing (as he does and must) with the aid of writing materials and with deliberation, creates his own language as he proceeds, the unlettered singer, ordinarily composing rapidly and extempore before a live audience, must and does call upon a ready-made language, upon a vast reservoir of formulas filling just measures of verse. These formulas develop over a long period of time; they are the creation of countless generations of singers and can express all the ideas a singer will need in order to tell his story, itself usually traditional[21].

Within the narrative of *Beowulf*, a poet is described composing in exactly this way in order to celebrate the deeds of the hero:

> One of Hrothgar's thanes blithely began
> To recite and recount Beowulf's bravery.
> He was a man endowed with words,
> His memory mindful of many an old
> Song, stored with a stock
> Of ancient stories. To tell an old tale
> New words he would weave, appropriate
> And pleasing, artistically linked,
> Suiting the subject, verbally varied,
> Cleverly composed, and sweetly sung[22].

Although as Caie points out the word 'text' was not available to the Anglo-Saxons, the concept of verbal art as something 'woven' was natural and familiar to them, and their terms for writing were often artisanal in association[23]. When scribes copied Anglo-Saxon poems into the earliest surviving manuscripts, most of which lie at some chronological distance from the initial composition, they were translating into the terms of a literary society the vestiges of an oral and artisanal culture, where the poet was a 'shaper' who composed and sang, and where our familiar distinctions between art and craft, technique and technology, did not exist. The great Old English devotional poem *The Dream of the Rood* survives in a manuscript copy, but also in variant fragments carved into a stone cross (the Ruthwell Cross) and on a small jewelled crucifix (the Brussels Cross)[24]. Here even the most intensely devotional writing inhabits a material world.

Nonetheless, it is at its most material and technical, at the point where writing really is weaving and constructing, that mediaeval literature also identifies writing as one of the most ineffable and numinous of activities, a fundamentally religious practice. Here also we find the most extreme polarisations between the transient and the eternal, the iterable and the immanent, together with the most ardent attempts to reconcile them into a single totalising vision of incarnate universality.

Characteristic of the mediaeval vision in Western Christianity is the idea of the world, or 'nature', as a text, a great script written by God, and corresponding to the formally written text of the scriptures. In order to document this universal text, mediaeval writers sought to collate and unify the whole of universal knowledge. As Jesse M. Gellrich puts it, there was a 'commonplace attempt to gather all strands of learning into an enormous Text, an encyclopaedia or *summa*, that would mirror the historical and transcendental orders just as the book of God's Word (the Bible) was a speculum of the Book of His Work (nature)'[25]. Gellrich shows, following Levi-Strauss, that this macro-text performed functions similar to those of mythology in primitive societies, totalising and classifying the lineaments of the known world.

In pursuit of this aim mediaeval thinkers found themselves grappling with issues of language and representation that have become the key problems of modern critical and cultural theory.

They could observe that language is variable, fluid, changeable; that there was always a gap between representation of the world in language or art, and the nature of the world itself; and that somehow the eternal was contained, figuring itself in the impermanent, eternity manifesting itself through change. This led some scholastics to develop semiotic theories that seem to parallel the work of post-structuralist and deconstructionist thinkers of today.

> When the mediaeval sign is defined as a tripartite structure – a *signum*, 'sign', that is divided into a *signans* ('signifying') and a *signatum* ('signified') – the work of Saussure comes to mind; and when Augustine imagines the cosmos as a vast 'script' written by the hand of God, in contrast to his own pale, flawed imitation of it, modern readers may see the deconstructive project of Derrida 'prefigured' (p. 21).

On the other hand the Middle Ages did not conceive of reality as a matter of signifying practice. Change was always relative to permanence, signification to eternal truth:

> Although these possibilities may be intriguing, they should be pursued only in full appreciation of the extent to which signs and signification, as they were explored in *grammatica* (the first discipline of the seven liberal arts) and in the hermeneutics of Scripture, remained committed to a larger intellectual preoccupation with stabilising the sign, moving it out of the realm of potential arbitrariness, and tracing utterance back to a fixed origin, such as the primal Word spoken by God the Father (p. 21).

This is exactly the 'logocentric' view of language and meaning that Derrida deconstructed. Though we can review mediaeval initiatives in linguistic theory in the light of deconstruction, we cannot say that their methods of analysis established any significant subversion to the totalising and logocentric model of Christian theology (see Gellrich, *Idea*, p. 22). In mediaeval thought the 'Book' is a model of containment, since it incorporates and interprets everything. 'Writing' and 'signifying' were compatible with that totalising project; whereas for Derrida, 'writing' (*ecriture*) is at odds with the book and essentially different from it: 'the idea of the book, which always refers to a natural totality, is profoundly alien to the sense of writing. It is the encyclopedic protection of theology … against the disruption of writing, against its aphoristic energy, and … against difference in general'[26]. Nonetheless, as later discussions will show, there is a fundamental continuity between Derrida's project of perpetual deferral, and the mediaeval habit of predicating everything on an absent centre, the eternal *Logos* that is the invisible source of all words.

I have dwelt briefly on these examples from ancient and mediaeval critical practice since they seem to me to exemplify all the central problems of modern textual theory, and come to seem in the context of contemporary debates surprisingly modern in their implications. For example, we can trace the origins of much contemporary textual debate – particularly the controversy over whether a text is a corrupt degeneration of a perfect and recoverable artistic vision, or an irredeemably flawed remnant of an irrecoverable utterance – to the different practices that operated in the libraries of Alexandria and Pergamum in the fourth century. The Alexandrians recorded all the variants in different manuscripts of Homer's poems, which in turn reflected the textual variance of oral transmissions, and posited, on the basis of Platonic ideas, an ideal Homeric text of which the variants were a corrupt representation. The grammarians of Pergamum in Asia Minor by contrast took a Stoic view of text, holding that writing, like all worldly activity, was inherently imperfect, and that individual utterances, particular texts, should be held to be as complete and as perfect as they ever can be, even in their very singularity and idiosyncrasy[27]. Greetham correctly observes of the Alexandrian school that 'the eclectic school of critical editing is a modern derivative of this Platonist approach to text' (Greetham,

Theories, p. 50); and clearly the work of post-eclectic textual theorists and practitioners has more in common with the practices of
Pergamum, and could be described as Stoic rather than Platonic
in character.

What I find most interesting about mediaeval textual practice
is that both these conceptions of text are continually in play, and
efforts are continually being made to resolve their contradictions.
In a sense we are always struggling to recover the creative synthesis of mediaeval culture, where writing and thinking about
writing were essentially practical, imbued with an artisanal
attachment to physical processes of making; yet at the same time
wedded to the transcendent. In the example given below Pierre
Bersuire imagines both the body of Christ and the body of the
Christian as one book, Christ through the Incarnation being
inscribed into the skin of the believer. The sequence of images
recalls those articulations of creativity with which I began, but
they are both more concrete in depicting the physical processes of
book manufacture, and more confident in reading through the
lineaments of worldly writing the letters of an eternal truth[28].

> For Christ is a sort of book written into the skin ... That book
> was spoken in the disposition of the Father, written in the con-
> ception of the mother, exposited in the clarification of the
> nativity, corrected in the passion, erased in the flagellation, punc-
> tuated in the imprint of the wounds, adorned in the crucifixion
> above the pulpit, illuminated in the outpouring of blood, bound
> in the resurrection, and examined in the ascension.

We will return continually to such 'materialist' realisations of the
immaterial, such textual 'incarnations'.

❧

As I will show in the next chapter, textual theory as it relates particularly to Shakespeare, and notably from the late nineteenth
century onwards, is imbued with these controversies. Textual

theory in general has enacted in the last decades of the twentieth century what D. C. Greetham calls an 'inversion' comparable to Marx's inversion of Hegel. The basic parameters of New Bibliographical editing, which consist of a belief in the supremacy of the author as generator of the text, the assumption that surviving documents are likely to represent corrupted vestiges of the authorial utterance, and a confidence in the ability of scholar and editor to recover from the surviving textual traces what the author actually wrote, have been turned upside down by the work of bibliographical theorists such as D. F. McKenzie, Jerome McGann and Roger Chartier. Just as Marx insisted that matter, not spirit, is the real substance of the world, so modern bibliographers have looked to the 'material text' rather than to the original authorial utterance or 'idea' as the 'real foundation' of textuality, 'making the very post-lapsarian contingencies of the text, its negotiations with its own history, as the *base* of textual operations, and by therefore making authoriality, and especially authorial intention, into merely a "function" (or the *superstructure*) of this history rather than its *raison-d'être*'[29].

Like the Stoics of Pergamum, the modern bibliographers predicate their approach to text on the basis that it is what it is, its potentialities for meaning circumscribed by its material format and physical characteristics, and not susceptible of restoration or improvement. The originating authorial vision, Shelley's 'fading coal' of inspiration[30] that dies before the text takes life, is beyond recovery. Instead of seeking to emulate a text-that-never-was, the authorial text imagined as complete and perfect in itself, bibliography now accepts textuality as a history of change:

> The textual condition's only law is the law of change. It is a law, however, like all laws, that operates within certain limits. Every text enters the world under determinate sociohistorical conditions, and while these conditions may and should be variously defined and imagined, they establish the horizon within which the life histories of different texts can play themselves out. The law of

change declares that these histories will exhibit a ceaseless process of textual development and mutation – a process which can only be arrested if all the textual transformations of a particular work fall into nonexistence. To study texts and textualities, then, we have to study these complex (and open-ended) histories of textual change and variance (McGann, *Textual Condition*, p. 9).

By abandoning the notion of degressive bibliography and recording all subsequent versions, bibliography, simply by its own comprehensive logic, its indiscriminate inclusiveness, testifies to the fact that new readers of course make new texts, and that their new meanings are a function of their new forms. The claim is no longer for their truth as one might seek to define that by an authorial intention, but for their testimony as defined by their historical use (McKenzie, *Bibliography*, p. 20).

There is a new emphasis here on the iterability of texts, no longer viewed negatively as a process of corruption and decline, but seen positively as an exhilarating history of the continual making and remaking of texts. This emphasis derives in part from a recognition that, if the material conditions of text – calligraphy or typeface, papyrus, vellum or paper, page layout and design, binding, cover – contribute significantly to its meaning, then that meaning must be influenced by a continually changing physical form. This may be from one technology to another – from stone to papyrus, scroll to codex, book to computer file; or simply through iteration – reissue, reprint, revision. But there is also in both McKenzie and McGann a new emphasis on the role of the reader in remaking text.

Any history of the book – subject as books are to typographic and material change – must be a history of misreadings ... Every society rewrites its past, every reader rewrites its texts, and, if they have any continuing life at all, every printer re-designs them (McKenzie, *Bibliography*, p. 16).

Reading does not leave a text as it was found, but alters all:

> Different readers bring the text to life in different ways. If a poem *is* only what its individual readers make it in their activity of constructing meaning from it, then a good poem will be one which most compels its own destruction in the service of its readers' new construction. When the specification of meaning is at one with its discovery in the critical practice of writing, the generative force of texts is most active (McKenzie, *Bibliography*, p. 17).

Textual variance and iterability, and the capability of the reader to remake text, are seen as contributory or even collaborative factors in the process of textual change. Here the bibliographical emphasis on the text as a site where shifting physical forms effect variable meanings, meets the post-structuralist critical focus on reading as reconstruction, re-making.

> But texts do not simply vary over time. Texts vary from themselves (as it were) immediately, as soon as they engage with the readers they anticipate. Two persons see 'the same' movie or read the 'same book' and come away with quite different understandings of what they saw or read ... the differences arise from variables that will be found to reside on both sides of the textual transaction: 'in' the texts themselves, and 'in' the readers of the texts' (McGann, *Textual Condition*, pp. 9-10).

Here McGann points out that when read, text is clearly changed into something else; and as text, is itself involved in a process of continual alteration. 'Writing', as Greetham notes, 'requires repeatability' (Greetham, *Theories*, p. 35). Iteration alters. McKenzie also sees textual change as determining, and yet compounded by, the plurality of readings:

> For better or worse, readers inevitably make their own meanings. In other words, each reading is peculiar to its occasion, each can be at least partially recovered from the physical forms of the text, and the differences in readings constitute an informative history (McKenzie, *Bibliography*, p. 10).

The centrality of the reader as a co-contributor to the writing of text has been foregrounded particularly in discussions of the new technologies, where text becomes information in order to become text again. As George Landow puts it, computer-based textuality 'leads to an entirely new conception of text', which 'demands new forms of reading and writing, and [has] the promise radically to reconceive our conceptions of text, author, intellectual property, and a host of other issues ranging from the nature of the self to education'[31].

Literary scholars tended to think, as they moved fairly easily in the 1980s from typewriter to word-processing and then to more extensive uses of the computer and the internet, that the technological change in which they were implicated was simply an extension of print, a continuous expansion of the Gutenberg Galaxy. But a more sophisticated awareness of issues in information technology has disclosed the fundamental differences between text as it is manifested in physical writing, including typing, and text as it is represented electronically on a computer screen.

> An electronic text is a series of electronic impulses which can be stored on a variety of media. These impulses have only two states, on and off, usually represented as 1 and 0, but so complex are the patterns which can be built up by these two states that all texts in all languages of the world can be 'written' in them. The internal, machine representation of text as electronic signals can be read only by machine; these signals have to be translated by the computer into a human-readable version which can be displayed or printed before they can be read by the eye. An electronic text, therefore, does not have a material existence in the way a book does[32].

Although as Kastan observes, electronic text, consisting as it does of particles of matter, cannot be considered in any way less 'real' than print (Kastan, *Book*, pp. 112-13), it is certain that reading in this environment is a different experience, since the 'text' is an invisible electronic entity that has to translate itself into a condition of legibility. Or as Landow puts it, 'The reader always encounters a virtual image of the stored text, and not the original version itself' (Landow, *Hypertext*, p. 19).

Kastan emphasises the material, physical differences between print and electronic technologies in terms recalling my earlier discussion of writing as work, practice, craft:

> The relative fixity of ink on a page gives way to the fluidity of pixels on a screen. All the previous technologies of writing involve more or less permanently marking the environment; cutting, brushing, pressing words into a medium chosen to receive and preserve them. Electronic texts work differently, both technologically and ontologically; their elements of meaning are 'fundamentally unstable' (Kastan, *Book*, p. 114).

The law of change that for McGann defines the textual condition is far more self-evident in information than in print technology, since, as Michael Joyce puts it, 'print stays itself, electronic text replaces itself'[33].

Kastan's phrase 'fundamentally unstable' is quoted from a striking discussion of these issues by Jay David Bolter, in which the key characteristics of the electronic text are defined as instability, iterability, what he calls 'restlessness'. The electronic text

> is the first text in which elements of meaning, of structure, and of visual display are fundamentally unstable. Unlike the printing press or the mediaeval codex, the computer does not require that any aspect of writing be determined in advance for the whole life of a text. This restlessness is inherent in a technology that records information by collecting for fractions of a second evanescent electrons at tiny conjunctions of silicon and metal. All information, all data, in the computer world is a kind of controlled movement, and so the natural inclination of computer writings is to change, to grow and finally to disappear[34].

This formulation suggests something of the fearful autonomy of information technology, that apparent capability of technology to operate beyond the will and intention of the user that arises from its sheer intellectual complexity, and is redolent of social anxieties about the powers of science[35]. In practice all that has happened here is that certain illusions about power, control and intentionality have been exposed as illusory. The 'instability' that post-structuralist criticism finds to be characteristic of the text is here self-evident as characteristic of its ontological as well as its hermeneutic existence. As Peter Donaldson puts it of hypertext:

> Multimedia hypertext reconfigures the relationship between an authoritative cultural source (a Shakespeare play) and its belated, aesthetically and culturally divergent versions, changing the ways we think about such matters as 'the original text', and its reproduction in 'authoritative' versions and productions. Much that has been written about hypertext assumes that the computer will be an ally of the contemporary literary theories that unseat the 'author', spread meaning out into a web of traces and associations, and change the relation between cultural centre and margin[36].

However, another approach to information technology, also espoused by Bolter, is to see it as empowering rather than disenfranchising the reader:

> The text as text only exists for the reader after it has first been recreated by the machine, and every act of reading the text is a new act of re-creation. This is not, of course, a phenomenon only of electronic text, as every new reading of a text in any form is a new act of re-creation, but it is true of electronic text physically as well as intellectually; the machine is interposed between text and reader as a physical necessity[37].

Hypertext, in its interactive nature, can be said to empower the reader 'by turning the reader into an author' in a process where 'the reader calls forth his or her own text out of the network, and each text belongs to one reader and one particular act of reading'

(Bolter, *Computer, Hypertext*, p. 6). Writing on Shakespeare, Peter Holland explicitly nominates the reader as an 'author' in the environment of hypertextual writing:

> Hypertext is essentially an activity of writerly reading, making the reader an author in the investigation of the routes, the navigation of the hypertext corpus ... Hypertext enables us to reconsider the whole notion of the intellectual status authorship confers[38].

⁂

All these considerations can be gathered into some kind of resolution by a focus on Tom Stoppard's *The Invention of Love*[39], which is something of a rarity, a play about textual criticism. It concerns the life and death of A. E. Housman, a major figure in the history of textual scholarship, and explores the contradictions of a life in which the sentimental poet and the rationalist scholar, the frustrated lover and the irascible Classics professor, strangely co-existed. The play begins with Housman, recently deceased, arriving at the River Styx. Charon the ferryman raises one of the play's key themes by indicating that he was told to expect both a poet and a scholar, and has naturally assumed this to be two people. The dead Housman has to explain that he purports to be both (Stoppard, *Invention*, p. 2). At some points the younger and the older Housman (AEH) appear on stage together, and between them act out this contradiction. Housman expresses the ambition of making his mark by writing, as Horace had phrased it in his '*exegi monumentum aere perennius*'[40], a monument more permanent than bronze. AEH asks if this is to be as poet or scholar, since one cannot hope to be both.

AEH   Poetical feelings are a peril to scholarship. There are always poetical people ready to protest that a corrupt line is exquisite...

HOUSMAN   But it is, isn't it? We catch our breath at the places where the breath was always caught. The poet writes to his mistress how she's killed his love 'fallen like a flower at the field's edge where the plough touched it and passed on by'... I could weep when I think how nearly lost it was ... that flower, lying among the rubbish under a wine-vat, the last, corrupt copy of Catullus left alive in the wreck of ancient literature (Stoppard, *Invention*, p. 36).

In fact the distinction will not hold, since the young Housman and the old, the youthful enthusiast for poetry and the scholar who called textual criticism 'not a sacred mystery', but 'purely a matter of reason and common sense'[41], are one and the same. The scholarship is in any case classics, a scholarship of ancient poetry, and despite himself the old Housman is lured into revealing, through the language of classical poetry, his true attachments to poetry and to love. He begins with the familiar quasi-scientific and common-sense definition of textual criticism as a science like botany or zoology. At the same time since the survival of writing is dependent on copying, and subject to the inaccuracy of human fingers, textual criticism can only aim at approximation. But still reason and common sense are the guiding principles of bibliographical scholarship (Stoppard, *Invention*, p. 38). Then rising into the full flow of that ritualistic excoriation of other scholars which is so characteristic of Housman's critical writing (his 'Adversaria'), AEH suddenly shifts to an entirely different tone, which leads him into reciting his own translation of Horace's '*Diffugere Nives*'[42]:

AEH   If I had my time again, I would pay more regard to those poems of Horace which tell you you will not have your time again. Life is brief and death kicks at the door impartially ... Seasons and moons renew themselves but neither noble name nor eloquence, no nor righteous deeds will restore us. Night holds Hippolytus the pure of stain, Diana steads him nothing, he must stay; and Theseus leaves Pirithous in the chain the love of comrades cannot take away (Stoppard, *Invention*, p. 39).

The love of Pirithous and Theseus, who could not rescue his

comrade from the underworld, serves in the play as emblematic of Housman's unrequited passion for his university friend Moses Jackson. In the play's second act the twenty-two-year-old Housman, not yet an academic, defines scholarship as 'useless knowledge for its own sake'. Although already confident in his ability to ferret out hidden corruption (he is sure of what Horace did and did not write), it is the poetry, and the poets' 'invention' of love that really counts. Against the robust academic confidence of his older self, the young Housman asserts a belief in the random and accidental survival of poetic riches, miraculously enduring the wholesale destruction of a much larger cultural heritage, the wreck of ancient literature:

HOUSMAN   ...have you ever seen a cornfield after the reaping? Laid
flat to stubble, and here and there, unaccountably miraculously
spared, a few stalks still upright. Why those? There is no reason.
Ovid's *Medea*, the *Thyestes* of Varius who was Virgil's friend and considered by some his equal, the lost Aeschylus trilogy of the Trojan
war ... gathered to oblivion in *sheaves*, along with hundreds of Greek
and Roman authors known only for fragments or their names alone
– and here and there a cornstalk, a thistle, a poppy, still standing ...
(Stoppard, *Invention*, pp. 72-3).

Those miraculous survivals (and incidentally our ability to revive them through translation) are what matter, not the futile attempts of scholarship to establish what an author really wrote. AEH extrapolates this critical position to a philosophy of life:

AEH: You think there is an answer: the lost autograph copy of life's
meaning, which we might recover from the corruptions that have
made it nonsense. But if there is no such copy, really and truly there
is no answer (Stoppard, *Invention*, p. 41).

AEH is ultimately reconciled to the Stoic position, accepting the permanent value of chance fragments in place of an attempt to reconstruct the lost totality.

A E H   In the Dark Ages, in Macedonia, in the last guttering light from classical antiquity, a man copied out bits from old books for his young son, whose name was Septimius; so we have one sentence from *The Loves of Achilles*. Love, said Sophocles, is like the ice held in the hand by children. A piece of ice held fast in the fist...
H O U S M A N   Love it is, then and I will make the best of it (Stoppard, *Invention*, p. 43).

As AEH knows only too well, in that romantic aspiration he signally failed, leaving the kind of empty space a writer like Stoppard can fill with sustained re-imaginings. All the key issues that pertain to 'textual Shakespeare' are explicated here: the complex relations between poetry and scholarship; the rationalist attempt to construct order out of evidence that in the end amounts only to accidental, miraculous survival; the final acceptance that there is no 'lost autograph copy' that would, if rediscovered, answer all our questions and resolve all our problems. Instead there are only fragments, documents, texts, that choke us with an awareness of what we have lost, while simultaneously prompting activities of reconstruction, re-imagining, translation, that can fill empty space with words and music[43].

Fire and Ice

Sophocles said
That love's like ice
Held fast in the fist
Of a child's warm hand.
Squeeze it tight,
And it slips through the fingers;
Open your palm
And it melts, evanescent,
Absorbed in the empty air.

Michelangelo made
A statue of ice
That stood for a day
Then lapsed into liquid
A pool on Pietro's floor.

Yet it's more near to me now
That shimmer of shards
Than David's abstracted gaze
Or the Mona Lisa's
Mockery smile.
Sophocles' line
Lies on my lips
Tasting of snowflakes
Echoing silent speech.

Lovers never forget
The chill in the palm,
Cold's shiver on shrinking skin
The dampness where love has been.

CHAPTER TWO

Shakespeare

ॐ

I N   C O M M O N   W I T H all textual studies, Shakespearean bibliography has concerned itself with the key questions listed in
the first chapter: what does this text mean? Who wrote it? What is
the status of this text? What are its physical characteristics? How
is it read? What is the role of the editor? The problematical nature
of this history in the case of Shakespeare lies in certain peculiari-
ties of the documents on which it is based. These are printed
texts, none of which appear to have had any authorial involve-
ment in their production, and which lie adjacent to, though
intimately engaged with, a separate cultural activity, that of dramatic production. These printed texts, though the primary
source of our modern editions, are clearly, in a historical sense,
secondary sources, since they follow and in some way or other
record, imitate, document, a corresponding theatrical performance or series of performances. The published text tends to be
presented as a post-performance version of the dramatic text 'as
it hath been diuers and sundry times lately acted'[1].

It is not impossible that a particular printed text might have
substantively corresponded very closely to the theatrical manuscript or copy on which the performance was based. But simply
by virtue of its having been developed through a distinct and

discrete process of cultural production, printing, it would, even if every single word were exactly the same and in the same order, be bibliographically different. The evidence and the probabilities actually point in quite the opposite direction, indicating clearly that these texts changed substantially and repeatedly through the processes of manuscript composition, copying for theatrical use, setting by a printer, revision in the printing house, re-setting for a re-issue, and preparation for a new edition such as the First Folio of 1623. 'The Shakespeare re-membered in the printing-house is inevitably something other than Shakespeare'[2].

Thus bibliography's first question (since in the case of Shakespeare the preliminary question 'what does this mean?' will already have been referred, for good or ill, to the arbitration of criticism) presents immense difficulties. Who wrote this text? Let us ask it of, for convenience, *Hamlet*, or rather of the three printed and published texts of that play that appeared in 1603, 1604/5 and 1623 respectively. The problem is not that Shakespeare may not have written these texts (there is really very little evidence to support the many 'disputed authorship' theories) but rather that they cannot be the texts that he wrote. We can say this with confidence simply on account of their distance from the action of authorship and the evident absence of the author from the process of publication; the extent of change that inevitably takes place where a text goes through a complex process of cultural production; and the substantial differences between the three texts. It is one thing to affirm that these texts, or at least one of them, bear(s) some intimate relationship with 'what Shakespeare wrote', and quite another to assert that this is actually it. As Roger Stoddard points out, whatever it is that authors do, they do not write books [3]. Immediately we are up against the still vexed bibliographical question of how exactly these printed texts came into being, and where the author stands in relation to them. From a very early stage in the editing of Shakespeare, scholars set themselves the task of identifying and correcting, in the early printed texts, inaccuracies that could be attributed to Elizabethan printing practices (which entailed in themselves processes of amendment, as subsequent editions like the much-corrected Second Folio were prepared for the press). They then attempted to reconstruct, from the fallible evidence of these printed texts, the manuscripts that lay behind them. Applying these principles could produce, it was believed, an edition that approximated as closely as possible to what Shakespeare himself actually wrote, and can be assumed to have wished (if he'd cared) to see published. Shakespeare's 'intended' text was assumed by definition to be not exactly (or in some cases not at all) what was to be found in the actual early printed texts themselves, since most scholars were agreed that these were very unreliable witnesses to the manuscript versions from which they must have derived.

The methodology can be found explicitly defined as far back as Nicholas Rowe's edition of 1709:

> I must not pretend to have restor'd this Work to the Exactness of the Author's Original manuscripts. These are lost, or, at least, are gone beyond any Inquiry I could make; so that there was nothing left, but to compare the several Editions, and give the true Reading as well as I could from thence. This I have endeavour'd to do pretty carefully, and render'd very many places intelligible, that were not so before[4].

Rowe's method was ostensibly to collate as many available texts as he could find and, where variant readings appeared, to judge for himself what seemed likely to be the 'true reading'. The result of this editorial process must be a conflated text, combining features of different printed editions. It will not be the same as any of the printed versions, since it is designed to approximate not to them but to another 'text', that which lay embodied within the author's manuscript but was already, by Rowe's time, irrevocably lost.

In practice Rowe's edition was based almost wholly on a reprint of the 1623 Folio, the Fourth Folio, and he collated only a few late seventeenth century quartos. But by stating explicitly that the extant texts could not be identical with Shakespeare's writing; that the contents of the manuscript could only be inferred from the printed record; and that an editor should compare his 'copytext' with earlier printed sources, Rowe 'established the basic conditions for editing Shakespeare that still pertain' (Kastan, *After Theory*, p. 98).

૩ઠ

The eighteenth century view that the surviving printed texts are pale imitations of what Shakespeare wrote, or intended to write (the texts having been corrupted, in Pope's words, 'by the ignorance of the Players, both as his actors, and his editors', and by the many 'blunders and illiteracies' of the first publishers), became the dominant view. Indeed, at least in editorial practice it survives as such, although it has been rigorously challenged, to the present day. Its great florescence was in the 'New Bibliography' of the early twentieth century.

The main source for New Bibliography was a form of textual analysis that derived in the later nineteenth century from classical and biblical studies, and took as its objective the establishing or 'settling' of texts. Documents were studied, analysed, compared and evaluated with a view to fixing the true form of the texts they contained beyond dispute, and thereby finally and permanently securing their meaning. Particularly important was the 'stemmatic' method of textual analysis developed by Karl Lachmannn for use on classical models. This posited for any text a genealogy or family tree enabling the scholar to work back through the accumulating errors of repeated copying to the manuscript that lay as near as possible to the writer's original words. Scholars welcomed this method as providing a more objective means for the editor to make decisions about textual cruces and what appeared to be misreadings by copyists. Since in many cases the manuscript was a copy taken at some considerable distance from the author (the oldest manuscript source of Catullus is fourteenth century, some fifteen centuries after his death) it is not surprising that classical editors felt relatively free to alter their sources[5].

Lachmann's method was devised for the interpretation of manuscripts, but Shakespearean scholar W.W. Greg applied it indifferently to printed texts. The study of Shakespeare's text became mainly a matter of analysing the printed records in order to identify and correct those inaccuracies that were assumed to have entered the texts through the vagaries of Elizabethan and Jacobean printing practice, and the conditions of theatrical writing. These practices of textual scholarship were formulated in strongly 'scientific' terms, and aimed at discovering the physical reality of texts as a basis for positing their meanings. Greg defined the method of this 'New Bibliography' as one that

> Lays stress upon the material processes of book-production, concerning itself primarily with the fortunes of the actual pieces of paper on which the texts were written or printed.
>
> Bibliographers have in fact brought criticism down from ... the heights of aesthetic and philosophical speculation to the concrete familiarities of the theatre, the scrivener's shop, and the printing house[6].

But despite this emphasis on materiality in the form of 'concrete familiarities', the ultimate objective of New Bibliography's search was less the 'concrete' and 'material' than something much closer to 'aesthetic and philosophical speculation': a vanished historical primary source, what Shakespeare actually wrote. The printed record was assumed to be in all cases at some distance from the authorial 'original', and in many cases a corrupt representation of it. Hence the New Bibliographic editor's task was explicitly defined as to 'strip the veil of print from the text'[7] in order to perceive its underlying reality.

Thus the New Bibliographers consolidated a narrative of textual history in which a stable and coherent authorial text, embodied somewhere in a lost manuscript, was 'corrupted' in the process of entering the printed state. The language of textual scholarship became pervaded, possibly by virtue of its roots in Augustan high culture, possibly by its proximity to biblical studies, by a morally charged lexicon of corruption and illegitimacy, purification and redemption. To be born into print was necessarily to carry a stigma of corruption. Scholarship could, however, reconstruct from these perishable materials a form of the text (the modern edition) that would redeem its fallen state and restore it to the condition of perfection it possessed at the point where it left the author's hand. In this context 'editions offer themselves as reconstructions of the play that the author wrote before it suffered the inevitable contamination of playhouse and printshop' (Kastan, *After Theory*, p. 62).

Certainly prior to the 1980s, the dominant conception of those early modern texts was the basic belief underpinning New Bibliographical editing, that they all stood in similar but differential relation to a lost authorial manuscript. The editorial approach most closely associated with W.W. Greg and Fredson Bowers conflates evidence from different texts in order to emulate a lost original. The assumption is that the true text, once embodied in Shakespeare's manuscript, gave rise to the various printed versions that we find in history. Although some texts would be considered closer to the putative authorial manuscript than others – e.g. Q2 *Hamlet* as distinct from Q1 or F – any of them might bear traces of the lost original (this applies even to the so-called 'Bad Quartos', which are still by some held to be tertiary sources, deriving not directly from the manuscript but indirectly via a performance version). Editing a play was therefore a matter of choosing which of the available texts, Folio or 'Good Quarto', approximated most nearly to the imagined manuscript, using this as 'copy-text', and then supplementing it by appropriating material from other texts. Where multiple contemporary texts exist (as they do for nineteen plays of the canon) the texts are sorted according to their imputed 'authority' and then subjected to a process of conflation and consolidation, whereby a particular copy-text is added to or subtracted from to arrive at 'the most authoritative possible texts of Shakespeare ... his own manuscript versions just as he meant them to stand'[8].

New Bibliography still remains the basis of much modern Shakespeare editing, although scholars working in the more advanced editorial projects are increasingly rejecting its principles. It was New Bibliography's search for the content of the 'manuscript', and a remarkable unanimity about what that manuscript might have contained, that produced relatively uniform and unitary editions out of the multiplicity of printed texts from which the modern editions are compiled. A more recent revision of New Bibliography, that of G. Thomas Tanselle, supplies alternative terms but adheres to the basic theory. The single uniform entity (e.g. *King Lear*) is here conceived as the 'core' or essence of the 'work', and variant texts are assimilated or rejected as they approximate or deviate from that 'core'. The 'work' is an ideal category, of which any individual text can only ever be an imperfect representation. The 'real work' can be perceived, like one of Plato's forms 'hovering somehow behind the physical text'[9]. Like Greg before him, Tanselle aspires to remove the integument of 'text' in order to get closer to the 'work' that the text adumbrates but never fully embodies.

This orthodoxy is gradually losing its hold, though as Barbara Mowatt comments, it still remains the foundational belief of much Shakespeare editing:

> The belief of Bowers and the other New Bibliographers remains current orthodoxy among Shakespeare editors, as one can see from the textual introductions to the standard Shakespeare editions, where the editorial rationale is inextricably linked to the editor's view of 'the manuscript' seen as lying behind the chosen early printed text[10].

Mowatt further observes that even the apparently alternative editorial policy, most strongly associated with the Oxford editors, of choosing as copy-text the text most closely associated with the theatre (e.g. F1 *Hamlet*, supposed to derive from a theatre copy, rather than Q2) still presupposes an authorial manuscript in the form of the mis-named 'promptbook' (p. 132). David Scott Kastan, developing a point made by Paul Werstine, points out that recent studies of extant theatre copies show that they contain none of the characteristics attributed to them by editorial speculation (Kastan, *After Theory*, p. 65). To some extent the Oxford Shakespeare enterprise, by its definition of the text as constitutive only of a particular theatrical moment, and in its acceptance of non-authorial elements (e.g. '*Macbeth* adapted by Thomas Middleton') led the way towards a text- rather than an author-centered editorial focus, and Oxford editor Stanley Wells has certainly expressed a preference for multiplicity, for single editions of discrete texts. The Oxford edition is also however closely associated with 'revision theory', discussed in more detail below. Essentially a branch of Lachmannian stemmatics, revision theory assumes that variant texts represent successive stages of authorial revision. It remains firmly attached to the authority of the author[11].

Mowatt goes on to demonstrate that this traditional view of the relation between printed text and manuscript is underpinned by a number of fallacies. One is that some texts carry a visible signature of authority marking them as more authentic (i.e. closer to the manuscript) than others, whereas in fact the early modern *Hamlet* text was in the seventeenth century 'as problematic as it is today':

> It existed, as it does today, in three printed forms that relate to each other in strange and interesting ways. Each claims to be an authentic text, but none carries any guarantee of authenticity, even though manuscripts of the play were available at the time (Mowatt, 'Problem', p. 134).

The other 'equally large fallacy' is the belief that manuscript copies, if they existed or were discovered, would solve the problem of stabilising the texts. Evidence from early modern manuscripts, even holographs written by authors like Middleton or Donne, actually suggests the opposite: that manuscripts were, if anything, even more unstable, iterable, in continuous alteration, less trustworthy, than printed texts.

> Instead of considering the possibility that each version may represent a printing of one of the many manuscript copies of a play circulating in the early 1620s, editors continue to try to link each version to a particular holograph. I would argue that it is this clinging to illusions about 'prompt-books' and 'authorial manuscripts' that blinds us to the possibility that there may have been a large flow of manuscript copies of Shakespeare's plays, copies marked by the idiosyncrasies of manuscript transmission, idiosyncrasies that would inevitably have made their way into the printed copies (Mowatt, 'Problem', p. 136).

As the influence of 'New Bibliography', at least at the level of textual theory, has weakened, another important strand of textual scholarship has come into corresponding prominence in Shakespeare studies. The methodology that has come to be known as 'the history of the book' derived initially from *historia litteraria*, the academic study of book-history, but has been strongly influenced by the French *Annales* school of historical writing, particularly in *L'Apparition du Livre* (1958) by Lucien Febvre and Henri-Jean Martin, which came into English in 1976 as *The Coming of the Book: the impact of printing 1450-1800*[12]. From this work comes the idea of *le rapport livre-societe*, the interrelationship between printed works and the society in which they are produced and circulated. The significant impact of this school of thought on modern critical studies can be recognised, as discussed in Chapter 1, in the work of Jerome McGann, which displaces the locus of 'authority' from the author to society. Effecting what Greetham calls a quasi-marxist inversion of author-centred editing, McGann revises the traditional view of the author as sole producer and guarantor (authoriser), of meanings that are then disseminated by secondary processes of distribution and exchange, and argues that the 'social nexus' which collaboratively generates and produces meaning is the real 'author' of the literary text. Although McGann wishes to recontextualise rather than replace the author, this approach to scholarship is consistent with some significant currents of modern literary theory, for example, the idea formulated by Barthes as 'the death of the author', that 'to give a text an Author is to impose a limit on that text, to furnish it with a final signified, to close the writing'[13]. Foucault took this further by arguing that the concept of the author itself is a strategy of containment, whereby meaning is limited, divided and constrained:

> The author does not precede the works; he is a certain functional principle by which, in our culture, one limits, excludes and chooses; in short, by which one impedes the free circulation, the free manipulation, the free composition, decomposition and recomposition of fiction[14].

While traditional bibliography has pinned textual studies firmly to the traditional concept of authorship, the 'history of the book' has in this way managed to bring textual theory much closer to modern theoretical criticism. It is increasingly acknowledged that the Shakespearean drama is best understood as a collaborative cultural activity within which the author played a significant but by no means an isolated part:

> The author certainly is not dead, but every act of writing is now understood to be inevitably compromised and fettered rather than some free and autonomous imaginative activity. An author

writes always and only within available conditions of possibility, both imaginative and institutional, and the text is realizable through (and inevitably altered by) the labors of other agents. Increasingly, textual criticism, if not editing itself, has attempted to uncover the full network of agents involved in the production of the text, restoring the literary work to the collaborative economies necessary for its realization and recognizing in the evidence of these collaborations not the causes of the text's deterioration but the enabling circumstances of its actualization, whether on stage or in the printing house (Kastan, *After Theory*, p. 67).

Barbara Mowatt aligns the 'radical destabilizing of the received Shakespeare text' (p. 138) with directions taken by contemporary criticism:

Today, many Shakespeareans ... see the plays as free from the process of filiation and (again to cite Barthes) read them 'without the father's signature'. They see them as subject not to interpretation but to explosion, dissemination: as woven from a 'stenographic plurality of signifiers', of cultural languages.

A similar shift in perception, a similar freeing of the text, occurs when critics place Shakespeare' s plays among other documents of the period – literary, historical, cultural – viewing them, in Barthes' language, as networks rather than organisms. Immediately the play is heard as separate, distinct voices, each voice making its claim, each fighting for its cultural and gendered place, instead of all being absorbed into the larger single voice that was for so long heard as Shakespeare's own (Mowatt, 'Problem', pp. 37-8, quoting Barthes, 'From Work to Text').

Hugh Grady has drawn a similar analogy between what he sees as the Oxford Shakespeare's revival of late nineteenth century textual 'disintegration' (the attempt to distinguish Shakespearean from non-Shakespearean elements in the texts) and the 'differentiation' of modern cultural studies[15]. Jonathan Goldberg notes the same convergence: 'post-structuralism and the new textual criticism coincide, historically – and theoretically. Both have called the criterion of authorial intention into question, thereby detaching the sovereign author from texts open to and constituted by a variety of intentions'[16]. It is no coincidence that the gradual consolidation of this position in mainstream criticism has taken place in the context of discussion around the variant Shakespeare texts. Once the influential New Bibliographical strategy of editing to emulate Shakespeare's manuscript is undermined, the traditional Shakespeare 'text' again disintegrates or de-composes into its constituent components, the original printed editions, and from there into the multiple contributory influences that constitute the 'collaborative economies' of the early modern theatre. At the level of front-line literary commerce this position has become accepted to a remarkable degree in terms of the ready availability of individual variant texts[17].

The plurality of accessible modern editions indicates a now much more firmly established understanding that the quarto and folio texts of *Hamlet, King Lear* and *Othello,* for example, provide valuable primary evidence about how these plays were produced, both as printed works and as texts-for-performance, in the collaborative economy of the Elizabethan and Jacobean theatres. The world of bibliographical and editorial scholarship is gradually coming round to accepting that the various early printed texts of Shakespeare's plays – the so-called 'Good' and 'Bad' quartos, and the Folio texts – should be considered as discrete and valid textualisations of artefacts that were never completed or finally stabilised, but continued to change and develop through a process of cultural production. It would not be an exaggeration to say that scholarly opinion has, over the last ten years, gravitated towards the view that every early modern printed text is a snapshot provisionally and temporarily fixing a particular stage in this process[18]. This constitutes a huge change in the way that texts are regarded, and as indicated the repercussions of the debate have had large implications for the publishing of Shakespeare texts.

ઝ૦

What then are the main features of this radically destabilised, thoroughly historicised, theoretically-oriented Shakespeare text of the twenty-first century? In order to appreciate the texts as historic cultural productions, one naturally needs first of all to see the variant early printings published, as they are now much more widely published, in the form of discrete and to some degree independent texts. Once they are present in the debate (even if the two texts of *Lear* are treated, as they are in 'revision theory', as both equally by Shakespeare, and therefore as both belonging to Tanselle's 'work'), the results of textual differentiation cannot help but draw attention to the specific historical circumstances of their initial cultural production, and to the fact that many more influences than the controlling direction of an authorial 'hand' were involved. In addition, if the plays are to be regarded as the collaborative products of a writing and theatre industry, one needs to see them in their historical context, foregrounded (as they were in the early printings) independent of the author, even to be received, in Barbara Mowatt's words, 'without the father's signature'. A play such as *The Taming of a Shrew*, which has never been accepted into the Shakespeare canon, is as valid and interesting a textualisation as *The Taming of the Shrew*, the text that appears in the First Folio. 'If the study and presentation of the text are designed to reveal the historically determined and meaningful collaboration of authorial and non-authorial intentions, there are no longer grounds on which one version of a text might be thought superior to another' (Kastan, *After Theory*, p. 67).

But more is involved in returning these texts to history and opening them to the illuminations of modern theoretical criticism than restoring their original independence. Where these variant texts are published in modernised form, or even in the partially modernised form of 'diplomatic reprint', much of their historical character is necessarily effaced. Modernisation in traditional editing entails far more than simply transcribing old spelling into modern orthography. Features of the old texts such as the frequent absence of act and scene divisions; the actual speech-headings used; aspects of grammar, punctuation and lineation, are all systematically expunged from them in a way that serves to 'idealize the activity of authorship, actively seeking to remove it from the conditions of its production' (Kastan, *After Theory*, p. 63).

All these characteristics are visible if the text is reproduced in photographic facsimile, and a number of influential scholars and critics have argued that it is in this form that the text lends itself most readily to both historical and theoretical interpretation, seeing the facsimile as that form of the text that preserves these examples of linguistic and typographical strangeness, those aspects of the early modern texts that insist on their historical difference. At the same time the facsimile makes these historical features available to criticism in ways that the standard modern edition occludes. Renaissance books operated, to use terms shared between early modernist Randall McLeod and Jerome McGann, by a different set of codes from their edited successor texts, and the modern reader needs to interpret such texts on their own terms, by reading and interpreting their own peculiar codes[19]. This view is summarised by David Scott Kastan as one in which: 'the unedited text, even in its manifest error, is the only and fully reliable witness to the complex process of the text's production and to the necessary resistance ... of its materiality' (Kastan, *After Theory*, p. 67).

So far though these critical and theoretical developments have not had the kind of impact one might have expected on the standard editions themselves. No doubt this is partly to do with the scale of the publishing enterprises involved, which are embedded in relatively massive institutional formations, and partly with the magnitude and longevity of the scholarly labour entailed in editing a play like *Hamlet or King Lear*[20]. But there is also in current thinking on these matters a curious circular return to the modernised standard edition. I have quoted a number of influential voices espousing new currents of textual theory. Yet each of them ultimately comes round to an interesting reconciliation with certain key features of the standard modern edition:

> In truth most of us will for the foreseeable future continue to read Shakespeare's plays and teach them in edited versions, in book form rather than off a computer screen, with spelling and punctuation modernised … If we must admit that in actuality there is no fully acceptable way to edit Shakespeare, at least no way to edit without losses that, depending upon one's interests and needs, will at times vitiate the advantages of the text's accessibility in whatever form it is presented, we must also admit that reading an edited text is a remarkably convenient way to engage the play … in reality there is no other way to engage the play, for from its very first appearance as printed text it has been edited, mediated by agents other than the author, and intended for the convenience of its readers (Kastan, *After Theory*, p. 69)

David Scott Kastan is a general editor of the Arden Shakespeare. Barbara Mowatt is a general editor of the Folger Shakespeare and, in the essay by her already quoted, goes on to discuss matters of editorial policy:

> Once one abandons the notion of the authorial manuscript behind the early printing, one is again and again left with the choice of reproducing, on the one hand, an early printing, with all its faults, and, on the other hand, the editorially, culturally constructed play …
>
> What does one do, for example, about the name of Hamlet's mother? … Most editors … use Q2 as the text on which to base their editions. Yet each edition names Hamlet's mother not as she was named in Q2, but as she was named in the Folio … They do

so, I suspect, for the same reason that Paul Werstine and I do in
the New Folger *Hamlet*: namely, because it is as Gertrude that she
exists and has existed for nearly three hundred years ... we allow
the 'Shakespeare' that is culturally constructed to outweigh the
Shakespeare that may be reflected in Q2 *Hamlet*, and name her
'Gertrude' (Mowatt, 'Problem', p. 142).

This example may be a relatively trivial point, but the editorial
strategy described indicates a reconciliation with the principles of
conflation, the role of the editor being always to make pragmatic
choices between alternative readings, rather than to respect consistently the historical integrity of a particular text.

The arguments that underlie this return to the standard conflated edition are important ones. The early printed texts are
'original' historical documents, with dates on them, that can be
located in a particular context of cultural production and
exchange. But does that mean that they are more authentic
records of the meanings generated in the seventeenth century by
their publication and performance, and therefore more reliable
guarantors of meaning for a historical criticism, than other extra-
textual kinds of evidence, or subsequent redactions, revisions,
editorial reconstructions?

A number of scholars have correctly observed that even the
facsimile gives only partial access to the nature of these texts as
they were produced and reproduced in early modern culture.
A facsimile edition usually has to choose one from among a range
of copies of a particular text that differ from one another as a
consequence of the practice of 'continuous correction' in the
printing house. A single edition cannot show this diversity of
copies, although variants can be marginally recorded in editorial
collation.

> Facsimile, for all its obvious ability to reproduce many of the
> significant visual characteristics of the original texts, performs,
> in both printed and electronic modes, its own act of idealisation.

> It reifies the particulars of a single copy of the text, producing
> multiple copies of a textual form that would have been unique
> (Kastan, *After Theory*, p. 68).

It is impossible to effect a return to an 'original' text, as any reproduction of a text is in some way a mediation[21]. Neither modern
printing and publication practices, nor modern methods of
decoding a text, can emulate or even imitate early modern book-
production and reading.

Jonathan Goldberg rightly argues that these texts were already
editions, copies not originals (Goldberg, 'Properties', p. 213):

> There never has been, and never can be, an unedited Shakespeare
> text. Textual criticism and post-structuralism agree therefore: we
> have no originals, only copies. The historicity of the text means
> that there is no text itself; it means that the text cannot be fixed in
> terms of original or final intentions.

Or as Stephen Orgel succinctly puts the same point:

> The history of realizations of the text ... is the history of the text [22].

Here 'realization' can refer to any number of cultural events that
participated in the history of a particular Shakespeare text. The
1608 Quarto of *Lear* was one such realisation, in printing and
publication. So was the Folio text, explicitly an edition, with
named editors who claimed privileged access to the original
manuscripts ('True Originall Copies'). But there were obviously
other realisations that have not left any comparable traces. There
were theatrical performances that can be assumed to have
differed from one another in ways that the two texts differ –
e.g. Globe performances may have used something like the Folio
text, while the recusant players who acted *King Lear* at Gowth-
waite Hall in Yorkshire in 1610 used the published Quarto – and
probably in other ways as well. Once the texts were in circulation
there were inevitably acts of individual reading and interpretation that also 'realised' the text in incommensurable acts of

cultural production. Since the story of King Lear circulated in a number of different versions, in prose and poetry as well as theatrical rendition, the Shakespearean texts and performances were obviously 'realising' some larger cultural apparatus that was being differentially and discrepantly realised within the culture as a whole.

In this post-bibliographic textual condition we have no basis for regarding, say, Q1 *Hamlet* as a better or worse, a more or less authentic, text than Q2 or F (and by the same token no basis for regarding F, as Wells and Taylor do, as more authentically theatrical than Q1), since we cannot relate any of them directly to that controlling authority 'the author'. Each version is an equally complex, overdetermined cultural product of the collaborative early modern theatre industry. Each may record the active participation of dramatist, actors, theatrical entrepreneurs, prompters, booksellers, compositors in the generation of theatrical and literary significance. Each reflects both authorial and non-authorial contributions in a synthesis sometimes impossible (even at the level of what appears to be error) to disentangle[23].

But exactly the same may be said of other 'realisations' normally thought of as falling outside the originating moment of cultural production: for example Restoration and eighteenth century adaptations and rewritings of Shakespeare's plays. Once this direction is pursued, it becomes difficult to object to modern editions of the texts, from the eighteenth century editors onwards, as not equally representative of historic 'realisations' of the text. For if Q1, Q2 and F are no longer in the traditional sense 'Shakespeare's', but (to use an equally convenient though less misleading shorthand), Trundell's, and Roberts's, and Heminge and Condell's, then in what ways are they different, other than chronologically, from Rowe's, and Pope's, and Warburton's; or even from Dryden's and Nahum Tate's?

Shakespeare's *King Lear* and Shakespeare's *Hamlet,* as their covers proclaim, turn out to be something less than truth in advertising. They are more properly Alfred Harbage's *King Lear* or Kenneth Muir's, Harold Jenkins's *Hamlet* or Maynard Mack's ... (Kastan, *After Theory*, p. 61).

Or as Jerome McGann puts it, editing is better understood as 'translation' than as a transparent representation of an original work (McGann, *Textual Condition*, p. 53). Provided that these attributions to the editor-translators are properly understood to reflect a quasi-authorial input into a textualisation that is just as historically specific, critically debatable and theoretically questionable as the early modern published texts, then they become in principle no less valid and valuable 'realisations'. It is only the dates that differ.

'If the *Mona Lisa* is in the Louvre, where is *Hamlet*?' F.W. Bateson's famously 'provocative' question is often quoted in discussions of textual theory with apparent approval[24]. But the distinction it makes is a difficult one. Bateson discriminates between a work of art that was physically executed by the hand of the artist, touched by his brush; and a work of art that has for us existed only in copies, at some remove from the artist's presence. It distinguishes between a work of art that is unique, inhabits its own physical space, and would be irreplaceable if destroyed; and one that exists universally in a vast multiplicity of copies, reproductions and performances. The assumption is that if the *Mona Lisa* were, for example, stolen (as it was, temporarily, in 1911)[25], then Leonardo's unique production would disappear from the possibility of common perception. It would be difficult to conceive of a comparable plan for stealing *Hamlet,* which has no such 'local habitation', but seems to exist only in a multiplicity of 'aery nothings'.

There is an easy answer to this problem, though in the end it is not a solution. We could say that *Hamlet* is 'in the British Library', or 'in the Folger Shakespeare Library', both of which house a number of valuable copies of the early printed texts, which in turn are the sole bases of the *Hamlet* we know. These could be stolen or destroyed. But they are by definition copies, not 'original' works by Shakespeare. The Shakespearean equivalent of the *Mona Lisa*, a work that had had physical contact with the writer's own ink-stained fingers[26], would be a holograph manuscript, no specimen of which exists. There is a sense, however, in which the distinction is too extreme. We do not doubt (unless we are Oxfordians or Baconians) that those printed texts are Shakespeare's 'work'. No one would claim that Milton did not write *Paradise Lost* because it was dictated rather than handwritten by the author[27]. By the time the plays of Shakespeare reached print, they had clearly absorbed the influences of many parties other than Shakespeare. But the same could be true of the painting. Did Leonardo mix his own paint, prepare his own canvas, apply the varnish? He certainly could not have designed the frame that now houses the picture, or be held responsible for any subsequent cleaning or other 'maintenance' that would manifestly alter the 'original'[28].

In fact, despite the ontological distinction between their respective modes of existence as text, both *Hamlet* and the *Mona Lisa* exist in exactly the same universal way, in the form of millions of copies distributed around the globe. The painting exists not solely within its own space in a Parisian gallery, but everywhere the image is circulated and reproduced. I have not seen it in the Louvre, but I would not therefore consider that I had not seen it at all. And if iteration alters, then the painting in the Louvre is not the painting executed by Leonardo, which was indeed already altered by recontextualisation by the time it was first exhibited to the spectator's recreating gaze.

When the painting was stolen from the Louvre in 1911, as a universal image and cultural icon it did not in any sense disappear. In fact, thousands of people (including among them Franz Kafka) flocked to view the blank space on the wall where the painting had been. At this height of modernism, the empty space from which the great cultural icon had disappeared may have seemed a more eloquent expression than its habitual familiarity[29]. Freud had argued in any case that what we see in the *Mona Lisa* and in its ambiguous expression is literally something unseeable, incestous desire for the mother.

We might say that a whitewashed wall is as good a screen as any for the projection of such unconscious human desire. But the blank space reflected back such possibilities of meaning only because it was previously occupied by the *Mona Lisa*. In the stage and film versions of the Broadway musical *Guys and Dolls*, a gangster called Big Jule gambles with dice from which the spots have been removed 'for luck'. His luck is guaranteed, since he remembers 'where the spots formerly were'[30].

It appears that the blank space behind the *Mona Lisa* was for at least a short time unconsciously accepted as the thing itself. When it went missing in 1911, it took twenty-four hours for anyone to realise its absence. An attendant who noticed it was not there thought it had been taken down to be photographed. The alarm was finally raised by a painter who had arrived to copy it.

For a Stoic or 'materialist' approach, which sees 'the history of realisations of the text' as 'the text itself' (Orgel, 'Authentic', p. 14), such copies are as much *Hamlet* and the *Mona Lisa* as the lost manuscript and the original painting. But do *Hamlet* and the *Mona Lisa* not also exist in a different way, one much more difficult to define, as the invisible source of their own copies? Somewhere there is a heart of silence, a blank space, that is uniquely the *Mona Lisa,* that is incommensurably *Hamlet* (in Emily Dickinson's words, 'Infinite enacted/In the Human Heart')[31]. Paradoxically such a space is constitutive and defining, yet also in Foucault's words 'a space into which the writing subject constantly disappears' (Foucault, 'What?', p. 102); or a vanishing point such as that identified by Derrida as 'the very origin of the destabilising moment'[32]. These originating spaces are not eternal, or immanent. They are certainly changed by those processes of cultural reproduction that recontextualise them and modify their essence; to quote Derrida again, 'the outside penetrates and determines the inside'[33]. The *Mona Lisa* was never quite the same after Marcel Duchamp adorned it with a Salvador Dali-style moustache. But however many copies are made, however many iterations occur, something endures, something alters yet remains itself.

This anecdote seems to suggest that we continue to need both Alexandria and Pergamum, both Platonic and Stoic conceptions of text. The altered 'copy' is certainly in a particular and local sense the 'text itself'. But what is it a copy of? *Prima facie* it is a copy of an 'original'. But in its altered state it must be an imitation not of the work, but of some potentiality within the work, something that lies even beyond the 'original', somewhere in that dark fertile space of human creativity from which both the artefact and its multiple potentialities of duplication derived. We cannot hope to reconstruct that Platonic essence, and our dealings with the text will always entail alteration. But that does not preclude us from believing in its existence. Both Greetham, and the anonymous author of *Exeter Book* Riddle 26 (see p. 56), sum up these paradoxes well:

> [T]he text is an ambivalent place and has been so from its beginnings in the language. It is, on the one hand, a place of fixed, determinable, concrete signs, a material artefact, and yet, on the other, an ineffable location of immaterial concepts, not dependent at all on performance transmission. It is, on the one hand, a weighty authority with direct access to originary meaning, and, on the other, a slowly accumulating, socially derived series of meanings, each at war with the other for prominence and acceptance. It is a place inhabited only by a sole, creative author who unwillingly releases control to social transmission, and it is also a

place constructed wholly out of social negotiations over transmission and reception. Each of these descriptions of text offers a different textuality and a different ontology ... (Greetham, *Theories*, p. 63).

Bibliotech

(Riddle 26, *The Exeter Book*)

He had it in for me, that certain someone
Who ripped off and stripped
The flesh from my skin,
Dunked me and dipped me,
Dragged me drowning, sopped
And sodden, sluiced and soaking,
Wet from the wash; stretched me out tightly,
Painfully pulled, pegged unprotected
In a searing sun, for days and days of
Dry desiccation, dehydrating
Drought. Then slit and sliced by the
Hard-honed gravel-ground keen knife's
Edge, fiddling fingers furled me in
Folds. A high-flying fowl's finest feather
Sucked up ink, scratched on my surface
A glittering stream of wood-dark dye.
Beyond the brown brim the plume
Plunged, dank and dripping,
Scratching and stabbing, scoring my
Sutures, tracing its track.

Was he the same one, my erstwhile enemy,
Who sought me and saved me from
Torture and torment, bound me about
With a bulwark of boards, tightly textured
From well-tanned hide, graced me with gold,
Twisted, tensile, brightest beauty of
Blacksmith's work? Was he indeed
My friend after all, that inscrutable stranger
Who turned me from textile to tell-tale
Text, blessing a skin with a god-given
Gospel, gracing a garment
With a gift of words?

CHAPTER THREE

Matter

꒰Ꙭ꒱

T HERE CAN BE little doubt that contemporary bibliography has invested most of its energies in the pursuit of fixed, determinable concrete signs, socially derived meanings and social negotiations over the transmission and reception of texts. Indeed, one of the key terms running through contemporary debates on textual theory and practice is 'materialism'. In one sense this is nothing new. As the adjective 'material', the word figured largely in the discourse of New Bibliography. But the concept of the text as a 'material object', and the value of 'materialism' as a relevant theoretical category in modern bibliography, derive at least indirectly from Marxism. Margreta de Grazia's 1988 article 'The essential Shakespeare and the material book' provided a theoretical critique of New Bibliography on the grounds that its claim to a 'materialist' methodology was in reality an illusion[1]. For all their preoccupation with the book as a physical object, with the 'material' processes of book-production, with the specific mechanisms and labour-processes by means of which books were produced, published and circulated, the New Bibliographers were ultimately dedicated to the thoroughly idealist aim of reconstructing, by inference from the evidence of surviving printed texts, the form and contents of Shakespeare's lost manuscripts. Modern bibliography has certainly found it convenient, in reviewing its antecedents, to invoke the name of Marx.

The theoretical problems addressed by de Grazia could already be detected within the critical vocabulary of New Bibliography itself. When W.W. Greg used the term 'material' to describe the method pioneered by New Bibliography, his 'materialism' seemed to rest on the philosophical certainties of nineteenth-century positivism. But this approach sat uneasily within a discipline that was after all a branch of literary criticism. When Greg defined his method in terms of 'the material processes of book-production'[2], these were presented as unproblematical categories, the appropriate tools of Housman's bibliographical common sense. Yet they were posited on a manifestly inappropriate mind/body dualism, in which theatres, bookshops and printing houses exist 'materially' on a separate plane, distinct from 'aesthetic and philosophical speculations'. This paradox is partly an effect of a scientistic rhetoric, by means of which New Bibliography claimed for itself the status of a science, rooted in empiricist particulars and rigidly bound by the exigencies of physical evidence. Both in respect of method (here the procedures by which texts are analysed and interpreted) and discourse (critical strategies of presentation and argument), New Bibliography sought a quasi-scientific status capable of dismissing criticism and theory as mere 'aesthetic and philosophical speculation', self-evidently inferior to the rigours of a scientific textual practice; while simultaneously retaining an awareness that critical judgement inevitably plays a very large part in the investigation of literary texts.

This positivistic materialism (shadowed by its binary opposite, subjectivity) was shared by other key figures in New Bibliography. Both Fredson Bowers and R.B. McKerrow operated with similar distinctions between 'objective' fact and 'subjective' judgement, between the 'textual object' and the 'taste and learning' of the editor. Bowers wrote:

Indeed, the heart of the method consists in supplying a *mechanical explanation* for all phenomena *mechanically produced* by the printing process whenever such an explanation can be arrived at on the *recoverable evidence*. On occasion such bibliographical evidence limits the number of possibilities open to the finishing touches of *critical explanation*, which must necessarily refer back to *values*, or *opinions*, as the basis for *judgement* (3, my italics).

Just as a 'mechanical explanation' of the process of 'mechanical production' is bound by 'evidence', so the iron discipline of scientific method circumscribes the influence of 'values' and 'opinions'. 'Judgement' should be firmly based on such robust 'evidence' rather than on the undisciplined subjectivity of 'values' or 'opinions'.

None the less, this positivist confidence in the reality of the object under scrutiny co-exists in New Bibliography with a pessimistic conviction that the available evidence consisted of a mere simulacrum, a copy of something infinitely more authentic, a corrupt imitation of a lost ideal form. This is really the case (see below for Gary Taylor's endorsement of this argument): there was a manuscript and there are printed texts that somehow relate to it. But when the focus of desire is so strongly on the lost original rather than on the surviving documents, the mechanistic language of materialism is likely to enter into conflict with its binary opposite, Platonic idealism. 'Reality' did not after all reside in the physical object we can know and explain by reference to mechanical laws, but in the lost manuscript, the unknown from which the known, the surviving physical object, derives. New Bibliographical method thus amounted in the end to this quest for the lost ideal, its ultimate aim being to 'strip the veil of print from a text' to reveal the characteristics of the underlying manuscript (Bowers, 'Textual Criticism', p. 869). The primary purpose of 'The essential Shakespeare and the material book' could be defined as that of exposing New Bibliography's idealism, and revealing within it an 'anti-materialist … strain in the study of the book as material object' (de Grazia, 'Essential Shakespeare', p. 71).

৯৫

A later essay that Margreta de Grazia published jointly with Peter Stallybrass, 'The materiality of the Shakespearean text' takes the debate several stages further[4]. Beginning with a recapitulation of the argument advanced in 'The essential Shakespeare and the material book', the essay goes on to elaborate the characteristic features of early printed texts, and provides a stronger indication of their attractiveness to modern theory. Here the older bibliographic 'materialism' of the New Bibliographers is synthesised with a new cultural 'materialism' to identify a transaction in which the physical materiality of the historical text is conceived as both resistance and opportunity, identity and relationship, text and context. In early modern texts

> … the features that modernisation and emendation smooth away *remain stubbornly* in place to *block* the illusion of transparency – the impression that there is some ideal 'original' behind the text.
>
> These features are precisely the focus of this essay: old typefaces and spellings, irregular line and scene divisions, title pages and other paratextual matters, and textual cruxes. Discarded or transformed beyond recognition in standard modern editions, they *remain obstinately* on the pages of the early texts, insisting upon *being looked at, not seen through*. Their *refusal to yield* to modern norms bears witness to the *specific history* of the texts they make up (de Grazia and Stallybrass, 'Materiality', pp. 257, my italics).

'Materiality' is both a matter of what the New Bibliographers called 'recoverable evidence' – in particular those physical objects, books and manuscripts, that were circulated through Elizabethan and Jacobean culture and that have survived for modern observation – and of the way such evidence has interacted with 'values' and 'opinions', factors inseparable from the reading of early modern (or indeed any) literary texts. Texts are both produced – with historical specificity, at an originating moment of production – and reproduced – iterably in an infinite number of cultural situations unforeseen by the witnesses of that originating moment. But there is a strong element of historical 'originality' that confronts the modern reader as a matter of resistance ('refusal to yield'): a physical identity of the text that speaks of historical difference, and resists contemporary appropriation. The emphasis here is on the obstinacy of the early modern text's bibliographic codes, physical features that 'remain in place' and are therefore not freely available for deconstructionist interpretation. Printed signs that 'block' the modern reader's inquiries and 'remain obstinately on the page' are by definition not open to reconfiguration at the observer's behest or the inquirer's whim. If historically generated and recorded signs, despite all our sophisticated strategies of reading and reconstruction, remain on the page, to be 'looked at, rather than seen through', then they not only constitute evidence of historical otherness; they also testify to the vital possibility of a cultural or textual identity that cannot be commandeered, a self that cannot be assimilated to the other[5].

This approach could be described as a 'dialectical' materialism, one that acknowledges both past and present, and facilitates transactions between an historic evidence and a modern agenda. But it is also inevitable that such a Marxist-derived, dialectical approach should find itself reviewing the nature of 'matter', and shifting from a mechanical materialism to a conception of the text as no longer an identifiable physical object with its own characteristic structure, but rather an element in a more general process of cultural production:

> We need, in other words, to rethink Shakespeare in relation to our new knowledge of collaborative writing, collaborative printing and the historical contingencies of textual production…if there is any single object between us and such a project, it is the sense that

the value of Shakespeare lies elsewhere, in the inner regions of the text rather than in the practices recorded on its surfaces, in what Pierre Macherey has termed the *'postulate of depth'*... But if we reject depth as the object of analysis, we will at the same time have to transform our notion of surface ... Perhaps a more helpful way of conceptualising the text is to be found outside metaphysics, in the materials of the physical book itself: in *paper*... paper retains the traces of a wide range of labor practices and metamorphoses ... The Shakespearean text is thus, like any Renaissance book, a provisional state in the circulation of matter (de Grazia and Stallybrass, 'Materiality', pp. 278-9).

Thus the 'specific history' of an early modern text, that which is deemed tenable by a materialist bibliography, is subsumed into a *general* history of early modern cultural process. As the passages previously quoted indicate, de Grazia and Stallybrass first offer a 'materialist bibliography' focused on the visual surface of an early printed text as accurately eloquent of its physical character. On this basis they seek to *read* it, rather than read *through* it. Here, however, they seem to reject this position in favour of a post-structuralist emphasis on textual transparency. The textual surface which first 'obstinately block[ed]' and limited the param-eters of interpretation suddenly becomes an open window on to the industrial and commercial processes of the early modern printing trade. Visual signs that first speak of identity, refusing to yield to appropriation, now point only outwards towards context and relationship, towards the 'diversity of labors' that constituted the productive process. The text still has a 'depth' to be plumbed by critical interpretation. But what the critic expects to find in those depths is not the plenitude of authorial presence, but the ambient and underpinning social infrastructure of which the text is a particular element.

۶

De Grazia and Stallybrass label their approach, with some justification, as part of a broader school of 'New Textualism'. But the roots of this version of materialism, and the theoretical difficulties it entails, lie in classical Marxism, where we find close correspondences with their analytical method. There can be little doubt that Marxism, albeit often in an obscured and attenuated form, is a major intellectual component of all modern cultural theory. As Derrida provocatively suggests, 'we are all heirs of Marx'[6]. And by referring back to Marx we can find a philosophical language capable of differentiating between the kind of 'mechanical materialism' employed by New Bibliography, and a 'dialectical materialism' more closely based on Marx's own discussions of the commodity in its relation to value, exchange and labour.

Marx's analysis of the commodity in *Das Kapital* proposes that an object possesses use-value (utility to others) only in so far as it contains the product of human labour. Uncultivated land, for example, can bear a price but has no use-value without the application to it of human labour. When objects as use-values are exchanged, however, they take on the character of commodities and appear to derive their value from that act of exchange rather than from the process of production. Utility thus seems to become a quality of the object, reflected in its price and exchange-value, rather than the result of a productive process:

> A commodity is therefore a mysterious thing, simply because in it the social character of men's labour appears to them as an objective character stamped upon the product of that labour; because the relation of the producers to the sum total of their own labour is presented to them as a social relation, existing not between themselves, but between the products of their labour. This is the reason why the products of labour become commodities, social

things whose qualities are at the same time perceptible and imperceptible by the senses[7].

The real transaction taking place in the exchange of commodities is a social relation between producers and consumers. Yet it is in the nature of the commodity to mystify that relation, and to hypostatise the commodity itself as an autonomous object:

> It is a definite social relation between men that assumes in their eyes the fantastic form of a relation between things. In order, therefore, to find an analogy, we must have recourse to the mist-enveloped regions of the religious world. In that world the productions of the human brain appear as independent beings endowed with life, and entering into relation both with one another and the human race. So it is in the world of commodities with the product of men's hands. This I call the Fetishism which attaches itself to the products of labour as soon as they are produced as commodities, and which is therefore inseparable from the production of commodities (Marx, *Kapital*, p. 51).

Marx's revolutionising of classical economics consisted largely of this redefinition of the commodity in terms not of intrinsic utility and value, but of the social and economic relations involved in its production and exchange. Marx thus shifted the focus of economic analysis from the mysterious, apparently autonomous object (the commodity) to the means of production (industry and labour), the relations of production (property and class) and the system of exchange (the market). Once these relations are properly understood, the fetishism of the commodity can become known, and all mystery should evaporate. This process of demystification is a precondition for the conquest of ideology, the overcoming of alienation and the return of human labour to humankind.

The close correspondence between this analytical model and that employed by de Grazia and Stallybrass should be clear. The theoretical method advocated is one in which the text is stripped of its mystery and spurious autonomy, and re-positioned as an element in a material process of production and circulation. The text may appear to possess, in its own right and as immanent qualities, depth, value and meaning. Traditional interpretative methods confront the text as autonomous, single and individuated, the direct utterance of authorial genius. An application of Marxist economic analysis reveals that this apparent autonomy arises from the character of that text as an isolable commodity, the printed book produced for sale on the commercial market. Where traditional bibliography would seek, by relating the text vertically to its authorial provenance, to invest it with the aura and ambience of mystery, materialist bibliography follows Marx (and Marxist-influenced post-structuralism), in relating the text horizontally to the historical conditions of its production.

This theoretical strategy would then appear to be an accurate 'cultural materialist' application of Marx's economic theory. But it is important to recall that the object forming the commodity does not, in Marx, simply disappear into an undifferentiated process of production. It still exists, identified by the possession both of material objectivity (an irreducible physical being that distinguishes it from other contingent or comparable objects); and even more significantly, it possesses 'use-value', a specific utility or range of capabilities conferred upon it by the economic and cultural apparatus within which it functions. The fact that a text is also part of a process of production and circulation does not eliminate that text's specific identity or its utility. The text that was printed, sold and preserved had a different physical identity and a different relationship from the general process of production, unlike those other textual forms that we have been accustomed, by the theory and practice of modern editing, to identify as analogous elements within a larger whole, as if all these micro-texts lay enfolded within the macro-text of the eclectic edition: the 'prompt-book', or the manuscript, or the script revised for a particular performance. This 'identity' of the text arises not from the ascription of authorial presence, or of an immanent 'depth' of meaning and value, but precisely from the text's original character as a commodity, with an exchange-value more manifestly marked than its use-value. Hence the particular historical significance of an early printed text consists in its individuation, its self-differentiation from the process of production and exchange of which it was a part. The theatrical performance sold to its spectators exhausts itself in the simultaneous moment of production and consumption: its physical form is concrete, immediate and transitory; its use-value and exchange-value are identical. What you see is what you get. The manuscript of an early modern play, despite the value it has accrued for modern scholarship and criticism, in its originating moment of production was linked more closely with the evanescence of theatrical performance than with the relative fixity and permanence of print. If it failed to achieve exchange value in print, and was exhausted by performance, the text becomes worthless except as paper. Theatrical manuscripts would often be converted to printer's waste and recycled as a book binding, their use-value and exchange-value parting company. Their surface and content may have been copied into print form but their material substance was reduced to raw material, with an attendant loss of textuality, pulp fiction.

These problems were focused with unusual clarity by the appearance, in a sale of literary material at Sotheby's in July 1992, of a leaf of 'manuscript' described in the auctioneer's catalogue as a 'fragment of a contemporary manuscript of an unrecorded Elizabethan or Jacobean play containing a scene very similar to one in Shakespeare's *Henry IV, Part One*.' The fragment corresponded to the scene known in modern editions as 2.1 of *1 Henry IV*. The verbal echoes and parallel action certainly make it as convincing an analogue as many other similar identifications. Sotheby's suggested that the unknown play from which the fragment derived might be a source or an adaptation – 'setting aside the tantalising

but tenable proposition that Shakespeare might have recycled one
of his own scenes himself'; and the catalogue prudently avoided
direct attribution of authorship by enclosing the bardic name in
cautious parentheses. Nevertheless, an implicit claim was made
for an 'originality' that takes us back beyond the corruptions of
print and publication to a pristine authenticity. Certainly the
expected price – £10-12,000 – seemed index-linked to a Shakespearean connection rather than to the work of some anonymous
Elizabethan hack dramatist[8].

The value placed upon such 'primary source' material by
modern scholarship (and reflected in the expected price of the
fragment at auction) contrasts starkly with the low estimate in
which such a manuscript was held within the historical conditions governing cultural production in the early modern period.
The fragment was found in the binding of a Geneva edition of
Homer's *Odyssey*, printed in 1586 and bound at Oxford around
1600. Evidently the whole play from which it derived was used by
printers as binder's waste – contemporary drama functioning as
scrap paper used to facilitate the publication of an ancient literary classic. Thus the manuscript could disappear as easily as the
performance into the undifferentiated continuum of productive
practices, and become lost to history. In some analogous way the
manuscripts of Shakespeare's plays also disappeared, and we
know them only from the books that were already copies of
something already lost.

De Grazia and Stallybrass are drawn towards two reciprocally
antagonistic propositions. First, we have a conception of the early
printed text as an 'original', a 'material book' constituting specific
'historical evidence'. Second, there is the post-structuralist view
that the early printed text was an undifferentiated element in a
process of production and exchange, plastic and iterable, its

material existence as vulnerable to discarding as the paper that went into the Geneva Homer. In one problematic a text is specific, individual, historic, declaring an irreducible individual identity. In the other a text is overdetermined, undifferentiated, unfixed, and eloquent only of the historical process of which it was a part. De Grazia and Stallybrass attempt in their essay to link a 'historical materialist' confidence in the reality of matter with a 'dialectical materialist' acknowledgement of the social and economic structures within which matter is both shaped and defined. But the more truly dialectical their approach, the less secure is their grasp of 'materiality'.

Post-structuralist historicism naturally conceives of a Shakespeare text as a 'signpost' pointing towards something greater and more complete than itself. For New Bibliography that 'other' was the authorial manuscript or the author's intentions. For post-structuralist 'New Textualism' it is the continuum of language, the process of history, or the system of cultural production. In each case we are to find the meaning and value of a text lying outside and beyond it, in some realm of inner depth or some outlying context, rather than materially inscribed onto its physical surface.

De Grazia and Stallybrass frequently reveal an implicit conviction that a 'text' is always larger than any individual textualisation. 'How many variants between texts of a given play', they ask, 'warrant the reproduction of the play in multiple forms?' (de Grazia and Stallybrass, 'Materiality', p. 26). Here the primary object is not an individual text but a 'play' that contains several component elements, among which may be a number of printed texts. Or again, 'The process [photography] that appears best suited for duplicating the material text ends up reproducing only one of its multiple forms' (de Grazia and Stallybrass, 'Materiality', pp. 261). Here the 'material text' possesses a transcendent unity greater than the printed texts that represent its various 'multiple forms'. As we have seen in the previous chapter, this comes as close to G. Thomas Tanselle's subordination of 'text' to 'work' as it does to Roland Barthes's inverted deployment of the same terms. In both cases that which is unique, concrete, particular, historically contingent, is perceived as part of a larger totality which is plural, general, implicit and intangible. Ultimately in this post-structuralist 'materialism', the printed text becomes a glass through which the great process of historical and cultural production and circulation can be perceived.

Discussing these same Marxist texts, Derrida shows how they paradoxically point beyond any simple conception of 'materiality'. The commodity manifests a displaced and distorted sense of identity. It appears to demarcate solidity and stability, an isolable individuality that invites secure possession. In fact, this impression is the misleading image the commodity shows in its own distorting reflection:

> There is a mirror, and the commodity form is also this mirror, but since all of a sudden it no longer plays its role, since it does not reflect back the expected image, those who are looking for themselves can no longer find themselves in it. Men no longer recognise in it the social character of their own labour. It is as if they were becoming ghosts in their turn ... The 'mysteriousness' of the commodity form as presumed reflection of the social form is the incredible manner in which this mirror sends back the image ... such an 'image' objectivises by naturalising. This is its truth, it shows by hiding ... (Derrida, *Spectres*, p. 156).

The commodity in question here is the apparently single, unmediated early modern text. What this text 'hides' by presenting that apparently solid identity is the network of relations within which it has always been involved. Thus Derrida shows that in positing for the commodity an unmediated 'use-value', Marx was guilty of the very fetishism he detected in the system of exchange, guilty of granting 'an origin to the ghostly moment'. Before exchange, Marx seems to say, use-value

... was intact. It was what it was, use-value, identical to itself. The phantasmagoria, like capital, would begin with exchange-value and the commodity-form. It was only then that the ghost 'comes on stage'. Before this, according to Marx, it was not there ... But whence comes this certainty concerning the previous phase, that of this supposed use-value, precisely, a use-value purified of everything that makes for exchange-value and the commodity-form? What secures this distinction for us? It is not a matter here of negating a use-value or the necessity of referring to it. But of doubting its strict purity (Derrida, *Spectres*, pp. 159-60).

In reality the commodity displays this spectrality before it encounters the relationship of exchange: ghostliness and immateriality are potentialities of its being, endemic to its very existence. From its indeterminable origin it is 'promised'

... to iterability, to exchange, to ... substitution, exchangeability ... the loss of singularity (Derrida, *Spectres*, pp. 160-1).

Considered as a commodity, the book that survives is no less ghostly, deferred, displaced, absent from itself, than the lost manuscript on which it was based.

In this way both New Bibliography, interested in textual surface but committed to spiritual depth, and post-structuralist 'New Textualism', unable to focus on textual surface as anything other than a transparent window on to the underlying depths of history, encounter one another finally as strange but compatible bedfellows. Both ultimately participate in that deflection of attention – from material text to textual material – earlier identified by Margreta de Grazia: 'When meaning and value are posited outside or beyond the text, its physical properties, even in their most ready form – the precise letters and words on a page – command little attention' (de Grazia, 'Essential', p. 70). But she herself has shown that meaning must always be sought 'outside' the text. In New Bibliography the orphaned text cries for its lost father, the manuscript. But equally in post-structuralist 'New Textualism' the text, facing dissolution in the acid solutions of history and culture, hungers to be reunited with the transcendent completeness of the unity, the 'play' or 'work', from which it has fallen, the historical process from which it has been abstracted. In both cases the historically contingent text gravitates towards something 'spectral', in Derrida's terms, something absent from itself, something 'ghostly'.

მ

A new textual theory must produce new kinds of editorial practice. Margreta de Grazia and Peter Stallybrass illustrate 'New Textualism' in practice by reference to two editorial enterprises: the Oxford Shakespeare (1986) and Michael Warren's *The Complete 'King Lear' 1608–23* (1989). The former printed two separate texts of *King Lear* (1608 Quarto and 1623 First Folio); the latter published no fewer than four separate texts under that same title, two Quarto texts (Q1 and Q2), and the 1623 Folio, in a loose-leaf format, together with a bound parallel text of F1 and Q1[9]. Such editions are deemed to exemplify a 'textual revolution', since they substitute for the traditional conflated or single control-text edition a *multiplicity* of texts.

> For over two hundred years, *King Lear* was one text; in 1986, with the Oxford Shakespeare, it became two; in 1989, with *The Complete 'King Lear' 1608–1623*, it became four (at least). (de Grazia and Stallybrass, 'Materiality', p. 255).

Progress is no longer measured retrospectively, as it was in the editorial culture initiated by the eighteenth-century scholars, and reconfirmed by New Bibliography, as a slow and gradual approximation to the *authorial* original; but prospectively, by the degree to which the modern edition can be seen splitting into modern textual forms that correspond to the original individually printed texts. The Oxford Shakespeare is acknowledged for its 'breakthrough' decision to print two texts of *King Lear*, while Michael Warren's unbinding of *King Lear* into two discrete Quarto and one Folio text is welcomed as a fuller celebration of textual multiplicity. Where facsimile editions inevitably 'confer a sanctity upon the particulars of the duplicated text, hypostatising forms that were quite fluidly variable at their publication',

> Michael Warren's *The Complete* King Lear *1608-1623* designedly resists this arrest by opening up the textual proliferation that was endemic to early modern printing practices (de Grazia and Stallybrass, 'Materiality', p. 261).

In the normal processes of early modern publication such texts were altered in the course of printing and before being finally bound; hence any modern print edition, whether conflated, copytext or facsimile, must inevitably reify as standard what in fact are particular features only of certain texts. But not only does Warren's edition secure greater historical accuracy in representing the documentary record: it also opens the texts up more readily to modern currents of critical theory and method. *The Complete 'King Lear' 1608-1623* is virtually a kit that would enable the modern post-structuralist or deconstructionist reader freely to manipulate the fragments of the various texts entitled *King Lear* to form any number of differential versions. Thus the resolution of textuality into distinct original constituents facilitates a critical dispersal of all textual elements – books, pages, lines, words – into raw textual material, open to contemporary 'strong reading', appropriation, de- and re-construction.

On the other hand, as de Grazia and Stallybrass admit, this delivery of a deconstructable text to free interpretation may well be an unforeseen consequence of these particular editorial experiments. Both the Oxford Shakespeare and the work of Michael Warren are, in fact, attached to a quite different theoretical position, one indeed that was given serious consideration even by the New Bibliographers themselves: 'revision theory', the view that some variant texts may represent authorial revision and may reflect changing authorial intentions.

৵

Revision theory accepts textual multiplicity, only to reconcile it with the integrity of the author. Shakespeare may not have written only one *King Lear*. He may have written two, and one is a revision of the other. The texts are different, as two children of different ages and the same parentage may differ: but both issue from the same parental source. For the proponents of the New Bibliography the answer to the problem of the dispersal of a work over several different incarnations was to reduce this multiplicity to uniformity, by privileging one incarnation and subordinating the other to it. From the late 1970s onwards the hegemony of this approach was systematically challenged by the proponents of revisionism, who proposed the separating out of individual textualisations, suggesting that such variations (or, at least some of them) may reflect distinct versions of a given text.

Although the revisionists have laid great emphasis on textual multiplicity, the source of this multiplicity has been seen as essentially singular: though *King Lear* may have two bodies, there is only one Shakespeare, the originator of both individual texts. But the coherence of that authorial construction is in practice guaranteed more by cultural and institutional than by bibliographical conditions. If the differentiation of texts into multiplicity occurs within a cultural project already framed by the 'author-function', Shakespeare, then any rediscovered polyvocality will quickly be assimilated to an authorial monotone. As previously noted, the 'document-based' Oxford Shakespeare operates on a convergence of theatrical influence and textual plurality that points well beyond the constricting problematic of the institutional context – the 'Oxford Shakespeare' – within which it was developed. Ideological commitment to that totalising authorial project entails a deprioritising of the texts as we find them in history: discrete, mutually independent, overdetermined by particular conditions of cultural production. Such a recognition of textual plurality should point towards a deconstruction of the mainstream editorial tradition, and an archaeological excavation of the 'real foundations' of that cultural edifice, the earliest printed texts themselves. But this will inevitably become suppressed within the determining framework of a primarily authorial construction. 'New Textualism' offers to return the texts to history and free them from the ideological constrictions of a canonical reproduction. But the impact is lost if the texts themselves are implicitly re-connected to the patriarchal source, silently re-inscribed within the ideological problematic of an authoritarian cultural apparatus. Revision theory, even in its new theatrically-inflected form of a directorial 'paratext' putatively supplied by Shakespeare, can still reconcile evidence of plurality between texts within the conceptual stability of an alternative author-function. Matthew Arnold's serenely detached master of a ready-perfected poetic speech, is replaced by Wells' and Taylor's restlessly-revising, theatrically-engaged perfectionist playwright[10].

The Oxford editors made it clear, by deriving their individual play-texts from single sources, by printing alternative texts of *King Lear*, and by confessing to some degree of regret that the project could not in this respect have been more ambitious, that they acknowledge a wider applicability for the general principle of textual plurality. But since that aspiration remains firmly located within the hypothesis of authorial revision, it points not towards liberation of texts from canonical colonisation and authorial sovereignty, but towards the juxtaposition of multiple texts re-inscribed into a relationship of parallelism and reciprocal interdependence. 'I should like to see,' says Stanley Wells, 'double editions of all other plays where there are significant differences between the early witnesses to the texts'[11]. Ideally, then, a reader or theatre worker should be offered not a multiplicity of *discrete* texts, but an opportunity to compare an early with a revised version, or an authorial draft with a theatrical adapted script. Texts in this model are related not horizontally and diachronically to historical conditions of production and contexts of cultural appropriation, but vertically and synchronically to one another, and to their 'onlie begetter'[12].

This problematic clearly acknowledges the influence of other determining factors, especially those involved in theatrical realisation: however, the final explanation of a text's mobility is located not in theatre or history or cultural context, but in the controlling mastery of authorial, or rather dramaturgical, intention. The *Textual Companion* to the Oxford Shakespeare defines the processes of canonisation in a biological metaphor which invokes the operations of nature rather than the constructions of artifice. A play, like a child, is the product of two parents, 'born of the fruitful union of a unique author and a unique society'. Careful to acknowledge the limits of authorial mastery, the editors none the less elaborate here a metaphorical fantasy which validates a rigid and exclusive conception of canon as an ideological totality:

> Like children, works of art acquire a being independent of those who conceived them. We may judge and interpret and enjoy a poem or person, without knowing the author or the father. But poems, like persons, come in families… In this sense a 'Complete Works' is the literary equivalent of a family reunion, the gathering of a clan of siblings…. In recognising the existence of such literary families, we need not accept any exaggerated theoretical estimate of the power of one parent – the 'author' – to impose successfully and consistently his or her intentions upon the children: we simply accept that each parent had some influence, often unconscious, commonly unpredictable, upon the maturing of each individual creation[13].

However prudently hedged about with qualifications, the metaphor remains questionable in its privileging of a particular sociological form of the family. Patrilinear, consanguinous, formed from the creative coupling of a clearly identified father ('Shakespeare') with an abstract female other ('society'), tightly sealed in its legal definition of membership, a particular ethnocentric conception of family structure is here hypostatised as universal. The metaphor operates to contain an appropriate interest in the diversity of offspring within a set of questionable editorial assumptions – all texts receive their signature of legitimacy from the authorial father; qualifications for membership, based on a community of blood, must be decided by an attestation of legitimate title; bastard offspring (such as 'Bad Quartos') are firmly placed outside the parameters of the family structure.

The textual scholar, who appears here in the guise of a family solicitor or real-estate lawyer, can prosecute his business of determining composition and inheritance, secure in the conviction that the canonical family is a formation of nature, not a construction of art. When Heminge and Condell, dedicating *Mr William Shakespeares Comedies, Histories, & Tragedies,* offered the plays to the patronage of the Earls of Pembroke and Montgomery – 'We have but collected them, and done an office to the dead, to procure his orphanes, Guardians' – they were invoking, in the same metaphor as the Oxford editors, a strikingly different, adoptive and non-biological, form of the family.

De Grazia and Stallybrass point out that the revisionists offer the possibility of textual multiplicity with one hand, only to snatch it away again with the other, as this multiplicity is referred back to the unifying figure of Shakespeare, the single authentic source of textual polyvocality:

> The recognition of multiple texts and variant passages is compromised by a theory of revision that ends up unifying and regulating what it had dispersed and loosened; all intertextual and

intratextual variants are claimed in the name of a revising Shakespeare (de Grazia and Stallybrass, 'Materiality', p. 279).

Once again, there is a stress here on the materiality of the text, the
conditions of its production and on the displacement of 'Shakespeare' as a unifying force, the sole guarantor of meaning and
coherence. But in the concluding paragraphs of their article,
where the authors offer a particular celebration of Warren's *Complete 'King Lear' 1608–1623*, this attachment to the concrete and
particular gives way to a larger preoccupation with the general
and symbolic:

> The collected facsimiles of Warren's *The Complete 'King Lear'*
> *1608–1623* open up a vastly wider range of textual possibility with-
> in the seventeenth century itself, both among different printings
> and among different forms of the same printing. Its three
> unbound *Lears* (Q1, Q2, and F1), each succeeded by either uncor-
> rected or corrected pages, allows, indeed coaxes, the reader to
> assemble any number and combination of pages (de Grazia and
> Stallybrass, 'Materiality', pp. 282–3).

The essay concludes with a strong affirmation of the creative possibilities open to a reader equipped with such apparently infinite
textual possibilities:

> Perhaps we should imagine ourselves critically positioned in this
> great bibliographical divide … unstitched like Warren's loose
> pages – in the space of historical difference. It might take our
> minds off the solitary genius immanent in the text and removed
> from the means of mechanical and theatrical reproduction. This
> genius is, after all, an impoverished, ghostly thing compared to the
> complex social practices that shaped, and still shape, the
> absorbent surface of the Shakespearean text. Perhaps it is these
> practices that should be the objects not only of our labors but also
> of our desires (de Grazia and Stallybrass, 'Materiality', p. 283).

Warren's decision to print these texts in a loose-leaf format is
taken as indicative of a metaphorical unbinding of the text, an

opening up of the text to the free play of assemblage or disassemblage, subverting (in Foucault's terms) the tendency of the authorial principle to impede the 'free circulation, decomposition, and recomposition of fiction'[14]. The loose-leaf format encourages the reader to assemble any number and combination of pages, to make and remake his or her own *Lear*(s). It should be noted that this assessment fails to acknowledge the real difficulties entailed in constructing unilateral textualisations from printed pages, which by virtue of their material technology explicitly resist such manipulation, holding their words, sentences and paragraphs firmly in linear sequence – difficulties that are to some degree resolvable via technological solutions such as hypertext. Nonetheless, there can be little doubt that ultimately in their handling of this great textual debate, de Grazia and Stallybrass gravitate towards a 'creative', post-structuralist vision of a self-multiplying *Lear*, the infinitely variable states of which might serve as 'the objects not only of our labors but also of our desires'. 'Materiality', and the need to 'rethink Shakespeare in relation to our new knowledge of collaborative writing, collaborative printing and the historical contingencies of textual production' (de Grazia and Stallybrass, 'Materiality', p. 278) are linked to a post-structuralist delight in the unbound, the unstitched, the sign in free and unanchored infinite play. The authors leave their own reader faced with a programme advocating both a scholarly engagement with the materiality and material conditions, 'the historical contingencies of textual production', and with an image of the critic realising his or her desire in the free play of an indeterminate and decidedly *im*material text.

Post-structuralist 'New Textualism' may set out to gather the text as a material object into temporary focus but will inevitably tend to be driven by its theoretical commitment to a deconstructive logic (as in the formulations of Orgel and Goldberg), to disperse the text into immaterial process. The true logic of a post-structuralist bibliography points in fact not towards the individual textualisation recognised as material form, but towards an eclectic embracing of the relationships between texts (whether in the comparative form of a parallel-text edition, or in the loose-leaf carnival of Warren's boxed *King Lears*), and of the interpretation of texts with one another. Here again, there is then no hindrance to acceptance of the traditional conflated edition as a valid space of textual free play. Margreta de Grazia and Peter Stallybrass, like Kastan and Mowatt, go some distance in this direction:

> If, as we have argued, there is no 'original', the later editions cannot be accused of a falling off and away, for there is no fixed point from which such falling could be measured.... There is no intrinsic reason *not* to have a modernized, translated, rewritten 'Shakespeare'. In an important sense, that is all we *can* have, because the material signs of early modern quartos and folios will themselves necessarily mean differently when read within new systems of textual production (de Grazia and Stallybrass, 'Materiality', p. 279).

The post-structuralist truism that there is no possibility of recovering original meaning (because the sign derives its signifying capability entirely from the structural context of its contemporary reading) is here expanded to a concession that the material signs themselves might just as well be manipulated, translated, modernised, since the end result of either process – the modern reading or the modern manipulation of the ancient text – will in any case be a contemporary appropriation. If the history of readings of the text is the history of the text, then why prefer an earlier form to a modern permutation? Employing very similar deconstructionist terms and concepts in the course of a critique of the Oxford Shakespeare, Brian Parker has inferred from the same theoretical premises a preference for the traditional conflated edition which, by providing the reader with a geological formation of overlapping textual variants, offers a complete packaged experience of textual multiplicity: 'it seems to me that a

conflated edition, that makes no claims to authority and questions its own readings in adjacent footnotes, can come much
closer to the exhilaration of postmodernist "bricolage"[15]. For
post-structuralist 'New Textualism' there is no essential difference between one kind of textualisation and another. The
theatrical performance, based on a provisional script; the printed pages of an early modern text, in production incessantly
modified by the practice of 'continuous correction'; the conflated modern edition; the parallel-text version; the 'Shakespeare
Unbound' of *The Complete 'King Lear' 1608-1623* ... each enacts
its own particular and variant contribution to the metanarrative
of cultural production.

I will close this section with a striking passage from Gary Taylor's
introduction to the Oxford *Textual Companion*, in which he
draws for illustration on the work of a modern dramatist. Here
we see the bibliographer literally entangling his own thoughts
with the substance of a dramatic medium and ultimately being
drawn rather deeper than anticipated into the activity of another's imagination.

> In a famous passage in Harold Pinter's *The Homecoming*, Lenny
> the pimp memorably and at length describes his encounter with a
> woman who was 'falling apart with the pox'. At the end of his
> story, the listener asks, 'How did you know she was diseased?'
> Lenny answers, 'I decided she was.' An editor, in emending,
> decides that a text is diseased; such decisions may be mistaken.
> But we know that every early printed edition of Shakespeare's
> plays is more or less diseased; every compositor and every scribe
> commits errors. Corruption somewhere is certain; where, is
> uncertain. We also know that Shakespeare's texts were composed
> on paper by an author before they were composed in type by a
> compositor. The lost manuscripts of Shakespeare's work are not
> the fiction of an idealist critic, but particular material objects

which happen at a particular time to have existed, and at another particular time to have been lost, or to have ceased to exist.

Emendation does not seek to construct an ideal text, but rather to restore certain features of a lost material object (that manuscript) by correcting certain apparent deficiencies in a second material object (this printed text) which purports to be a copy of the first (Gary Taylor, 'Introduction' to *Textual Companion*, p. 6).

Some of the most interesting insights into textual theory are to be detected, as we have seen, in the language used by bibliographers and editors when explaining their positions. In this chapter I have unpicked the industrial and scientific language used by the New Bibliographers; Gary Taylor's parable of the collected works as a family reunion; and the terms in which de Grazia and Stallybrass deploy a language of solidity and resistance, which ultimately attenuates into a decidedly immaterial vision of cultural process, perceived from an invisible 'space of historical difference'.

Here Taylor refines New Bibliography by extending the status of 'materiality' from a feature of the surviving printed documentation to a characteristic of the missing manuscript. It is reasonable to claim that some kind of manuscript copy must have preceded the printed text, and that such manuscript copy must have once existed as a 'material' object. Indeed, it is not absolutely beyond the realms of possibility that such lost materials could re-surface, as did the fragment in the binding of the *Odyssey*. But as many scholars have subsequently observed, that undeniably material object may not in any case have been the authorial manuscript. When editors construct a text by deduction, 'correcting' the printed texts to make them resemble what they seem in their error to have attempted to convey, they are certainly speculating on what might have been the characteristics of a certain material object. But what really existed as the immediate source of the printed copy may or may not have been *that particular type* of material object. 'Correction', however wisely and carefully done, of imputed corruption, may in fact lead back only to something that was already an altered copy and not back to Shakespeare's own inky fingers.

So there is a certain wilfulness in this editorial method which Taylor almost seems to celebrate via the example quoted from Harold Pinter's *The Homecoming*. In this analogy the text is imagined as a woman, irredeemably corrupt and diseased. Just as the pimp claims to be able to diagnose by sight the symptoms of venereal disease, so the editor guesses at corruptions within the body of the (here implicitly female) text. The appropriate editorial practice to adopt when confronted with such degeneracy is suggested by the subsequent drift of Lenny's speech, which Taylor does not quote:

> I clumped her one …and there she was up against this wall – well, just sliding down the wall, following the blow I'd given her… So I just gave her another belt in the nose and a couple of turns of the boot and sort of left it at that[16].

To pursue this analogy we would have to assume that what the female text lacks in purity, the male editor will beat into her. Although this could hardly be said to characterise the editorial practice of Stanley Wells and Gary Taylor (neither of whom personally bears very much resemblance to Pinter's Lenny!), what is offered here metaphorically, and therefore at the level of theory, is an intimidating object-lesson in how to handle a text.

It seems unwise to simply 'sort of [leave] it at that'. In the Pinter text this apparent soliloquy is one side of a dialogue between Lenny and Ruth, a woman of some mystery who appears to be his brother's wife. Lenny's statement is a characteristically perverse assertion of macho defiance in the face of a searching interrogation by Ruth, who is much more than a mere 'listener' in this exchange. The statement is a move in an elaborate 'status-game' between man and woman, each vying for discursive power over the other. Ruth's question is not an innocent request for information but a cutting riposte to Lenny's macho posturings, a sly demonstration that he had, by his own account, no means of knowing that the woman was 'falling apart with the pox'. Lenny's insistence on the incontrovertibility of his assertion is a kind of defensive wilfulness, an arrogant refusal to heed question or entertain doubt. It is certainly a strange basis on which to found a theory of editing. We may well find ourselves obliged here to take the woman's part, and to put the question again: 'How did you know she was diseased?'

The question goes to the heart of the editorial tradition. On what basis should we assume that 'corruption is everywhere', since the only possible measure of such corruption, the authorial manuscript, is not there to be consulted?[17]. The imputed 'materialism' of this editorial policy is precisely the same as that of New Bibliography, a materialist methodology devoted towards the idealist end of stripping the Platonic 'veil of print' from a text to reveal the immanent form of the underlying manuscript. The object of which we can have direct knowledge, the printed text, is judged to be corrupt by conjectural reference to the object of which we can by definition have no direct knowledge, the uncorrupted (but non-existent) manuscript. The procedure is self-contradictory, since the historical document is being compared with an 'original' that can be speculatively reconstructed only from the evidence of the historical document itself.

A.E. Housman acknowledged that this circular argument was indeed the basis of Lachmann's theory:

> This state of affairs is apparently, nay evidently, paradoxical. The MSS are the material upon which we base our rule, and then, when we have got our rule, we turn round upon the MSS, and say that the rule, based upon them, convicts them of error. We are thus working in a circle, that is a fact which there is no denying; but as Lachmann says, the task of the critic is just this, to tread that circle deftly and warily; and that is precisely what elevates the critic's business from mere mechanical labour[18].

This conviction that 'error', rather than potentially productive change, was endemic to textual transmission by copying is eloquently expressed in Stoppard's *The Invention of Love* by the character Benjamin Jowett, Master of Balliol, who describes the textual legacy of the classics as the result of 'corruption breeding corruption'[19]:

> ... certainty could only come from recovering the autograph ... anyone who has a secretary knows that what Catullus really wrote was already corrupt by the time it was copied twice, which was about the time of the first Roman invasion of Britain: and the earliest copy that has come down to *us* was written about 1,500 years after that. Think of all those secretaries! – corruption breeding corruption ...

Setting aside the relatively unproblematical category of manifest error, what both Housman and Taylor call 'corruption' is to some degree what modern bibliography terms 'social negotiations over the transmission and reception'[20] of texts. If this is corruption, then our obligation is to embrace it, as Flaubert's St Julien embraced the leper, in trust and in faith; since this is all, for the moment, we can hope to have[21].

The Scholar to his Text

(Catullus, Carmina, XLIII)

My compliments, madam. Yes, that's you,
With your huge snout, and your club foot,
And your eyes like piss-holes in snow;
And your stubby mitts, and your slobbering gob,
And your lolling tongue that no one, not even
The most enamoured and ardent admirer
Could ever possibly describe as even
Remotely resembling anything like
Elegant.

Yet, in these parts, they praise you as
Pretty! And liken my lovely
Lesbia to you!

Oh, what a stupid
Century! What ignorant, idiotic,
Tasteless times!

CHAPTER FOUR

Confluence

෧

IN THIS CHAPTER I wish to pursue for some distance the exhortation from Margreta de Grazia and Peter Stallybrass that we should focus on the historical contingencies of textual production. In the case of Shakespeare this implies, as an immediate imperative, the decomposition of conflated modern editions into the various discrete, and to some degree incommensurable, textualisations that were produced by those historical contingencies in the late sixteenth and early seventeenth centuries. A general recovery of such textualisations, as they existed before their colonisation by the modern edition, was at that point in time (the early 1990s) clearly a priority. Only when these documents had been at least partially recovered could we begin, as de Grazia and Stallybrass recommended, to look *at* rather than *through* them, to distinguish and discriminate each text's particular and historically contingent capability for the production of meaning.

The *Shakespearean Originals* series of individual texts, diplomatically edited by myself and Bryan Loughrey, was devised at exactly this time precisely to satisfy something of this demand[1]. The basic editorial principles of the series, though widely misunderstood, were very simple and straightforward. The series aimed to provide readily accessible texts both of plays traditionally attributed to Shakespeare, and of non-canonical plays associated with the Shakespeare corpus (such as the anonymous *The Taming of a Shrew*), in a format which differed on the one hand from that of the modern standard edition, and on the other from that of the photographic facsimile reproduction. We wanted to preserve from those 'originals' (i.e. the surviving printed texts of the plays as they were published in both quarto and folio volumes between the 1580s and 1623) certain structural features, certain theatrical characteristics proper to early modern play-texts, and as much as possible of their dramatic and poetic language. So we chose to retain the frequent inconsistency of Act and Scene divisions, and the complete absence of location directions and line numbering; the actual stage directions and speech-headings provided in the texts, as distinct from the frequently interpolated, amended and standardised apparatus to be found in many modern editions; and the original spelling, punctuation, marks of emphasis and actual lineation of verse. We also published the texts under the titles conferred on them when initially printed, since these are often more elaborate and informative than the generic titles established by the modern editorial tradition. '*King Lear*', for example, differs markedly in its implications as to the focus of the play from '*M. William Shakespeare HIS true Chronicle Historie of the life and death of King LEAR and his three daughters*'[2].

At the same time we wanted these new editions to be as freely accessible as the standard modern editions. We wanted them published cheaply in paperback so as to render the texts, with those structural, theatrical and linguistic features retained, easily and widely available for the purposes of teaching, performance and research. We therefore took the decision not to aim at facsimile status, but instead to convert the original printing into modern typography, and to remove orthographic features (such as long 's') which might present an obstacle to some less advanced readers.

These two objectives were to a degree in conflict, as was stated in the 'General Introduction':

> In some senses we have embarked upon a project of textual archaeology, and the logic of our method points towards facsimile editions ... [but] since we wish to challenge the hegemony of standard editions by circulating the texts within this series as widely as possible, we have aimed at 'diplomatic' rather than facsimile status[3].

It was made quite clear from the outset that these texts, though far less intrusively edited than most, were nonetheless offered as modern *editions* and not facsimiles. There was no attempt to reproduce original pages, or to imitate exactly the lineation of prose passages, or to retain catchwords, or to copy irregular running titles. The specimen facsimile pages provided at the end of each text were there specifically to show the reader how *different* these partially modernised texts were from the material 'originals'. Each diplomatically-edited text (which despite a degree of modernisation was still at the time much closer to its source than any other generally-available twentieth century edition), was deliberately framed within the parameters of a modern page, and within the format of a light, readable, usable and affordable paperback.

In addition to the objectives listed above, we also wanted to publish, as discrete editions, the variant textualisations which throughout a long editorial tradition had been consistently either merged with one another to produce a conflated hybrid edition, or formally segregated into 'good' and 'bad' texts. We were determined both to disentangle the texts merged by conflation (e.g. the 1604 and 1623 versions of *Hamlet,* or the 1608 and 1623 versions of *King Lear*); and to give the so-called 'Bad Quartos' an independent status and validity equal to that ascribed to other quarto and folio texts traditionally adjudged to be 'Good'. Our strategic emphasis here was signalled in the series title by use of the generic and descriptive 'Shakespearean', rather than the attributive and authorising 'by Shakespeare'. 'Shakespearean' was carefully employed as an alternative to, not a confirmation of, authorial assignation: the texts were offered as texts 'of or pertaining to Shakespeare' rather than as 'Shakespeare's' texts.

The title *Shakespearean Originals: First Editions* was intended to adumbrate these principles as clearly as possible. The series rejected the theoretical basis of most modern editing, New Bibliography's search for 'authority' in the authorial presence, and for 'authenticity' in the lost authorial manuscript. It recognised the early printed texts explicitly as 'editions', already when first published sufficiently removed from the 'author' to render that relationship problematical. And it acknowledged the unique value of the early quarto and folio texts as the concrete historical documents on which all modern reproductions must inevitably be founded. The main objectives of the series were thus: the recuperation of discrete textualisations, and their liberation from canonical authority; the introduction of historic textual variety to a wider audience of students and scholars; the acknowledgement of early printed texts as reliable historical documents, the only 'originals' that exist; the opening up of pedagogic and theatrical possibilities released by the provision of accessible and usable editions that retain in their foreground some at least of the linguistic and dramatic traces of the 'originals'; and the interrogation of modern editorial traditions and their ideological underpinnings.

The earliest printed texts (the various quartos and the 1623 Folio), the unique 'first editions' of Shakespeare, are after all the only 'originals' we are ever likely to have. However, their 'originality' lies not in any claim to direct authorial provenance but in a recognition that texts individually shaped by multiple cultural influences authentically constitute the true nature of

Shakespearean drama. As was made clear in the 'General Introduction' to the series:

> We therefore present within this series particular textualisations of plays which are not necessarily canonical or indeed even written by *William Shakespeare, Gent.,* in the traditional sense ... The editors of *Shakespearean Originals* reject the claim that it is possible to construct a rehabilitated text reflecting a form approximating Shakespeare's artistic vision. Instead we prefer to embrace the early printed texts as authentic material objects ... (Holderness and Loughrey, *Tragicall Historie*, pp. 8–9).

Where these principles and objectives were recognised and understood, the value and utility of the texts were correspondingly acknowledged by a broad selection of eminent critics, scholars and directors, who commended precisely those aspects of the series outlined above. The following endorsements were provided on request:

> Editions of Shakespeare from the eighteenth century on have been haunted by the spectre of what Shakespeare really wrote, and various tactics of discrimination between, or conflation of, quarto and folio materials have been the stock-in-trade of Shakespeare editions ever since. We can never know what Shakespeare wrote; the only originals we have are the various printings of the plays. *Shakespearean Originals* makes these more readily available to a wider audience than the usual scholarly printings of these texts allow. So doing, the series performs an invaluable service. (Jonathan Goldberg)

> By making early quarto versions of Shakespeare plays available in highly readable and affordable texts, the Harvester series is performing an important service for scholars, students and the general public – for anyone fascinated, rather than repelled, by the variability of early printed texts. (Leah Marcus)

Shakespearean Originals is a godsend in the classroom, and I wonder how I taught *The Shrew* or *Henry V* before they were available. Holderness and Loughrey's discreetly edited and user-friendly texts allow students to confront the silent editorial choices and conflations of texts which are the invisible ideological infrastructure upon which the institutionalised reception of 'the Bard' is built. The editors have carefully avoided substituting any dogma of their own for those we get in other versions of Shakespearean texts, which makes their sensibly-priced volumes a pleasure to recommend to students, and a joy to use. (Lisa Jardine)

These intriguing playtexts suggest a Shakespeare of the rehearsal room, rather than the bardic authority of modern times. Because of their early conventions of spelling and punctuation – very clearly presented in modern type – these texts offer a startlingly fresh reading experience, while allowing students insights into scholarly questions of textual transmission and historical context. (Alan Sinfield)

I find it monstrous that pedants for all these years have ignored what are the very first performance texts of Shakespeare's plays known to us. They give an extraordinary insight into the workings of theatre on the run, providing abundant proof, if any were needed, of the natural organic growth of a play. (Michael Bogdanov).

And published reviews of the series sounded similar notes of enthusiasm for the project[4]:

This new series is essential reading for all serious students of Shakespeare (Eric Sams).

A valuable new series ... succinctly outlines the way Elizabethan texts have been gradually transformed by their successive editors (Christine Dymkowski).

Clearly, the wish is to free readers, actors, directors, and all of us from accumulated editorial tradition, and return us instead to the plural and contested texts in which the plays of Shakespeare and his contemporaries were originally presented ... I believe firmly

> that there is a place in our pluralistic world for modern edited texts, especially where they work to undo the mistakes of past editors. But I also have no hesitation in urging that unedited originals be brought into play as a means of recovering a sense of the past as accurately as we can. (David Bevington).

In these comments it is possible to recognise *Shakespearean Originals* as a pioneering initiative pursuing directions the scholarly consensus has subsequently followed. But at the time such acknowledgement was by no means universal. On the contrary, *Shakespearean Originals* became the object of a substantial degree of misunderstanding, misrepresentation and hostility and was widely misconceived as an extension of the very editorial tradition it sought to undermine.

Many critics assumed that the series concerned only the so-called 'Bad Quartos' and was established to claim on their behalf the imprimatur of Shakespearean authorship. D.C. Greetham stated in *PMLA* that the texts were presented as containing 'evidence of direct authorial presence'. Janet Dillon, writing in *Shakespeare Quarterly,* argued that *The Tragicall Historie of Hamlet Prince of Denmarke* claimed the First Quarto as 'Shakespeare's real *Hamlet*'. Jonathan Sawday found in the series a 'touching belief in the authenticity of the early printed editions of Shakespeare's plays'. Lois Potter assumed that *Shakespearean Originals* was established to 'further the cause [i.e. the authorial claim] of the Bad Quartos'; and Rosalind King and Nigel Alexander considered that the series aimed to present 'bona fide Shakespeare versions'. This critical tendency began as early as the summer of 1992, when A.R. Braunmuller, in a seminar discussion at the International Shakespeare Association conference in Stratford, went out of his way to 'reject the series title and its claim to present "what Shakespeare originally wrote"'[5].

In some ways the reception of the series was conditioned by its innovative character and by a degree of what would now be called 'aggressive marketing' in its public profile. When the first

Shakespearean Originals editions (*The Tragicall Historie of Hamlet Prince of Denmarke,* and *A Pleasant Conceited Historie, Called the Taming of a Shrew*) appeared in 1992, some of their first critics paid more attention to advance publicity and to back-cover blurbs than to the editorial principles and critical apparatus of the texts themselves. The phrase targeted by Braunmuller, 'what Shakespeare originally wrote', appeared only in a promotional leaflet, circulated by the publisher in 1992, and had no foundation in the theoretical manifesto of the series as articulated in the General Introduction. King and Alexander based their inference about the series as an extended authorial canon on the publisher's back-cover blurb of *The Tragicall Historie of Hamlet Prince of Denmarke.* Lois Potter's remark seemed to be an all-too-common misconception of *Shakespearean Originals* as exclusively a series of Quarto, or even 'Bad Quarto', texts, a misunderstanding partly based on the phrase from that same back cover, 'the earliest known editions of Shakespeare's plays', and on the appearance of two so-called 'Bad Quartos' as the pilot volumes. Jonathan Sawday, true to the superficial methods of this tradition, also quoted from the back cover, challenging the 'publisher's commitment to raising "fundamental questions about the authenticity of these texts"' and the intention to promote a '"radical departure" from other editions of Shakespeare currently available'. Dillon's source for the phrase about 'Shakespeare's real *Hamlet*' is not the edition but 'the Harvester catalogue's description' of it (Dillon, 'Is There?', p. 74).

Some of the promotional material distributed by Harvester Wheatsheaf did indeed, it is true, render possible a range of misleading and inaccurate interpretations: that the series was concerned exclusively with re-editing the so-called 'Bad Quartos'; that we believed the earliest texts, including the 'Bad Quartos', to be closer to Shakespeare than later contemporary textualisations; and that we wished to confer some kind of authorial claim on such early texts. These possibilities for misconstruction were compounded by a feature on the front page of the *Times Higher Education Supplement* in June 1992, written as is customary by a *THES* journalist on the basis of the promotional material and on a telephone interview with me, which certainly, though unwittingly, gave a distinct impression that the series was privileging the 'Bad Quartos', the 'earliest known editions', as closer to Shakespeare: 'The new texts are part of a series deliberately based on the earliest known editions of Shakespeare's plays, versions often dismissed and ignored by Shakespearean scholars'[6]. Obviously the only texts that could be described as 'dismissed or ignored' by the editorial tradition would be the 'Bad Quartos'.

These misconstructions were, however, corrected in a letter from the General Editors of the series published in the *THES* the following week[7]:

> The governing principle of the series is not that the so-called 'Bad' Quartos are to be preferred to other, later texts: but that all the original printed texts of Shakespearean drama – whether 'good' Quarto, 'bad' Quarto or Folio – are to be preferred to modern editions. We have a particular interest in the 'Bad Quartos' because of their historical marginalisation, and the series is launched with a group of such texts. But our main concern is simply to put all these 'originals', good, bad and ugly, into circulation ... One of our main theoretical aims is precisely to break with the tradition – uniform throughout Shakespeare scholarship, not excluding 'revision' theories – of regarding these texts as variants of a single absent original – Shakespeare's lost manuscript, the bibliographer's equivalent of the intentionalist fallacy ... We are also determined not to draw the texts into the theoretical environment of a single authorial source ... We are emphatically not claiming the imprimatur of Shakespearean authorship for the bad Quartos or for any other dramatic text; but rather publishing the plays, in the light of modern critical theory, as in effect author-less – or more exactly, as overdetermined products of the collaborative cultural conditions of the Elizabethan theatre industry.

We were frankly surprised, given the manifest discrepancies

between the promotional material and publicity on the one hand, and our explicit editorial theory and policy on the other, that so much attention was paid to publicity materials; and even more surprised by the extent to which even the promotional material itself could be so systematically misread. Janet Dillon, for example, picked on the same point in her *Shakespeare Quarterly* discussion of *The Tragicall Historie of Hamlet Prince of Denmarke*, citing not the text or its introductory matter, but advertising copy: 'The title of the series makes a claim for authenticity, a claim central to the way the texts are advertised both on the covers of the books themselves and in the hype of the publisher's catalogue ... Clearly "authenticity", to borrow the quotation marks of the book's own blurb, is the point at issue' (Dillon, 'Is There?', pp. 74-75). 'Authenticity' obviously was a point at issue, which is why the quotation marks were there to be borrowed. The conviction that the series consists of a collection of quartos or even of 'Bad Quartos' outlived even the subsequent publication of both 'Good Quarto' and Folio texts (see the 1995 editions listed in Note 1). Jonathan Sawday, for example, carelessly listed the titles of the 1995 texts, which included Folio versions, as evidence that we sought to recover 'the pre-Folio world of the Shakespearean text' (Sawday, 'Beam me up', p. 24).

Editors clearly have to take responsibility for what is said in promotional material, even when what it says is not quite what they would have wanted to say. But there is surely something dubious about conflating editorial judgement and marketing hyperbole. Similarly, it ill befits one of the editors of a series such as *Shakespearean Originals*, which promotes ideas of multiple authorship and cultural overdetermination, to protest against the 'corruptions' introduced by printer and publishing house! On the other hand, it still seems reasonable to have expected commentators to pay more attention to matters of editorial principle, textual theory and critical debate than to promotional material.

It was striking to note how many times commentators objected not only to the claims apparently made in the publicity, but to the very act of promoting 'the much-hyped paperback series *Shakespearean Originals*' at all[8]: '[T]he texts are advertised' complains Janet Dillon, 'both on the covers of the books themselves and in the hype of the publisher's catalogue' (Dillon, 'Is there?', p. 75), as if Harvester were the first publisher to advertise its products. There may well have been some unspecified resistance to the pressure of a new product on what Jonathan Sawday called 'an already saturated market' (Sawday, 'Beam me up', p. 24). The suggestion of excessive or disproportionate publicity ('hype') is tenuous, if Harvester's promotional operation were to be compared with those of major academic publishing houses such as Routledge, Oxford, and Cambridge to which the series offered a puny measure of competition. Nonetheless the innocuous, if potentially misleading, leaflets of a relatively tiny series were widely seized on and condemned as boastful 'hype', when the massive promotional profiles of the *Oxford* or *Arden* Shakespeares seemed to be unquestioningly accepted as natural features of the publishing landscape.

If the limited promotional exercise mounted around the series aroused such hostility, presumably that was because it was judged to be making extravagant and unreasonable claims. Despite the errors of the promotional exercise, I would still affirm, even at this distance, that we were doing something 'original' in producing and circulating, in accessible and user-friendly format, texts that were neither standard modern editions nor facsimile reproductions; attempting to carve out a new space in the editorial and publishing tradition, a 'niche' subsequently identified by David Bevington as 'a genuine and useful space between fully annotated editions on the one hand, and photographic reproductions on the other' (Bevington in *Shakespeare*

Quarterly). At the time we believed this aspiration, one that has since been pursued by many other publishers (and by the extensive provision of online electronic texts on the Internet) to be remarkably uncontentious. No one, we thought, however committed to the necessity for 'improving' original texts, and however passionately convinced of the 'badness' of the 'Bad Quartos', could possibly object to the aim of rendering such representations accessible, in the form of cheap and readily available paperback editions, to the student, the teacher and the general reader.

Looking back from the standpoint of the present, it is much clearer now that the controversy of 1992-4 was generated more by the principles of the series than by imputed editorial incompetence (though that allegation was certainly made). Take for instance Brian Vickers' review in the *Times Literary Supplement* for December 1993. Here Vickers was not simply saying, as many assumed, that the series was badly edited (an assumption easily derived from phrases such as 'sloppy editing') but rather that it was wrongly conceived. In his view such texts should not have been published at all: 'An inexpensive paperback series of early Quartos would indeed be useful, but this is not it … It all needs doing again'[9]. Vickers further suggested that such texts were already sufficiently in circulation, in perfectly adequate and acceptable facsimile and edited forms. But although facsimile and edited texts did exist, as the 'Textual Histories' in the individual editions acknowledge, they were not then as generally available as *Shakespearean Originals* and as other parallel editions are today. Subsequently Janet Dillon confirmed the justice of our initial aspiration: 'Arguably, such access could be said to be available through existing facsimiles; but the price and format of these new editions does increase their availability' (Dillon, 'Is there?' p. 75n.)

The fundamental basis of Vickers' critique was therefore a defence of the traditional bibliographical judgement on the Bad Quarto of *Hamlet* as an unauthorised 'memorial reconstruction'

of a contemporary performance; and his deepest objection to the
Shakespearean Originals edition of *The Tragicall Historie of
Hamlet Prince of Denmarke* was that it failed to comply with this
traditional view of the text as the 'inauthentic' shadow of an
'authentic' original. The 1603 Quarto is, he argues, as Duthie and
Hart 'incontrovertibly confirmed', a memorial reconstruction,
based on performance, corrupted and contaminated, full of
senseless language and bad verse, and above all manifestly and
irrefutably inferior as a text to the 1604/5 quarto version and the
1623 folio text.

Most of Vickers's long review is taken up with defending the
'memorial reconstruction' hypothesis and the status of Q1 as a
corrupt, performance-derived 'Bad Quarto'. It was generally con-
jectured from the early twentieth century onwards that the First
Quarto was reconstructed from memory, possibly by one of the
actors who performed in it, and published without permission
of the author or his company. The Second Quarto (some copies
of which are dated 1604, some 1605) which bears on its title page
the description 'Newly imprinted and enlarged to almost as
much againe as it was, according to the true and perfect Coppie',
would then have been a publication by dramatist and company
of an authorised text. If that were the case, it would be reasonable to assume that the Second Quarto represents both
Shakespeare's 'intended' text and the version the company used
for performances.

Despite Vickers' robust defence, the 'memorial reconstruction'
theory is no longer the orthodoxy it once was, as subsequent
correspondence in the *TLS* (4 and 11 February 1994; 4 March
1994; 1, 8, 15 and 22 April 1994) abundantly demonstrated. And
many other scholars have shown that this use of the term 'Bad
Quarto' to identify a dramatic text supposedly reported or reconstructed from a theatrical performance permits a pervasive
strategic dispersion of the attribution of 'badness', from a
description of a particular mode of transmission (illegitimately

copied from a performance rather than derived from some supposedly more authoritative source such as authorial manuscript,
a scribal copy of the manuscript or an authorially 'approved'
prompt-copy) to ascriptions of artistic or even moral 'badness'
on the part of both the text and its conjectural producers[10]. Just
as ostensibly innocent bibliographical terms such as 'corruption'
and 'contamination' carry far too strong a charge of ethical evaluation for their signifying power to operate purely at the level of
objective scholarship, so a 'Bad Quarto' can readily be received
as not only bad in itself, but the product of bad men, the
unscrupulous Elizabethan 'pirates', the ubiquitous 'playhouse
thieves'. But since we have no means of knowing the extent to
which authorial influence (as distinct from the influences of
actors, theatre entrepreneurs, scribes, printers, pirates) uniquely
determined the shape and contents of the printed texts, we are
left with a self-evidently and irredeemably collaborative cultural production. As it is now widely agreed that the early modern
drama was a highly collaborative cultural form, such collectively
processed scripts would seem accurate and appropriate products of its collective methods. In practice, however, this general
acceptance of the 'Shakespearean' drama as a collaborative
rather than an individual cultural form has not finally dislodged
the rigid hierarchy of functions implicitly assumed by traditional editorial practices: what the writer writes, others (actors,
theatre entrepreneurs, scribes, printers, pirates) corrupt, mangle
and pervert to illegitimate uses. The privileging and hypostati-
sation of the authorial role is a retrospective anachronism; and
the pervasive assumption of hierarchical precedence between
the various functions an entirely inappropriate model of the
historical conditions of early modern culture (Shakespeare, for
one, belonged to at least three of the categories listed here:
writer, actor, entrepreneur). If 'corruption' could be purged of
its aura of moral transgression and translated as the collaborative, overdetermined productivity of the early modern theatre,

in which the authentically Shakespearean input fruitfully co-existed with a diversity of other influences, then Q1's validity as an 'original' text could hardly any longer be questioned.

Vickers nonetheless adhered to the memorial reconstruction theory, and to a designation of the text as 'Bad Quarto'. In his review *The Tragicall Historie of Hamlet Prince of Denmarke* is referred to as 'corrupt', 'rubbish', 'horribly jumbled', 'garbled', 'dross', 'contaminated', 'unintelligible'; and the pirate-actors responsible for expropriating it, and all others involved in its reproduction, are dismissed as 'inept'. This 'inauthentic' text stands in Vickers' theoretical model in sharp contradistinction to an 'authentic' text. Oddly, however, there seem to be three quite separate definitions of which text is the authentic one:

> The pirated version of *Hamlet* [Q1] came out in 1603, Shakespeare's company issuing an *authentic* version [Q2] in the following year … the 1623 Folio [F1] offer[ed] this almost complete edition as the *authentic* work of Shakespeare … Graham Holderness and Bryan Loughrey reject … all attempts by modern editors since the eighteenth century to establish an *authentic* text [my italics] (Vickers, 'Dogberry', p. 24).

Thus the quality of 'authenticity' is shared by three textualisations of this play: Q2, F1 and those modern editions that have sought – usually by merging Q2 and F1 – to re-establish Shakespeare's 'authentic' text of '*Hamlet*'. Q2 is assumed 'authentic' because closest to the authorial manuscript. The Folio collection is also however 'authentic' because the editors claimed it was based on Shakespeare's own papers. Yet Q2 and F1 are quite different texts. This confusion is worse confounded when a third text is claimed as 'authentic', this time the text that modern scholars 'establish' as an emulation of the manuscript original, the ideal text of *Hamlet* that appears in most standard editions. If Q2 and F1 are both 'authentic', why was it necessary for modern editors to 'establish' an 'authentic' text? Vickers attributes to Q2 and F1 a quality of 'authenticity' based on *OED* sense 6, 'really proceeding from its reputed source or author'. But another kind of 'authenticity', that defined in *OED* senses 3 ('reliable, trustworthy') and 5 ('real, actual, genuine') has to be inserted by the editor. It is the editor, acting as the author's agent, who confers authenticity and guarantees to restore the text to a form approximating Shakespeare's intended artistic vision, by correcting the errors introduced into its variant forms in the course of performance and printing. Here nothing much has changed since Nicholas Rowe.

Vickers' review is a reaffirmation of the very editorial theory, embodied particularly in New Bibliography, that the series was set up to destabilise. For him, the criminalised status of *The Tragicall Historie of Hamlet Prince of Denmarke* had already been settled beyond dispute; and the text itself was sufficiently available in texts appropriately framed by this orthodoxy. By way of illustrating these related points, Vickers recommends Howard Mill's book *Working with Shakespeare,* which addresses the Q1 text, and which contains in its 'specimen analyses' of the different texts of *'Hamlet'* an 'admirable comparison' likely to command 'wide agreement'[11]. In fact, Mills's book disqualifies both of Vickers's arguments. Enjoying a common access to all those old facsimiles and editions, Mills nonetheless employed, for his comparative discussion, the *Shakespearean Originals* edition itself, which he explicitly applauds and from which he quotes several pages. And he does so partly in order to challenge the categorisation of Q1 simply as a 'Bad Quarto'.

> The first Quarto is often dismissed out of hand as 'the Bad Quarto', quoted in Riverside's notes only to 'help the reader in appreciating its debased nature'. All power, therefore, to the editors of a 1992 reprint [i.e. *Shakespearean Originals*], which I gratefully use as my source, whose introduction 'attempts to view the play as a work of art in its own right rather than as an analogue to the received text'[12].

The primary objective of our edition of *The Tragicall Historie of*

Hamlet Prince of Denmarke – 'to make the play generally available, for the first time since the early seventeenth century, for the kind of practical experimentation and theoretical mobilisation which alone can genuinely test the validity of that scholarly consensus that has kept this play on the margins of editorial reproduction, critical debate and theatrical performance' – therefore appeared even then, at least from the example cited by Brian Vickers, on its way to being achieved.

∽

Subsequently however the series was criticised not for celebrating the inauthentic, but for *promoting* notions of 'authenticity'. In an essay published in *London Quarterly*, Jonathan Sawday draws a parallel between the editors of *Shakespearean Originals* and the 'Klingons', an atavistic warrior race featured in *Star Trek*[13]. *Shakespearean Originals*, he affirms, is based on 'a touching faith in "authenticity"', and its methodology is to translate modern editions of Shakespeare back into what he calls 'the original Klingon language [i.e. into early modern English]' (Sawday, 'Beam me up', pp. 23-4). He suggests that the texts carry the titles under which they were initially published rather than those generic titles they have subsequently accumulated in the course of modern editing, in order to confer on them a kind of antique period charm, an *ersatz* heritage comparable with the historicised artificiality of the replica Southwark Globe[14].

Sawday again quotes from sources such as back-cover blurbs, in order to illustrate this 'touching faith' in 'authenticity', which is defined as a pedantic focus on curatorial preservation, or artificial reproduction, of ancient historical objects. But the 'General Introduction' of *Shakespearean Originals* clearly defines the liminal status of the partly modernised texts reproduced, and describes them as based upon historical documents, and not invasively transformed. It further makes clear that the texts were not privileged one over another, nor merged to form a conflated hybrid, nor related vertically to the author as 'onlie begetter'.

One of our primary objectives was to contest the claim of the modern edition to represent an 'authentic' ('really proceeding from its reputed source or author') rendering of what Shakespeare actually wrote, or probably wrote, or would if left alone have really wanted to write; and to replace this conception of *absolute* authenticity, whereby the modernised edition aims to approximate a lost manuscript, with a more *relative*, historicist conception of 'authenticity' as denoting no more than a genuine documentary historical record, produced by 'historical contingency', which could reasonably be described as 'reliable, trustworthy', and 'real, actual, genuine'. Even the notorious blurb only claims that the original printed texts are 'the most "authentic" we have'; and there is surely nothing else which can claim *more* authenticity as evidence about early modern printed dramatic texts. 'Authenticity' here then is a descriptive term, indicating a material condition. These texts were the 'original' editions – i.e. they *were* published before later editions – and all subsequent editions *do* derive from them – since there was nowhere else, except editorial surmise, from which they could have derived.

As a bibliographical initiative, then, *Shakespeare Originals* has been from its inception criticised from all sides. The series was also challenged by some commentators particularly interested in the dramatic and theatrical issues raised by the reproduction of 'original' texts[15]. Janette Dillon's *Shakespeare Quarterly* essay 'Is there a Performance in this Text?' quickly became something of a *cause célebre*, and has been extensively cited as a useful 'antidote' to the 'excesses'[16] of *Shakespearean Originals*. Yet Dillon's essay generously acknowledges the value of the series:

The aim of the series, to make available in cheap paperback

these early printed versions of plays more familiar to students in conflated editions, is a worthy one … The value of *Shakespearean Originals: First Editions* lies in the extent to which the editors foreground difference and warn against the false idea of the singular text, often a conflated text pretending to be singular and authentic. The point that these editions underline, and from which there can be no going back, is the plurality of the extant material objects, the undeniable existence of, in the case of *Hamlet*, at least three texts of the play so different from one another that their difference should be recognised by the printing of separate editions. The appearance of *Shakespeare Originals* mark the end of the notion of correctness (Dillon, 'Is there?', p. 85).

On the other hand, Dillon sustains a polemical convention by questioning the publisher's promotional material, criticising evident inaccuracies and apparent errors, and then dispersing assumptions derived from the advertising copy across the series' critical parameters:

> The title of the series makes a claim for authenticity, a claim central to the way the texts are advertised … The slippery and undefined notions of authenticity and originality, which underwrite not only the advertising copy but also the general introduction to the series and the introductions to specific play texts, stands in urgent need of questioning (Dillon, 'Is there?', pp. 74–5).

Later in the article, discussing the quality of evidence supplied by early-modern title-pages, Dillon undermines the very method on which her critique is based. She rejects the claim to a performance history contained in the title page of the 1603 quarto of *The Tragicall Historie of Hamlet Prince of Denmarke*, on the grounds that 'Title pages are devised in order to sell books, not to make precise scholarly statements about the texts they preface' (Dillon, 'Is there?', p. 79). The original title-page of *Hamlet* has no status at all as evidence; yet it is legitimate to read the Harvester Catalogue's reference to 'Shakespeare's real *Hamlet*' as such a 'precise scholarly statement'.

The primary focus of Dillon's interrogation is on the particular status she imagines the series attributes to *The Tragicall Historie of Hamlet Prince of Denmarke*:

> The thrust of the editorial argument, as set out in the introductory material, is not towards a plurality of authentic texts but towards an insistence on the superior authenticity of Q1 (Dillon, 'Is there?', p. 75).

This assertion is incorrect. The critical introduction naturally, in the light of the text's historical marginalisation, argues for a revaluation. But that is not a revaluation vis-à-vis the other Jacobean texts of *Hamlet*, but against the modern editorial tradition. Nowhere does the introduction argue that Q1 has more value as a text than Q2 or F1; only that it is a *better* text in absolute terms than is generally acknowledged. Indeed, the 'Introduction' explicitly disavows such comparative judgements between 'original' texts[17]:

> In a hierarchical configuration of texts separated by principles of moral discrimination, priority is automatically given to those texts adjudged 'good'. On a level playing field of textual plurality, variant readings can be objectively compared and apprehended as different from one another, without any establishing of discursive hierarchy (Holderness and Loughrey, *Tragicall Historie*, pp. 22-3).

The main objective of the introduction to *The Tragicall Historie of Hamlet Prince of Denmarke* is to test a hypothesis. Since the text is generally accepted as a 'bad' text, how could it produce a 'good' performance? The problem arises, the introduction goes on to suggest, from a 'current diplomatic alliance of scholarship and theatre studies' (Holderness and Loughrey, *Tragicall Historie*, p. 13), which is put under some pressure when an effective performance arises from a text judged to be 'bad'. Dillon worries about this term 'diplomatic alliance', which seems to her to suggest 'a calculated interdependence for mutual profit'.

She goes on to point out that such 'alliance' between theatre and scholarship is 'not really so new', citing the instance of William Poel's 1881 production of Q1 '*Hamlet*'. Poel's production is actually discussed in some detail in the 'Introduction' to the edition; and the word 'diplomatic' was employed to foreground the historical relativity of that symbiosis of stage and study which clearly exists today, and is quite different from the equivalent relations in (to cite an extreme example) the Restoration and eighteenth century. The problem posed would not have been an issue in eighteenth century culture, where scholars were attempting to fix the Shakespearean text, while the theatres excelled in free adaptation and rewriting. When Nicholas Shrimpton saw a production of Q1 *Hamlet* at the Orange Tree Theatre in Richmond, he was shocked at the success of the performance because of his prior negative opinion of the play as a text[18]. If, on the other hand, it is accepted that the text is in its own right 'authentic', and possesses both historical and contemporary interest and value, then its capacity for performability will not surprise. The issue remains a paradox only for those who are convinced by practical demonstration of the text's performability, yet wish to retain the dismissive aesthetic category of 'Bad Quarto'. As editors we did not need to 'authenticate' the text by reinstating a theatrical 'authenticity factor' and, in fact, the edition attempted to show, by only a few illustrative examples (Holderness and Loughrey, *Tragicall Historie*, pp. 21-2) how the 'distinctive poetic' qualities of the play have remained unrecognised by a scholarship generally disposed to view the text as a garbled imitation of something better.

Dillon argues that *The Tragicall Historie of Hamlet Prince of Denmarke* theoretically eliminates the author only to re-authenticate the text by reference to the criterion of performance; and that Q1 is asserted to be, by virtue of its historical theatricality and modern performability, demonstrably superior to both Q2 and F1. But this is not the case. It is the common consensus that this text comes very close to actual Jacobean stage practice, which is why some of its striking stage directions ('*Enter Ofelia playing on a lute, and her hair downe, singing*'), together with other theatrical features, are frequently borrowed for modern editions and performances (examples listed by Irace, *The First Quarto*, pp. 20-3). Dillon makes much of the fact that the basis of that consensus is a general acceptance of the theory of 'memorial reconstruction', which in turn underlies the designation of 'Bad Quarto'. So the edition appears to be using symptomatic evidence derived from a theory it disavows. But those characteristics of the so-called 'Bad Quartos' that are consonant with the 'memorial reconstruction' theory – graphic and detailed stage directions, self-evidently theatrical devices (such as the complete Christopher Sly-frame of *The Taming of a Shrew*), a certain 'levelling' populism – could equally point to some other performance-related origin[19]. At the same time the edition explicitly states that F1 also bears many traces of playhouse influence, and even concedes that from the evidence of Q2's title-page, it would be reasonable to assume that the Second Quarto represents a version the company may have used for performances.

The main issue is not then, as it is for New Bibliography, the relation between text and author. All these early modern dramatic texts have been transmitted in printed forms which effectively *conceal* specific elements of indebtedness to their several and various contributors. The dramatist naturally played a central, even an 'originating' role in this process of multiple and collective 'authorship' (Holderness and Loughrey, *Tragicall Historie*, pp. 6–7). But if there is an 'authenticity factor' in play, it is neither the author as sole originator, nor the theatre as proxy-author: but rather that collective process of cultural production now widely acknowledged as the source of the drama, and whose precise causal configuration, and particular divisions of labour, remain to such a large extent hidden from us (Holderness and Loughrey, *Tragicall Historie*, p. 16).

Nor is it necessary to invoke a hypostatised and unitary conception of theatre to validate the text. Dillon argues that 'there is a slippage toward a more unitary notion of Jacobean stage practice which judges some texts as more authentic than others' (Dillon, 'Is there?', p. 77), producing a privileging isolation of Q1 *Hamlet*. But the edition says something quite different:

> It is becoming clear that within Elizabethan and Jacobean culture, around each 'Shakespeare' play there circulated a wide variety of texts, performing different theatrical functions and adopting different shapes in different contexts of production (Holderness and Loughrey, *Tragicall Historie*, p. 7).

The existence of three '*Hamlet*' plays is evidence supporting that theoretical premise, while to the post-Malone editorial tradition such variants testify only to the pristine unity possessed by the authentic original before it disintegrated into its constituent textual fragments. Differing texts arise from 'different contexts of production'; and although it is often difficult to link specific texts to particular contexts, the very fact of textual multiplicity disposes of any 'unitary' notion of 'the Jacobean stage'. Nor can it reasonably be said that the agency of 'historical performers' is occluded in an edition that explicitly acknowledges their determining, though indeterminate, contributions[20].

The initial emphasis throughout this chapter has been on the singularity of the individual play text, the specific identities it reassumes when partially restored to its originating context of production. This strategy of textual individuation is rendered necessary by the dominance of New Bibliographical principles in editorial theory and practice: and there is clearly something artificial, synthetic, about 'restoring' the texts, a term that now speaks of antiquarian refurbishment rather than of archaeological recovery. If we know that we cannot hope to return to the texts in a manner unmediated by their subsequent histories of production and reception, then releasing them in a form approximating more closely to their 'original' material character is as much a novel initiative as to combine the elements into a new eclecticism, or to rewrite the texts entirely into completely new forms. The whirligig of time brings in its revenges, and the old starts to look new again.

It is perhaps inevitable that an initiative in the re-individuation of texts long since incorporated into a tradition of combination should be mistaken for a strategy of idealization, a ring-fencing of such texts as the 'Bad Quartos' to accord them a more privileged status[21]. The very isolation of the historic text might seem calculated to suggest authorial authenticity, or a bid for canonical status. This remains unfortunate, for the required emphasis is precisely the opposite of textual isolation and singularity. What I had hoped we could achieve via *Shakespearean Originals* was something much closer to the de Grazia and Stallybrass focus on 'historical contingency': that is, a restoration of these texts not to uniqueness, but to the plural and multiple histories from which they derived. In divesting the texts to some degree of validation by authorship ('Shakespearean'), I had hoped that more readers might be enabled to experience them in terms of the multiple, collaborative authorship proper to a highly collectivised theatre industry; and to see in them, in the depth and thickness of their material textuality, something of their authorship by history.

We isolate, identify, individuate a text not in order to establish its purity but as in Derrida's 'Law of Genres', to find in it 'a law of impurity, a principle of contamination'[22]. The text is itself only in relation to what it excludes; its identity is defined by its relationships; its singularity by its difference; and its apparent autonomy by the 'confluence' of social, economic and cultural forces that permeate and transgress its material, immaterial body.

I take the word 'confluence' from a poem of Dante Gabriel Rossetti[23]:

The Love-letter

Warmed by her hand and shadowed by her hair
As close she leaned and poured her heart through thee,
Whereof the articulate throbs accompany
The smooth black stream that makes thy whiteness fair, –
Sweet fluttering sheet, even of her breath aware, –
Oh let thy silent song disclose to me
That soul wherewith her lips and eyes agree
Like married music in Love's answering air.

Fain had I watched her when, at some fond thought,
Her bosom to the writing closelier press'd,
When, through eyes raised an instant, her soul sought
My soul, and from the sudden confluence caught
The words that made her love the loveliest.

Rossetti attempts to show here an absolute unification of writer, writing, text and reader. The writing – 'the smooth black stream' that paradoxically beautifies the whiteness of paper – seems a direct expression of the woman's body, its fluid rhythm consonant with the 'articulate throbs' of her beating heart. But the material text, the paper on which the letter is written, is equally anthropomorphised, a 'sweet fluttering sheet' that seems an extension of both her skin and her breath; just as the writing, when pressed to her breast, interfaces directly with the secret writing of her heart. The letter's eloquence resides in its silence, its voicelessness, since it expresses that essence that the physical only signifies, the soul. The writing is plural, a commixture of the physical and the spiritual, a blend of sound and silence. But writing, reading, lips, eyes, meet on the site of the text and produce a perfect harmony, a 'married music'.

Towards the end of the poem the same harmonious unification and concordance of separate elements is called 'confluence', a flowing together that more accurately reflects the true plurality of this harmonious exchange. It is the text that brings together and distinguishes the inter-related elements, the letter that lies inside the poem, that piece of white paper signed with black ink. But it is also, of course, the poem we have just read, black on white, singularity in difference, black marks on a fluttering sheet that tenuously link, in a precarious harmony, Rossetti's dead, silenced voice with our living and listening ear.

Rossetti's wife, Lizzie, died in 1862. Just before her coffin was closed, he placed a manuscript book of poems between his dead wife's cheek and hair. The motive he gave to friends for the action was one of guilt: since many of the poems had been written during her suffering, when he could have been attending her, 'the solitary text should go with her to the grave'. In later years he attempted to recover these early poems from memory, but found himself unable to do so completely. Under persuasion from his friends, he agreed to the recovery of his manuscript from Lizzie's grave. Permission secured from the Home Secretary, the grave was opened at night, and the manuscript removed. Stained and mouldered from its proximity to a decaying corpse, it was dried and treated, and returned to Rossetti. He had the poems copied out and (it was believed) destroyed the manuscript[24].

Lizzie Rossetti literally left textual traces of herself in the material texture of that manuscript, since the manuscript participated in her own decay. The macabre 'confluence' that took place over those seven and a half years in Highgate Cemetery offers a striking comparison with the 'confluence' celebrated in 'The Love-letter'. While the poem presents a model of writing which acknowledges the collaborative nature of authorship, the story of the manuscript. illustrates even more forcibly how no piece of writing can stand alone, singular, pure[25]. Even a genuine holograph manuscript can exemplify the universal 'principle of contamination'. Like the only surviving manuscript believed to contain text in Shakespeare's handwriting, 'The Boke of Sir Thomas More', which is thoroughly contaminated by the confluence of collaborative authorship, the manuscript does not after all give us 'unmediated access', in Stephen Greenblatt's words, 'to the astonishing forge of imaginative power that was the mind of the dramatist'[26]. Elsewhere Greenblatt writes poignantly of the way in which writing carries traces of authorial influence, and yet simultaneously frees itself from its own legacy, exposes it to the influence of other lives:

> The written word has strange powers: it seems to hold on to something of the very life of the person who has written it, but it also seems to pry that life loose from the writer, exposing it to vagaries of history and chance (Greenblatt, 'General Introduction', p. 71).

Disintegration

(Riddle 24, the *Exeter Book*)

A worm wolfed my words.
Funny it felt, queer and uncanny
That a clemmed creepy-crawly
So easily swallowed my phrases and
Paragraphs, sayings and
Sentences, rapturous rhythms and
Paeans of praise, by the simple expedient
Of papyrus-pulping, vellum-devouring,
Munching the membrane they stably sat on,
Pinned where I put them, my well-chosen
Words. Though I know that he's not
That nifty night-stealer
One whit the wiser for his verbal
Voracity, I flinch when I feel
The worm that awaits in a papery
Dark to devour destructively
Lips and loquacity, speech with skin.

PART TWO

Textual Practice

CHAPTER FIVE

Texts and Contexts:
King Lear

ॐ

T HE LONG-RUNNING debate about the two texts of *King Lear* has generally been framed within the parameters of revision theory. But consideration of the relations between the two texts, and of the 1608 Quarto as a text in its own right, can lead us towards more interesting reflections on the interactions of text and culture.

The bibliographical story of *King Lear* is sufficiently well-known. What modern readers and audiences know as Shakespeare's *King Lear* is a composite construction[1] formed by the merger of two distinct original texts, the First Quarto (Q1), *M. William Shakespeare: his true chronicle historie of the life and death of King Lear and his three daughters*, published in 1608; and *The tragedie of King Lear*, published in the first collected edition of Shakespeare's plays, *Mr William Shakespeares Comedies, Histories, & Tragedies*, the First Folio of 1623 (F1)[2]. It was not until the 1970s that a new approach began to surface, initially in Michael Warren's famously controversial paper submitted to *PMLA*, which suggested that the two texts represented distinct, independent versions of the play, and that between them Shakespeare had systematically revised it. This implies that in terms of authorial relationship, both texts would possess equal authority. A few years later similar arguments appeared in Steven Urkowitz's *Shakespeare's Revision of 'King Lear'* and Peter Blayney's *The Texts of 'King Lear'*, and the 'two-text hypothesis' was theoretically established by *The Division of the Kingdoms: Shakespeare's two Versions of 'King Lear'*, edited by Gary Taylor and Michael Warren[3]. But the most significant contribution was the decision of the Oxford editors to implement the 'two-text' theory into textual practice in the Oxford *Complete Works* which offered the reader both *The History of King Lear* (based on the 1608 Quarto text) and *The Tragedy of King Lear* (based on the 1623 Folio text). Wells declared subsequently that 'once the hypothesis of revision is accepted, conflation becomes a logical absurdity ... I believe that the conflated text has had its day'[4].

Thus the Oxford Shakespeare gave credit and currency to the multiplicity of at least one Shakespeare play. On the other hand, as the previous chapter has shown, the editors in no way questioned the centrality of the author. Warren, Urkowitz, Wells, Taylor and other revisionists did not produce an 'indeterminate Shakespeare'[5], since in revision theory Shakespeare becomes something very like a determining principle, a guarantor of authority and meaning. The author remains the fixed and stable point through which a clear relationship among multiple texts can be drawn.

Other editions of the Quarto text are based on the same theoretical premises. *'King Lear': A Parallel-Text Edition,* edited by René Weis (1993) again links the two texts inextricably together within the greater metacategory of 'Shakespeare's *King Lear*': 'The most uncontroversial and perhaps the most sensible position to adopt about the two *Lears* is to submit that they are two states of the play, and that all the material they contain is by Shakespeare.'[6]. This assumption justifies publishing the two original texts in facing-page parallel form, signalling that each is a separable element of a greater whole, and drawing attention to the similarities and differences between them. Parallel-text presentation is actually only one step away from conflation, since although the discrete texts are discriminated, they are separated out only to the extent of a double page, still held firmly together and fixed into an inescapably comparative relationship with one another. Indeed, Weis explicitly salutes the traditional conflated editions that his own publication might be understood to supersede:

> While it seems unlikely that a conflated text of *Lear* can in the future form a satisfactory basis for discussion, conflated *Lears* (as currently available in a number of excellent single editions by Muir 1989 and Hunter 1972, and in prestigious complete Shakespeares such as the Alexander, Riverside and Bevington texts) will undoubtedly continue to inspire readers and audiences (Weis, *Lear*, p. 5)

Weis, in practice, adheres very closely to the principles of the mainstream editorial tradition. His texts are modernised, collated with reprints, and emended by reference to one another. Both are divided into acts and scenes, though in the original publications F is so divided, and Q is not. Speech headings are regularised ('EDMUND' is substituted for '*Bastard*'); stage directions are filled out or even interpolated (where Q gives '*a letter*', and F no direction at all, both Weis texts show ['*Gives Gloucester a letter*']). Q is not given its original title, but printed under the title invented by the Oxford editors, *The History of King Lear* – a title which, balancing exactly with the Folio's *The Tragedy of King Lear* – confers on the two texts a perfect though quite inappropriate symmetry, 'stabilising' (in Paul Werstine's useful phrase) 'both texts in opposition to each other'[7].

A further text of Q1 *Lear* appears as part of the New Cambridge Shakespeare series, edited by Jay L. Halio, and published under the title *The First Quarto of 'King Lear'*. This publication represents a significant departure from the norms of revisionist practice, since the text is not only incorporated into the Shakespeare canon (a move effected by the Oxford edition and by the editions of Warren and Weis) but published individually as a discrete text; discriminated from the standard series format by a separate sub-series title (*Shakespeare: the Early Quartos*), but none the less accorded a place within the great Shakespearean whole. Stanley Wells's individual Oxford text of *King Lear* is an edition of the Quarto.

Brian Gibbons, General Editor of the New Cambridge Shakespeare, provides a brief prefatory note to the *Early Quartos* sub-series, indicating a rationale for the inclusion of such 'abbreviated', 'reported' or 'playhouse adaptation' quarto texts: 'These early quartos are not chosen as copy-texts for modern critical editions and are not readily available, though indispensable to advanced students of Shakespeare and of textual bibliography'. The volume editor Jay L. Halio cites[8], as his theoretical credentials, revision theory and the 'two-text hypothesis':

> This edition of *King Lear* has been designed as a complementary text to the Folio-based edition published in the New Cambridge Shakespeare … this edition accepts the two-text hypothesis; indeed, that hypothesis is the main justification for bringing it to print.

The text presented in *The First Quarto of 'King Lear'* is wholly modernised and regularised, with the original format relineated and repunctuated according to principles established by modern editions of conflated or 'good' texts. Halio's text employs, albeit in parenthesis, the familiar stage directions interpolated by eighteenth-century editors – '*Aside*' for 'What shall Cordelia do?', '*Gives him a letter*', '*Strikes him*', and so forth. Act and scene divisions, introduced in the Folio and standardised by the editorial tradition, but notably absent from the Quarto, are also included. Speech-headings are not those of the Quarto, most strikingly in the consistent conversion of '*Bastard*' to 'EDMUND'. There can be little doubt that these editors are acting as co-authors, producing Wells/Taylor, Weis or Halio versions of *King Lear*, in much the same way as the editors of ideal-text editions.

৵৹

The title *M. William Shak-speare: his true chronicle historie of the life and death of King Lear and his three daughters*, whoever composed it and attached it to the text, calls attention precisely to some of the differences between the two early printed versions[9]. By contrast with the Folio title, the austere *The Tragedie of King Lear*, which seeks to contain the text within a distinct genre, Q1's title invokes a more diverse generic background, claiming the play for serious historiography ('true ... history'), legendary historiography ('true chronicle') and fairy tale ('King Lear and his three daughters'). It is in that character of generic diversity (common to both original texts but in some ways more manifest in Q), and not in a changing of authorial mind, that we should seek for the basis of textual plurality.

In keeping with its generic diversity, the narrative origins of the Lear plays disclose an extraordinary variety, which in turn influenced subsequent reproduction of the play in the post-Restoration theatre. Any production of *King Lear* seen in a theatre between 1681 and 1823 would reveal the language of the play entirely rewritten, and even the basic plot radically dissimilar to the familiar Shakespearean action. During that 142-year period, Cordelia's reluctance to marry did not remain a mystery: she was already in love, with Edgar. There was no trace of the Fool, a central figure for modern criticism of the play. Above all, the play was no longer a tragedy. Within seventy-three years of its original publication in 1608, it had acquired a happy ending. Cordelia and Edgar manage between them to defeat the powers of the older daughters and to restore Lear to his throne.

Neither Lear nor Cordelia die in this version. Cordelia is instead rescued, first from rape and then from hanging, by her lover Edgar. The play ends with Edgar renouncing any claim he might as victor have over the kingdom, preferring to join Cordelia in a romantic retirement. The closing lines of the play – familiar to us from modern editions as Edgar's:

> The weight of this sad time we must obey;
> Speak what we feel, not what we ought to say.
> The oldest hath borne most: we that are young
> Shall never see so much, nor live so long [10].

– for a century and a half reappeared in a radically altered form, though still spoken (as in the 1623 edition) by Edgar:

> Our drooping country now erects her head,
> Peace spreads her balmy wings, and Plenty blooms.
> Divine Cordelia, all the gods can witness
> How much thy love to empire I prefer!
> Thy bright example shall convince the world
> (Whatever storms of Fortune are decreed)
> That truth and [virtue] shall at last succeed [11].

'Succeed' hints there at a double meaning, with the primary sense 'emerge with success' further suggesting 'inherit power by succession'. This play could be described as a political romance, concluding with a particular kind of 'happy ending', entailing the restoration of a previously abdicated monarchy.

Nahum Tate, author of this adaptation, was writing after exactly such a 'Restoration' in 1660. But he was also deploying the standard contemporary practice of regarding Shakespeare's plays as texts to be adapted and rewritten, virtually translated into what was considered the more polished and civilised language of the day. From the perspective of the later seventeenth century, Elizabethan drama appeared to be the product of a relatively uncivilised culture, strong on genius and imagination, short on taste and correctness. To a writer like Tate, the dramatic writings of that earlier period seemed works of pure 'Nature' – 'a Heap of Jewels, unstrung and unpolisht ... dazling in their Disorder' [12] –

and the modern poet's job was therefore to polish and restring the stones into an orderly configuration. But even in such a context, where free adaptation was regarded as an appropriate way of reproducing earlier texts, Tate's alteration of *'King Lear'* from tragedy to comedy, and the strikingly long period of currency and popularity enjoyed by that adaptation, still seem remarkable.

The most obvious change introduced is that of the happy ending, which helps to convert the dramatic action from tragedy to romance: from a narrative in which innocence and weakness are mercilessly punished along with the guilty, to one in which virtue and proper sentiment are rewarded with romantic reconciliation and the restoration of legitimacy. Despite the contemporary popularity and esteem accorded Tate's adaptation (Dr Johnson preferred it to Shakespeare's) in modern criticism it has been ridiculed as a travesty of Shakespeare – 'notorious', 'infamous'. The adaptation has earned, according to James Black, 'more scorn than commendation' (Black in Tate, *History*, p. xv), a view exemplified by Maynard Mack: 'Tate's *Lear* invites ridicule, and deserves it'[13]. Such a view is perhaps inescapable, if we compare them, in historical retrospect, with the Shakespearean drama taken as the 'original' of which Tate's adaptation was a corruption, the norm from which Tate manifestly deviated.

This is not, however, the only way of looking at it. Shakespeare did not invent the 'King Lear' story. It was, on the contrary, a traditional historical legend with a long ancestry, existing in a large number of different retellings, some of them in Shakespeare's time relatively recent. The versions of the story most likely to have influenced the 1608 and 1623 dramatic versions are (i) the reign of Lear recounted as part of the history of early Britain in Holinshed's *Chronicles*; (ii) the story as narrated in Book 2 of Spenser's *The Faerie Queene*; (iii) an anonymous play entitled *The True Chronicle Historie of King Leir*, performed in the 1590s and published in 1605. The most striking feature of these different legendary and historical narratives, from the perspective of a comparison between Shakespeare and Tate, is that all these versions tell the same story as Tate's adaptation. The 'King Lear' story is a historical romance narrative of restoration, in all versions but those exemplified by the two Shakespearean texts. It is so in Holinshed's version:

> Herevpon, when this armie and nauie of ships were readie, Leir and his daughter Cordeilla with hir husband tooke the sea, and arriuing in Britaine, fought with their enimies, and discomfited them in battell … and then was Leir restored to his kingdome, which he ruled after this by the space of two yeeres, and then died, fortie yeeres after he first begun to reigne[14].

And in Spenser's:

> The wretched man gan then auise too late
> That loue is not, where most it is profest,
> Too truely tryde in his extreamest state;
> At last resolu'd likewise to proue the rest,
> He to *Cordelia* to him selfe addrest,
> Who with entire affection him receau'd,
> As for her Syre and king she seemed best;
> And after all an army strong she leau'd,
> To war on those, which him had of his realme bereau'd.
>
> So to his crowne she him restor'd againe,
> In which he dyde, made ripe for death by eld,
> And after wild, it should to her remaine:
> Who peaceably the same long time did weld:
> And all mens harts in dew obedience held[15].

If Shakespeare's *King Lear* is taken as a starting-point, it appears that Tate distorted the original (with what seems to modern witnesses quite inexplicable success) and that the original was then permanently restored to the theatre in the nineteenth century. When modern dramatists undertake similarly free adaptations of Shakespeare, their rewritings do not replace the 'original' but parallel and complement it. The Shakespearean norm remains in place, to exercise a salutary and corrective influence on any manifest deviation. But Tate's adaptation took place when the play was a bare seventy-three years old, and when both the unassailable Shakespearean reputation, and the stable Shakespearean text, were yet to be consolidated (the first edition of Shakespeare's works – other than simple reprints of the 1623 Folio – that of Nicholas Rowe, was not published until 1709). Prior to Shakespeare's play, the 'King Lear' story existed as a historical narrative with a long development stretching from the Middle Ages to the early seventeenth century. Tate was, if anything, actually 'restoring' the 'Lear' story's original shape and generic character after its 'distortion' by Shakespeare.

This evidence provides a different way of looking at the same process. During the greater part of its history, the 'Lear' story took the form of a historical romance ending in restoration. For a brief period between the first decade of the seventeenth century and 1681, the story appeared and achieved currency in the Shakespearean form, as a tragedy. It was then restored by Tate to its original romance form, in which it persisted until 1838 (with at least one scene surviving as late as 1860 [see Foakes, *Lear*, p. 85]). Thereafter, with the consolidation of Shakespeare's prominence as Britain's national dramatist, the Shakespearean text became accepted as the only fictionalised version of the 'Lear' story to retain any enduring artistic value.

The modern reader approaches this problem from a perspective predetermined by the location of Shakespeare's play as a fixed point of reference. But an attention to the broad field of cultural production from which the *King Lear* texts emanated would suggest that the Shakespearean dramatisations cannot be disentangled so easily from the narrative materials that went into their making. Narratives and dramatic plots never exist as pure story; they are always narrated and dramatised. Narration and dramatisation confer upon a particular telling or retelling the characteristics of a specific genre, the shaping structure of a certain cultural conventions, a guiding framework of cultural rules that enables the reader to orientate him or herself in relation to the overall pattern and local details of the plot. A plot is never separable from its genre, from the particular configuration of conventions into which the story is located. The 'King Lear' story demonstrates a range of narrative and dramatic possibilities, and in each manifestation the chosen convention is overtly foregrounded.

> Leir the sonne of Baldud was admitted ruler ouer the Britaines in the yeare of the world 3105 ... (Holinshed, quoted from Muir, *Lear,* p. 234).

>> He had three daughters, first and eldest hight *Gonerell:*
>> Next after hir, my sister *Ragan* was begote:
>> The thirde and last was, I the yongest namde *Cordell* ...[16].

> ### Kent.

> I thought the King had more affected the Duke of *Albany* then *Cornwall* ... (*true chronicle historie,* p. 71).

Holinshed's perspective is that of the historical chronicle, impersonal, objective, matter-of-fact. John Higgins's first-person narrative foregrounds the folk-tale structure of the 'Lear' story, pointing up its distinct resemblance to archetypal fairy tales such as that of Cinderella. The Shakespearean version, dramatic not narrative, plunges the spectator *in medias res,* while simultaneously recapitulating a dramatised action already in progress.

The 'Lear' story thus manifested a range of narrative and generic capabilities up to and including the Shakespearean dramatisations. It could be narrated as historical romance, ending in restoration and unity; or it could be dramatised, as it is in both Shakespearean texts, as tragedy, culminating in the deaths of Lear and Cordelia. The full historical legend contained both possibilities, which is why it could function as a source for such differential narrations. In the traditional versions, including those of Holinshed and Spenser, the romance history of Lear's restoration was followed by a tragic sequel. Lear survived his own restoration to sovereignty by only a few years. He was succeeded by Cordelia, who reigned for five years as 'supreme governesse of Britaine'. After her husband's death, her nephews (the sons of Gonorill and Ragen), 'disdaining to be under the government of a woman', rebelled against and imprisoned her. Cordelia was 'laid … fast in ward, wherewith she tooke such grief, being a woman of manlie courage, and despairing to recouer libertie, there she slue hirselfe' (Holinshed in Muir, *Lear*, p. 237). In Spenser's version Cordelia is less 'manlie', and hangs herself merely from weariness of long imprisonment[17]. The tragic sequel to the traditional chronicle history was thus incorporated into the Shakespearean versions, though as assassination rather than suicide.

The fact that the Lear story came to Shakespeare saturated with the varied colourings of these discrete genres, history, romance and tragedy is acknowledged as a fact of cultural transmission. But it is one thing to admit such generic eclecticism and catholicity of sources as typical of Shakespeare's method of working: quite another to see this plurality of provenance as unsettling the artistic unity of the final product. Kenneth Muir, for example, acknowledging some of the play's apparently dubious origins, none the less could not wish the fault undone, the issue of it being so proper:

> It is likely that the old play gave Shakespeare the idea of writing on King Lear; but he had long been familiar with the versions of Holinshed and Spencer, and also with *The Mirror for Magistrates*. As we have seen, he was cheerfully eclectic in his use of sources, combining details and phrases from each. On the one hand he rejected the happy ending of *King Leir*, and gave form to its formlessness; on the other hand he rejected the undramatic elements of the versions of Spenser, Holinshed, and Higgins, in which the defeat and the suicide of the heroine come as an epilogue

irrelevant to the story of Lear himself. The suicide of Cordelia would have been intolerable to a sensitive audience, and her murder necessitated the punishment of the guilty: Goneril and Regan could not be suffered to escape, if Cordelia were to die; and Lear could not, without anti-climax, be restored to the throne. Out of a moral story with a happy ending and an irrelevant, despairing epilogue, Shakespeare created a homogeneous tragedy (Muir, *Lear,* pp. xxxvi-xxxvii).

In Muir's view, whatever Shakespeare did to the traditional Lear materials would have been justified in the outcome: he could not put a foot wrong. But why should a tragic reworking of a narrative of restoration be so obviously and inevitably superior to a romance version, and why should a pattern of restoration necessarily prove an anti-climax? Dr Johnson thought the romance of restoration superior to the tragedy, and Tolstoy found the *True Chronicle Historie of King Leir* less, not more, formless than Shakespeare's play. Why should the subsequent fate of Cordelia be deemed 'irrelevant' to the story of Lear, unless Lear's history can be conceived of without Cordelia? Why should the heroine's suicide be 'intolerable', and who says Shakespeare's theatre had a 'sensitive' audience? The traditional narrative is castigated as a 'moral story', yet Muir's own *Lear* is virtually a cautionary tale of guilt and inevitable punishment.

R.A. Foakes in the revised Arden 3 edition considers exactly the same evidence of multiple sources, but draws quite a different conclusion:

What we know of Shakespeare's wide reading and powers of assimilation seem to show that he made use of all kinds of material, absorbing contradictory viewpoints, positive and negative, religious and secular, as if to ensure that *King Lear* would offer no single controlling perspective, but be open to, indeed demand, multiple interpretations (Foakes, *Lear,* p. 107).

❦

The three most significant generic contexts influencing the Lear-plays are history, romance and tragedy. As a historical legend, the Lear story acquired traces of a historiographical context that manifested themselves throughout the play texts. As exemplified in Holinshed, the Lear tale is a historical narrative of legitimacy, power, political authority and military struggle: a story of a kingdom divided, invaded and reunited. Though clearly the King Lear texts are not historical in the same sense as a play like *The Life of Henry the Fift*, the texts none the less connect with seventeenth century historiography, and remain available for historical reinterpretation[18]. In the early seventeenth century history was also a matter of myth and legend, and therefore available for reproduction in that contemporary political language that invoked 'mythical charters' of the past to legitimise and sanction modern configurations of power[19].

Contingent upon the legendary dimensions of the Lear tale was a strong element of romance, manifest in the versions of Spenser and *The True Chronicle Historie of King Lear*. Within the framework of a historical and political narrative that could be understood either diachronically, as reconstruction of the past, or synchronically, as indicative of the present, the Lear plays generate folk tale and romance motifs of banishment and exile, recognition and return, disguise and mistaken identity. The courtly and romance language of the 'division' scene begins as ritualised ceremony but slides unexpectedly into genuine pastoral discourse:

> Fairest *Cordelia* that art most rich being poore,
> Most choise forsaken, and most loved despisd,
> Thee and thy vertues here I ceaze upon,
> Be it lawfull I take up whats cast away
> (*true chronicle historie*, p. 78).

A fundamental romance archetype, the abandonment to chance of a royal child and her acceptance, dowerless, by a royal suitor, is enacted in the course of a few lines. Other romance elements include the story of Kent, a loyal courtier banished for honest speaking who re-enters his master's service in disguise; and the Gloster subplot, with the good brother disinherited by deception, disguised as a beggar until the time is ripe to return for single combat and the offer of a kingdom. A precursor of the play's climax, and a provisional fulfilment of its romance pattern (soon to be overtaken by tragic calamity), is figured in a reversion to the chivalric romance of the duel between Edgar (who appears, from nowhere, the stereotypical anonymous challenger) and his brother Edmund.

The '*King Lear*' plays locate themselves firmly into the typology of tragedy: and it is in this respect that the 'Shakespearean' Lear texts resemble one another more closely than they resemble any of the other narrative versions. Neither of the two texts betrays any ambiguity on this point: Cordelia is executed, Lear dies. But the distinctive character of the Lear tragedy is that in its contradictory relationship with its narrative sources, it is quite unlike any other 'Shakespearean' tragedy. If that distinctive willingness of the Shakespearean Lear texts to read their sources against the grain introduces into the texts some residual conflict with the ancient lines of the romance-narrative, then even the ostensibly uncontroversial category of tragedy might become complicated and problematical. We already have two Lear plays: but are there even within the space interpolated by this bifurcation further discrete Lear stories, locked in conflictual interplay?

While much discussion within the two-text debate, concerned as it has been to trace a trajectory of authorial alteration, has focused on traceable or speculative discriminations between different states of the texts' development, little attention seems to have been paid to possible correlations between the texts' significant divergences and their separate generic dimensions. Where the texts of the Lear play, in other words, differ substantially one from another, it is likely to be along the axes of, or the sutures joining, those historical, romance and tragic narrative influences that constitute their iterable and volatile textuality. This in fact is the case, and can be illustrated briefly by reference to: differing treatments of the war, where one text clearly dramatises civil war and the other foreign invasion; separable representations of Cordelia's homecoming, in particular the inclusion in Q1 of the scene reporting Cordelia's return to Britain (*true chronicle historie*, p. 130); and the strikingly dissimilar versions of the final tragic conclusion.

In both texts Cordelia's return has the objective of intervening, in what is already a situation of violent civil discord, on behalf of the king and against the forces of her sisters. The issue of discrepancy between the texts centres on whether Cordelia brings a French army with her: whether, in other words, the pro-Lear alliance formed between Albany, Gloster (later Edgar) and Cordelia, involves the military intervention of a foreign power. 'ther's a division betwixt the Dukes' says Gloster in both texts; but in Q1 this is followed by 'Ther's part of a power already *landed*', where F1 gives 'already *footed*'. Q1 openly and consistently identifies the French army as a player in the action; where F1 with equal consistency omits such allusions, and throws the emphasis on internecine conflict and civil war. The relevant Q1 passages include:

> [*Gon*] Wher's thy drum? *France* spreds his banners in our noyseles land,
> With plumed helme, thy state begins thereat
> Whils't thou a morall foole sits still and cries
> Alack why does he so? (*true chronicle historie*, p. 129).

> [*Alb*] ... for this busines
> It touches us, as *France* invades our land
> Not bolds the King ... (*true chronicle historie*, p. 144).

Neither of these references has any counterpart in F1. Where Kent initially broaches the prospect of open civil war, the texts diverge in the same way. Q1's version elaborates on the imminent French invasion:

> ... there is division,
> Although as yet the face of it be cover'd,
> With mutuall cunning, twixt *Albany* and *Cornwall*
> But true it is, from *France* there comes a power
> Into this scattered kingdome, who alreadie wise in our
> Have secret feet in some of our best Ports, (negligence,
> And are at point to shew their open banner.
> (*true chronicle historie*, p. 111).

While F1 reduces this to the ambiguous or evasive[20]:

> There is diuision
> (Although as yet the face of it is couer'd
> With mutuall cunning) 'twixt Albany, and Cornwall:
> Who haue, as who haue not, that their great Starres
> Thron'd and set high; Seruants, who seeme no lesse,
> Which are to France the Spies and Speculations
> Intelligent of our State.

The scene of Cordelia's return, which occurs only in Q1, reports the landing of a French army accompanied by both Cordelia and the French king, who then returns to France leaving his general 'Monsier *la far*' in charge.

These variations thus represent a substantive textual difference in each play's recyling of the historical Lear legend. Earlier scholars suspected the influence of censorship, with Q1's representation of a foreign invasion toned down, on censorial instruction, to F1's domestic civil war. Greg thought the motif of foreign invasion presented a 'patriotic dilemma', suggesting that the nation could not save itself but had to be liberated by a foreign ally; and Madeleine Doran argued that the Folio made cuts in the Quarto text precisely to alter the nationality of Cordelia's military 'powers'[21]. The leading revisionists, however, have rejected this view, arguing that the diminution of France's role derives from 'an altered dramatic vision of the last half of the play'[22]. René Weis also agrees with this position, citing Taylor's suggestion that F produces 'a more benevolent impression, one more clearly personified by Cordelia herself', and concurring that the more benevolent version is the revised one, the one representing Shakespeare's ultimate intentions and considered judgement (Weis, *Lear*, p. 31).

All these arguments around censorship and revision remain inconclusive, relying as they do on unproven assumptions about agency and development – that is, that an authorial agent deliberately modified Q1, in response either to externally imposed pressure of censorship or to internally generated possibilities of artistic reconstruction, to produce the 'revised' Folio text. Such arguments need working assumptions about the rationale for any general or particular change: and here these assumptions seem particularly questionable. Arguments from censorship assume the French invasion to have been, in Greg's words, a 'ticklish business'. But why should the representation of civil war, in a play printed in 1608, have seemed more acceptable than that of foreign invasion? As Gary Taylor points out, the Jacobean administration had if anything more to fear from the former than from the latter (Taylor, 'Monopolies', p. 80). Equally, however, revisionist arguments have assumed that the depiction of a state healing its own civil discord by internal subjugation of injustice presents a more 'benevolent' image than that of one requiring assistance from a foreign ally. This presupposes that such a healing process does actually take place, an assumption that rests more securely on critical tradition than on the textual evidence.

These debates are none the less not without interest,

acknowledging as they do the irreducible differences between the discrete textualisations. The revisionist proposition that from the ambiguities of Q1, F1 consolidates a mature and tragic vision, can be seen to reinforce the reciprocity of the two texts as a canon in miniature, enacting that classic Shakespearean trajectory from tragic despair to enlightened resignation. Some sacrifices are none the less entailed in this attempt to rescue the integrity of authorial vision. An interpretation that emphasises the possibilities of national regeneration must place much more emphasis on the battered male survivors of the civil conflict – Albany, Edgar, Kent – than on Cordelia, the good daughter who reappears only to suffer defeat and ignominious death. But Cordelia's strength is defined in the Quarto very much in terms of the military power she leads. In the battle scene (modern editions 5.2) Cordelia in Q1 is announced as leading both the French army and the British king: *Enter the powers of France over the stage, Cordelia with her father in her hand.* In F1 both the French presence and Cordelia's priority have been reduced: *Enter with drum and colours Lear, Cordelia and soldiers over the stage.*

The revisionist arguments that express a preference for the Folio version's diminution of the French invasion entail a distinct complicity with both authorial intentionality, and with a conservative critical agenda that invests its desires in the surviving male protagonists of the tragedy. The Quarto text more sharply and painfully foregrounds the incommensurable discrepancy between the promise of Cordelia's return, and its manifest failure, as both the heroine and her imported army endure defeat.

Another way of putting the distinction between differing representations of the war, would be to say that the geopolitical worlds of F1 and Q1 are equally incommensurable. The world of the Quarto text is more obviously the terrain of romance, where both geographical place and national boundaries are relatively ambiguous and undefined. Value and significance are invested in the person and the cause, rather than in whatever detailed political arrangements currently pertain; the plays do begin, after all, with the arbitrary division of a map along the lines of personal idiosyncrasy and family preference. What is important in Q1 is not the nationality of the 'powers' Cordelia brings, but that she reappears empowered, as the potential saviour of the romance narrative. F1, we might say, has introduced into its geopolitics more modern sensitivities about national boundaries, mapping the integrity of the modern nation state onto the romance fluidity of Lear's Britain. In doing so, the text curtails some of the potencies available within chronicle romance to strengthen and centralise the representation of Cordelia.

The most substantial difference between Q and F texts concerns precisely this configuration of Cordelia, the French army and romance convention. The scene, familiar from conflated editions as 4.3, in which Kent and a Gentleman discuss Cordelia's return from France, appears only in the Quarto text. The scene is virtually a preface to the following section in which Cordelia herself converses with a Doctor. Cordelia's return is therefore first reported and described before she herself appears to the audience. The convention of narrative report allows for the full intensity of an iconographic idealisation of Cordelia, in which she is represented both sentimentally and heroically: a virtual force of passion, and a source of discipline and control; both dutiful daughter, and warrior queen:

> (of griefe.
>
> *Kent.* Did your letters pierce the queene to any demonstration
> *Gent.* I say she tooke them, read them in my presence,
> And now and then an ample teare trild downe
> Her delicate cheeke, it seemed she was a queene over her passion,
> Who most rebell-like, sought to be King ore her.
> (*true chronicle historie*, p. 130).

Although focused on powerful emotions, the text immediately draws analogies between person and state, individual feeling and political context. Cordelia is both monarch and rebel, not only in terms of her emotional control. She is also the daughter who 'most rebell-like' defiantly subverted the authority of the King. She is 'queene' of France but is here as a pretender, seeking political control over Britain; and therefore a 'rebell' to the legally constituted (though manifestly unjust) authorities of the kingdom. She is out to restore a fallen king whose personal weakness corresponds in inverse ratio to her evident strength, a powerful queen hoping to prop up an enfeebled monarch. Metaphorically the 'passion' that is figured as a 'King' is also Lear himself, whose initial banishment of his daughter is thus formulated as a 'rebell-like' usurpation of true moral sovereignty.

The subtle play of this political vocabulary articulates a complex configuration of meanings around legitimacy, restoration, force and authority. In the following scene Cordelia attempts to clarify her cause by disentangling these ambiguous valencies:

> (ward.
> *Mes.* News Madam, the Brittish powers are marching hither-
> *Cord.* Tis knowne before, our preparation stands,
> In expectation of them, ô deere father
> It is thy busines that I go about, therfore great *France*
> My mourning and important teares hath pitied,
> No blowne ambition doth our armes in sight
> But love, deere love, and our ag'd fathers right…
> (*true chronicle historie*, p. 132).

In dutiful compliance with her romance heritage, Cordelia here offers 'love' as a transcendent value, occluding the political and military motives attaching to her mission. Where the Gentleman's metaphors invest Cordelia with an aura of power that is both impressive and dangerous, she herself explicitly disavows any 'rebell-like' intentions, reassuring the audience that this is no act of territorial aggression, but a mission of mercy, a crusade of liberation. The military power of France is merely an adjunct to the irenic aspiration of Cordelia's filial duty; indeed the military commitment itself is initially motivated by compassion rather than anger:

> ... great *France*
> My mourning and important teares hath pitied ...
> (*true chronicle historie*, p. 132).

It is no reflection on the purity of Cordelia's represented motives to observe that the balance of moral and political values in her language presents genuine difficulties. Invasions are often presented as necessary acts of liberation, and a pacific sanction often conferred on military violence. But the effort visible here to subjugate passionate indignation to the discipline of a serene patience remains problematical for all that. In Cordelia's behaviour, as depicted by the Gentleman, we witness a powerful struggle between compassion and rage:

> Faith once or twice she heav'd the name of father,
> Pantingly forth as if it prest her heart,
> Cried sisters, sisters, shame of Ladies sisters:
> *Kent,* father, sisters, what ith storme ith night,
> Let pitie not be beleeft there she shooke,
> The holy water from her heavenly eyes,
> And clamour moystened her, then away she started,
> To deale with griefe alone. (*true chronicle historie*, p.131)

The linguistic violence visible and audible here in those strong verbs – 'heav'd', 'prest', 'shooke' – testifies to a suppressed anger that is sharply at odds with the image of tearful feminine sympathy. Even the 'holy water from her heavenly eyes' joins with the more demonstrative 'clamour' to mollify ('moysten') her righteous indignant anger. Just as in the play's opening scene Cordelia's silence was used as a sharp-edged weapon, so here she does not retreat into private grief but actively 'start[s]' aside in order to master her own emotions, 'To deale with griefe alone'.

The reporting Gentleman remains committed to a project of idealisation that disallows the presence within Cordelia's emotional range of that violence of anger that so pervades the emotional world of the play, and is the source of both insanity and vicious, vindictive cruelty. His Cordelia remains the supreme master-mistress of her own passion:

> *Kent.* O then it moved her.
> *Gent.* Not to a rage, patience and sorow streme,
> Who should expresse her goodliest you have seene,
> Sun shine and raine at once, her smiles and teares,
> Were like a better way those happie smilets,
> That playd on her ripe lip seeme not to know,
> What guests were in her eyes which parted thence,
> As pearles from diamonds dropt in briefe,
> Sorow would be a raritie most beloved,
> If all could so become it (*true chronicle historie*, pp. 130-1).

Those proper feminine and filial feelings are figured by natural metaphors of flowing water, beginning with Cordelia's spring of weeping ('an ample teare trild downe'), modulating through the 'streme', the 'sun shine and raine' of merging patience and sorrow, and moving to a formal sacralisation of this liquid diction in 'holy water'. The Gentleman's idealising emblematisation permits Kent overtly to declare that absolute distinctiveness of virtue and vice that is structurally characteristic of the radiant world of romance:

> *Kent.* It is the stars, the stars above us governe our conditions,
> Else one selfed mate and make could not beget,
> Such different issues … (*true chronicle historie*, p. 131)

The 'reporting' technique of the scene permits a focus on the production of reality in language, as other interpreters reproduce Cordelia in their own preferred form. The text delivers a different Cordelia, one in whom the emotional tension between daughterly compassion and indignant anger is paralleled by the tension within her cause, between the potentially violent subversiveness of invasion and usurpation, and the proper observation of filial duty. Though modern critics have sought to martyr Cordelia on the altar of female virtues, making of her a pattern of patience and obedience, within the Quarto text there remain strong traces of that 'woman of manlie courage', the Cordelia of historical romance.

As this scene appears only in the Quarto, the standard revisionist method of comparative analysis has been unavailable to scholars, and the textual differentiation therefore relatively uncontroversial. Whatever of Cordelia is represented and produced in this scene, whether that be the saintly female martyr or the empowered romance heroine, is by definition not to be found in the Folio. As Grace Ioppolo says:

> 4.3 does not merely serve to 'emblematize' Cordelia but deliberately and majestically extends the direction of her character which the Quarto has been building for four acts. She is represented as the strong queen and the loving daughter, and her roles merge as she acquires the power to act as one of the play's moral spokespersons ... Because the Folio lacks these lines ... it weakens the establishment of moral strength in Cordelia by reducing her at this point in the play to a supporting character rather than a fundamental one[23].

The 'emblematized' and idealised image of Cordelia is precisely what our dominant critical traditions require. Purged by idealisation of the potent and dangerous associations of otherness (foreignness, manliness, militarism) that collect about her in the Quarto, Cordelia's virtue is ready to withstand the otherwise terminal obstacles of military defeat, capture and execution, as her redemptive and sacrificial virtues are split off into a hypostasised realm of indissoluble purity. This is certainly what is done to her in the speeches of Kent and the Gentleman. It is attempted again by Lear himself, as the defeated contenders are led off the battlefield; though the warrior courage of Cordelia's resentment and indignation breaks through the strategies of idealisation within which patriarchy attempts to confine her:

(incurd

> *Cor.* We are not the first who with best meaning have
> The worst, for thee oppressed King am I cast downe,
> My selfe could else outfrowne false Fortunes frowne,
> Shall we not see these daughters, and these sisters?
> *Lear.* No, no, come lets away to prison …
> Upon such sacrifices my *Cordelia*,
> The Gods themselves throw incense …
> (*true chronicle historie*, p. 146).

And it is done to Cordelia over and over again, in those acts of critical interpretation that seek to replicate the patriarchal idealisation of the Quarto's Gentleman.

Above all, this scene is the strongest link to the old romance narrative from which the Shakespearean tragedies derive. With the scene intact, we have a play in which the discrepancy between traditional happy ending and modern tragedy is stretched to a painful tension, as the dramatic action seems to be moving literally in two quite opposite directions. With Lear's insanity, the torturing of Gloucester, Edmund's success, the text rushes towards the supremacy of disaster. With Cordelia's return, the arrival of allied troops, the continuing determined passive resistance of Kent and Edgar, it turns away towards the once-familiar happy ending of restorative romance. In the Folio version that tension is necessarily reduced by the absence of this particular scene. In the Quarto it remains obstinately in place, disrupting generic uniformity and consistency of tone. It has even been suggested that this element of the play must to its first audiences have raised expectations that the drama would play out towards the familiar happy ending: an expectation that must have terminated in a most bitter and cruel disappointment. Certainly for modern readers, as John Turner puts it, 'the play (unlike any other Shakespearean tragedy) leads us even when we know it well, to ache after that happy ending implicit in its ancient storylines' (Turner, *Play*, p. 95).

કર્

Just as the dominant editorial tradition has been founded on an attempt to restore by collation, conflation and emendation a textualisation approximating to a lost 'original', so the dominant critical tradition addressing the Lear plays as tragedy has evaluated them within an interpretative context governed by a search for the play's moral philosophy. From G. Wilson Knight's view of *King Lear* as a parable of Christian sacrifice and spiritual regeneration, to Jan Kott's perception of the play as depicting the ethical vacuity and moral exhaustion of the modern world[24], '*King Lear*' has been expected to deliver some kind of authorially intended and deliberately composed world-view. In the course of the debate around revision, the editorial and critical agendas have become interestingly intertwined. Since the founding modern critical debate (1930-70) produced an interpretative spectrum largely concentrated on the play's moral philosophy, but ranging widely from 'optimistic' to 'pessimistic' readings, it seemed inevitable that bibliographical comparisons between the 1608 and 1623 texts should also focus on variations within the same interpretative field. Thus the textual debate, with its enforced concentration on the relationship between the two texts, has tended to concern itself with the same problems of interpretation, and tried to assess how each text scores on the same scale of values – is '*King Lear*' an uplifting affirmation of the possibilities of spiritual redemption, or a bleak invocation of an empty universe? Do the gods of the play throw incense on sacrifice, or wantonly kill men and women like flies?

If the obvious variations between the texts are attributed to authorial revision, and both 1608 and 1623 versions contained within the great metacategory of the 'author', then each text can be expected to embody and express a distinct, though clearly iterable, authorial perspective. Revisionist bibliography, in short, needs the concept of authorial intention; and the debates discussed above also make full use of other problematised critical concepts such as Bradleian character-study and the pseudo-Aristolean conception of tragedy as an immanent aesthetic form.

The focus on 'character' seems to reflect a critical conservatism, but has been justified by the argument that textual variations (usually involving the addition, subtraction and differential allocation of 'lines') affect characterisation more obviously than other aesthetic categories. Gary Taylor thus observes of the 'two-text debate', that 'much of the argument has involved alleged differences in the presentation of character. Character criticism is, of course, intellectually unfashionable at the moment, but studies of pervasive imagery and themes could hardly be expected to differentiate two strata of composition'[25]. The presence within the *King Lear* two-text debate of 'unfashionable' Bradleian character-criticism can be demonstrated from a series of discussions addressing the variations or alterations in the textual presentation of Albany and Edgar, and their influence on each text's conclusion. The final speech of the play, though common to both texts, is spoken by Albany in Q and by Edgar in F. The debate was initiated by Michael Warren in his 1978 paper on 'Quarto and Folio *King Lear* and the Interpretation of Albany and Edgar'. Gary Taylor pursued this line in *The Division of the Kingdoms,* his comparative discussion of the roles of Albany and Edgar framed within the same assumptions about tragedy as an ethical discourse, and focusing particularly on the dramatic conclusion of each text: 'To Michael Warren's admirable account of the Folio's magnification of Edgar, largely at Albany's expense, I have nothing to add; but neither he nor Urkowitz remarks on the fact that Edgar fills the role of chief moral survivor much more comfortably than either Albany or Kent' (Taylor, 'Date and Authorship', p. 425). It is axiomatic to this argument that tragedy ends with a recomposition of social order and a re-establishment of moral integrity, directed or presided over by a key 'moral survivor'. Edgar seems to Taylor to fill that role admirably; he is 'a representative of moral continuity' (p. 425), whose strengthened role in the Folio 'naturally therefore strengthens the promise of moral continuity after the tragedy … Some sense of hope, transcendence, spiritual consolation, the Folio ending … offers us' (p. 427).

René Weis follows this tradition, arguing that the role of Albany is substantially weakened and Edgar's substantially strengthened, between Q and F. His particular evidence for Albany's progressive enervation is the absence from F of some speeches (*true chronicle historie*, pp. 128-9) in which he stands up to his wife, an exhibition of manliness and personal probity considered indispensable to the holding of public office: 'Albany needs to sever himself from Gonoril and a married life with her. If he is to bear the standard of decency and duty in the play and lead his people, he must spell out his rejection of Gonoril's evil and his past married life with her' (Weis, *Lear*, p. 1). The relative strengthening of Edgar's role indicates 'a wider conceptual transformation', in the course of which the revising Shakespeare shifted the ultimate conferral of moral power from the legitimate but poorly qualified heir, Albany, to the figure who claims power by right of suffering and moral growth. By virtue of 'the fact that Albany speaks the last lines in Q and Edgar in F … F would appear to play down the importance of Albany: after all, the concluding lines are very important here where the speaker assumes the mantle of the ultimate moral authority in the play' (pp. 7-8). The attribution of that status to Edgar is described by Weis as 'a radical and aesthetically conscious act', aligning power with virtue, and allowing the meek to inherit the earth.

It should however be apparent that both texts, though in F much more decisively than in Q, defy and defeat any expectation of restoration, recomposition or 'moral continuity'. In Q Albany offers the kingdom of Edgar and Kent as joint rulers:

> *Duke*: Beare them from hence, our present busines
> Is to generall woe, friends of my soule, you twaine
> Rule in this kingdome, and the goard state sustaine.
> (*true chronicle historie*, p.155)

As the sole surviving member of the aristocracy to whom Lear granted the divided kingdom, Albany should constitutionally inherit: but he appears not to want the job. There is already therefore a distinct sense, inconceivable in a historical drama but possible in a romance, that there is no recomposition: that monarchy itself has died with Lear, and that the kingdom exhibits a condition of what John Turner has called 'terminal collapse': 'We are left at the end not with dogma but with dead loss' (Turner, *Play*, p. 97).

Kent certainly declines the offer: his allegiance is to a lost world-order, an absolute attachment to 'a civilization lost with anguish for all time' (Turner, *Play*, p. 97). Albany's summing-up speech is not at all what might be expected from an agent of social reconstruction, but it does at least express some sense of human solidarity among the younger and surviving generation, symbolised by himself and Edgar. Kent, together with Lear and Gloster, belongs to a superseded generation, which vanishes together with the world it governed. Albany and Edgar remain to pick up the pieces. Albany's final speech is not, however, a formal declaration of reconstruction, the kingdom 'under new management', but an elegiac reflection on the incommensurability of that old lost world and what survives. Abandoning his formal attempt to restore order, Albany asserts that such political language is beside the point, and only the language of feeling remains valid. Edgar, in this version, says absolutely nothing (even less than Cordelia had said at the play's opening). His eloquent silence is a suitable testament to the sovereignty of emotion, but distinctly unpromising in a figurehead of government.

More decisively still does F insist on the finality of the king-dom's terminal collapse. Albany again offers the job of ruler to the only two available candidates: but this time both appear to decline. It seems to have escaped the notice of revisionist critics that in F, Edgar seems no more inclined to accept sovereign responsibility than is Kent. It is very clear that in both texts the language required by the situation, 'what we ought to say', is identified as that formal language of political recomposition that the survivors find so embarassingly inappropriate. The language of feeling, that transparent language Lear had discovered in his reconciliation with Cordelia, necessarily has the ultimate effect of deferring the moment of political restitution. Edgar's elegiac tribute to the authorities of Lear's vanished world co-exists with a humble and despairing expression of inadequacy. This is not what we have been taught by our critical traditions to expect from the final resolution of a 'Shakespearean tragedy'.

ॐ

> ... she's gone for ever.
> I know when one is dead and when one lives;
> She's dead as earth. Lend me a looking glass;
> If that her breath will mist or stain the stone,
> Why then she lives (Foakes, *Lear,* 5.3.257-61)

> O thoul't come no more,
> Never, never, never, never ...
> Do you see this? Look on her: look, her lips.
> Look there, look there! *He dies.* (Foakes, *Lear,* 5.3.306-7, 309-10).

What does Lear see in Cordelia's lips? The distinction between life and death, the living and the dead, is here proposed as absolute: Cordelia is 'dead as earth'. Yet having pronounced her dead, Lear looks for signs of life, for the faintest traces of breath, invisible and inaudible, that yet may mist the mirror, 'stain the stone'. If it be so, 'she lives'. The second speech repeats exactly the same paradox: 'thoul't come no more'; yet some motion about her lips, some stirring of breath or speech, seem to imply vitality.

Is Cordelia already dead, and the evidence of life merely the delusion of a mad old king, himself on the point of extinction? Or is she still barely alive, her actual death perhaps coinciding with that of her father? Lear's perception could hardly be trusted, if one were looking for a reliable clinical diagnosis; and the silence and inactivity of Edgar and Albany and Kent, who make no move to resuscitate her, seem to tell their own story. Lear's desire for Cordelia to survive, his yearning 'ache' for a romance resolution to the tragedy, is all that creates these imaginary vital signs. At the beginning of the play Lear looked to Cordelia's lips to speak a public declaration of love. But he did not listen, either to her speech or her silence; he was unable to grasp that Cordelia's lips would inevitably speak differently, that 'woman's desire would not be expected to speak the same language as man's'[26]. Now it is too late.

But 'life' may mean something different within the symbolic language of the drama from a pulse, respiration, continuing cerebral activity. What Lear feels from Cordelia's dead lips may be a breath that mists no mirror, a quickening spirit that transcends mortality, a sign of life everlasting. As Bradley and many critics after him have shown, the language of the play's closure overtly hints at redemptive, sacrificial, even specifically Christian meanings.

> This feather stirs, she lives: if it be so,
> It is a chance which does redeem all sorrows
> That ever I have felt (Foakes, *Lear*, 3.5.263-5).

'... if it be so', then Lear may die, as Bradley describes him, in 'unbearable joy'[27].

The supersession from about 1960 onwards of these redemptive interpretations of King Lear by bleak and nihilistic readings is a familiar history. Subsequent critics have proceedeed with an acute awareness of the extremity of this 'fierce dispute'[28], this 'dizzying fluctuation between contradictory meanings'[29] and have tended to find the play unstable and indeterminate, as

Stephen Booth puts it, 'unfixed'[30].

The two-text debate has clearly reinforced this tendency to see *King Lear* as multiple and pluralistic in its meanings. We could note for instance that the words 'Do you see this? Look on her: look, her lips/Look there, look there!', words on which whole redemptive theories have been founded, are not present in the Quarto text, appear only in the Folio. Adherents of revision theory would have to agree that here Shakespeare has 'changed his mind' by adding a reference to possible signs of life. But even if this were accepted, it takes us no nearer to definitive interpretation. The line is further evidence of redemption, even of immortality; or it is an even more cruel twist of tragedy's wounding knife, signalling an even sharper contrast between human hope on the part of 'impassioned clay' (Keats, p. 295) and the absolute finality of death; a 'cruel final delusion' or a 'blessed liberation' (Foakes, *Lear*, p. 75).

'We will not reach conclusion'[31] along these lines. It is perhaps surprising that accounts of the play were for so long so conclusive and definitive in their attempts to fix meaning. But such readings were based on the standard conflated text, while contemporary interpretations cannot but be aware of textual multiplicity. The quotations given above from *King Lear* omitted some of their edition's textual features.

> ^QO^Q thoul't come no more,
> Never, never, ^Fnever, never^F …
> ^FDo you see this? Look on her: look, her lips.
> Look there, look there! *He dies.*^F (Foakes, *Lear*, 5.3.306-7, 309-10).

The Arden 3 text is also a conflated edition but as this extract shows, it introduces a set of bibliographic codes that call the reader's attention to the text's hybridity. The sutures joining one text with another are not concealed, or partly disguised at the foot of the page as a collation, but obtruded upon the experience of reading. Instead of the invisible mending that normally stitches together the disparate materials of Q and F, Foakes's text boldly displays the joints, brackets, or hinges that weld the text together into a construction. They further adumbrate the activity of the editor as craftsman or artisan, a collaborator in the process of composition. He does not make the material from which the text is fashioned but, as the superior indicators show, he has decided or agreed that this is how it should be put together; the design of the piece is his. The raw material has itself in any case been produced by collaboration, at the very least of the author with himself in a dialogue between different and discordant aesthetic choices ('Two texts, two hands, two ways of listening', [32]), and more probably in a collaborative economy involving the activity of others[33].

Inside Foakes's text another kind of collaboration is signalled to the reader. In his list of acknowledgements to colleagues and predecessors, Foakes mentions 'the gracious librarians of the Shakespeare Centre Library in Stratford-upon-Avon', and

> especially Mary White, who became my wife; it was a joy to have her help and her sustaining presence while I was working on this edition (Foakes, *Lear*, p. xvi).

Mary White is evidently the same person who appears in the edition's dedication:

> For my beloved Mary
>
> *Thoul't come no more,*
> *Never, never, never, never, never ...*

From this we learn that underlying this text is a history of personal bereavement, to which Lear's words on the death of Cordelia give eloquent utterance. Mary is inside the text as a collaborator, a 'help and sustaining presence'; but also as an absence, a sign of loss. The 'joy' that accompanies the editor's remembrance of the 'gracious' gift of her (which perhaps echoes Bradley's 'unbearable joy'), co-exists with despair at an absoluteness of separation: 'Thoul't come no more'.

So it will always be. We love, and lose, and are lost. But we never lose what Stephen Greenblatt called our 'desire to speak with the dead'[34], a desire that is enhanced rather than annulled by any refusal on their part to answer. Dialogue is possible, in Greenblatt's terms, via those 'textual traces of themselves' that the dead leave behind. He is thinking here of writing; and relatively few of us leave behind the great poem, or novel, or even edition, that so readily facilitates that strange 'conversation' of speech with the dead, where textual traces 'make themselves heard in the voice of the living' (Greenblatt, *Negotiations*, p. 1). But if all writing is collaborative, then many more contribute to memorable utterance than have their names signed upon it[35]. Mary White was one such; but in this case her clearly substantial personal contribution to the work is acknowledged, since her husband had the grace to sign his edition with her name.

Thoul't come no more

(Horace, *Odes* IV.vii)

Snows slop to slush, but growing greenery graces the fields,
Trees toss their hair;
Streams subside, obedient to their banks, earth tilts
In a different direction;
Nature strips off, nymphs and graces unashamed bare
Their skin to the vernal air.
Hours devour the day, the days the year. Fair warning:
Nothing's immortal here.
Spring splits the ice-age, summer scorches spring;
Hard on the heels of
Apple-bearing autumn's profusion of fruits
Back comes the killing snow.
How quickly the crescent moon recovers lost light!
But when we go down
To the dark where the great and the good and the brave
Await us, dust we are, and dreams.
You can pray to the heavenly gods to add to tomorrow
The grace of another day;
Spend all your wealth on delighting your soul, and cheat
The avarice of heirs. But
When we shrink in the shade, and the dreadful judge
Delivers his verdict, there's nothing
Not eloquence, not birth, not virtue, nothing at all
Can bring us back here.
Pure as Hippolytus was, not even huntress Diana
Could drag him to light;
And loving Pirothous still sits in the dark, his chains unsheared
By Theseus' invincible sword.

CHAPTER SIX

Notes and Queries:
Macbeth

୬

A S THE PREVIOUS CHAPTERS have indicated, one has to feel sorry for *Macbeth*. A vast amount of scholarly labour, critical argument and publishing activity has over the last decade concentrated around the variant texts of Shakespeare's plays, and especially *Hamlet, King Lear* and *Othello*; such that 'plays' familiar for centuries in fairly standard conflated editions, have now replicated into a 'multiple-text' Shakespeare, compelling evidence of such cultural activities as revision, collaboration, co-authorship, and adaptation for performance. Standing aloof in solitary eminence from this superabundance of textualisation is *The Tragedy of Macbeth,* the only one of the four 'great tragedies' to lack any printed-text evidence prior to the 1623 First Folio. Since it is now widely accepted that variant texts, where they survive, are sufficiently different from one another to merit separate publication, and that evidence of textual multiplicity enriches rather than diminishes a play's reputation, a tragedy with only one text, without at least a 'Bad Quarto' to accompany it, seems to be at something of a professional disadvantage.

On the other hand, the singular Folio text of *The Tragedie of Macbeth* has frequently been treated by scholars as almost its own 'Bad Quarto': as a reduced, revised, restored, even 'ruined' text,

cut down from Shakespeare's original conception for performance, worked over and tinkered with by other writers, certainly
and identifiably by Middleton. And it is true that *The Tragedie of
Macbeth* bears some of the characteristics often associated with
'Bad Quarto' texts. It is short. It contains abundant evidence of
multiple authorship. It is full of linguistic obscurity and textual
cruces. It is characterised by a crowd-pleasing theatricality, visible
especially in the witches' song-and-dance routines. It displays
confused stage directions (e.g. Macbeth is apparently killed on
stage, but his head is produced from off). And so on.

Re-reading the introduction to an old edition like J. Dover
Wilson's 1947 text for the CUP 'New Shakespeare' series, we find
all these faults admitted, yet excused, since the play is regarded as
manifestly perfect in its received textual form. In a section sub-
titled 'The Three *Macbeths*', Wilson summarises the preceding
scholarly debate as essentially 'disintegrationist', concerned to
identify non-Shakespearean amendments and interpolations. The
Clarendon Press edition of 1872 queried some 300 lines as possibly non-Shakespearean; and the 'Arden' edition of 1912 regarded
167 lines as 'spurious'[1]. Accepting that the Folio text as it stands
represents an abridgement and adaptation of an earlier fuller
text, and that it contains traces of this chequered history, Wilson
quotes with some sympathy W.J. Lawrence's description of the
Folio text as the ruin of some 'vast and venerable Gothic cathe-
dral, tastelessly tinkered by an unimaginative restorer'[2]; but then
inclines to agree with Mark van Doren that the text is 'incomparably brilliant as it stands, and within its limits perfect'[3]. Wilson's
solution to this apparent contradiction is to broach an explanation that has become familiar as 'revision theory': that
'Shakespeare himself must be the chief abridger' (p. xxiii).

Wilson's 'three *Macbeths*' are: (i) an original version of the play
by Shakespeare, longer and fuller than the Folio text, of unknown
date; (ii) an abridgement of this play, also by Shakespeare, which
Wilson dates to 1605-6, and which became the Folio text and (iii)

a subsequent 'rehandling of this abridgement in turn by the "unimaginative restorer"', who was, of course, 'botcher' Middleton. Thus in a single ingenious argument Wilson accepts many of the principles of modern textual criticism – textual fluidity and variance, legitimate textual adaptation for the stage, multiple authorship, cultural collaboration – while at the same time fixing the Folio text of *The Tragedie of Macbeth* as uniquely authoritative, 'incomparably perfect', and indubitably Shakespeare's final intentions for the work.

Wilson's speculations about a very early Shakespearean *Macbeth* has not found much support. Most modern scholarship continues to relate the play via circumstantial evidence (Scottish history, witches, touching for the King's Evil and equivocation) to the early years of James I's accession, and specifically to the Gunpowder Plot. The modern consensus seems to be that distinct versions of *Macbeth* (any of which might have been, but apparently were not, captured by a particular printed edition), existed in 1604-5, when it was putatively played at the Globe as a topical drama; 1606, when it may have been performed before James and King Christian of Denmark at Hampton Court and 1611, when it was witnessed at the Globe by Simon Forman. The only version for which any substantive textual evidence exists, is that of the text integrated into the First Folio of 1623.

All that can be said for certainty, therefore, is that this history of textual iterability eventually generated one text that has survived, that printed in the First Folio. Although the topical references pointing to 1604-5 have become virtually unquestioned editorial reference points, they are all, as A. R. Braunmuller succinctly puts it, 'vague, circumstantial or undatable'[4]. The court performance of 1606 is an established part of theatre history, and it very probably occurred, yet there is no direct evidence for it at all. We know from references in other plays that the play was performed over this period and that its impact was considerable: but what happened to it between these various windows of performance opportunity, and the moment when the text was finalised into the 1623 textualisation, is anybody's (or rather everybody's) guess.

Evidence of the play's 'after-life' discloses a continuing history of radical change. The Padua prompt-book, a marked-up performance copy of the First Folio text, is dated by G. Blakemore Evans to around 1625-35, and may therefore reflect in its cuts and amendments pre-Restoration stage practice[5]. Scholars frequently note how short *Macbeth* is in comparison with the other great tragedies; and yet the Padua prompt-book shows us that it was still extensively cut in performance, especially around the Porter scene (2.3), the first interview with the murderers (3.1), the choric commentary of 3.4, and the long Macduff-Malcolm interview of 4.3 . After the Restoration Davenant's adaptation (published 1674) seems to have triggered the publication of the 1673 Quarto text of *Macbeth,* which prints in full the Middleton songs only cued in the Folio[6]. Once again, the text has changed. The story told by the concrete evidence of all these historical documents is a story of continual iterability. This history should urge caution on us when we make assumptions that the Folio text was the final and authoritative textualisation of '*Macbeth*', if what we mean by that term is the drama that was produced and circulated, performed and printed, seen and heard and read, in the early years of the seventeenth century.

In all this textual speculation there is one oddity. There is universal agreement that different versions of the play existed and that the isolation of the Folio text is a historical accident. A surprising number of variant versions of the play have been imaginatively reconstructed in editorial introductions, from such evidence as internal inconsistencies of the Folio text, and circumstantial references to topical events. These hypotheses, if finally unconvincing, indicate at least a powerful residual desire on the part of scholars and editors to possess other texts of *Macbeth,* such as those that are now so promiscuously available in the cases of the other 'great tragedies'. But there is one compelling piece of evidence that seems in this context to be undervalued, ignored or even overlooked. That is the fact that on Saturday 20 April 1611 a man went to the Globe Theatre on Bankside, paid his penny or twopence, watched a performance of Shakespeare's *Macbeth,* and subsequently wrote up his recollections in one of the few detailed eyewitness accounts of such a performance. Whether we ask the complex question 'what was *Macbeth* in 1611?', or the simple question 'what did Jacobean audiences actually see at the Globe on 20 April 1611 when they went to see a play called *Macbeth*?', a set of answers lies very readily to hand in the form of the substantial and detailed description by doctor and astrologist Simon Forman of the production he himself undoubtedly witnessed[7].

> In Mackbeth at the glod 1610 the 20 of Aprill [Saturday] ther was to be observed firste howe Mackbeth and Bancko, 2 noble men of Scotland Ridinge thorowe a wod the stode befor them 3 women feiries or Numphes And saluted Mackbeth sayinge of. 3 tyms unto him haille Mackbeth king of Codon for thou shalt be a kinge but shalt beget No kinges &c and then said Bancko What all to macbeth And nothing to me. yes said the nimphes Haille to thee Banko thou shalt beget kinges yet be no kinge And so they departed & cam to the Courte of Scotland to Dunkin king of Scotes and yt was in the dais of Edward the Confessor. And Dunkin bad them both kindly wellcom. And made Mackbeth forth with the Prince of Northumberland. and sent him hom to his own castell and appointed mackbeth to provid for him for he wold Sup with him the next dai at night & did soe. And mackebeth Contrived to kill Dumkin. & and thorowe the persuasion of his wife did that night Murder the kinge in his owne Castell beinge his guest. And ther were many prodigies seen that night & the dai before. And when Mack Beth had murdred the kinge the blod on his hands could

not be washed of by Any means. nor from his wives handes which handled the bloddi daggers in hiding them By which means they became both moch amazed & Affronted. the murder being knowen Dunkins 2 sonns fled the on to England the [other to] Walles to save them selves. they being fled, they were supposed guilty of the murder of their father which was nothinge soe. Then was Mackbeth Crowned kinge and then he for feare of Banko his old Companion that hre should beget kinges but be no kinge him selfe he contrived the death of Banko and caused him to be mur-dred on his way as he Rode. The next night beinge at supper with his noble men whom he had bid to a feaste to the which also Banco should have com, he began to speake of Noble Banco and wish the he were ther. And as he thus did standing up to derincke a Carouse to him. the ghoste of banco came and sate down in his cheier behind him. And he turninge About to sit down Again sawe the goste of Banco which fronted him so. that he fell into a great passion of fear & fury. utteringe many wordes about his murder by which when they hard that Banco was Murdred they Suspected Mackbet. Then mack dove fled to England to the kinges sonn And soe they Raised an Army And cam into scotland. And at dunstone Anyse overthrue mackbet. In the meantym whille macdovee Was in England mackbet slew mackdoves wife &children. and after in the battelle mackdove slew mackbet.

Observe Also howe mackbetes quen did Rise in the night in her slep & walke and talked and confessed all & the doctor noted her wordes.

Scholars have admitted that this is substantially the play recorded in the 1623 Folio text. But it does not seem to be, since there are obvious divergences, a literal description of a performance of the Folio text. Given the universal acknowledgement that *Macbeth* must have existed in radically different performed versions, it would seem natural to conclude that Forman's account con-structs something like a lost text of *Macbeth,* one of the numerous textual and performance versions that entertained Jacobean audiences from court to public theatre. But ranged against Forman's eyewitness testimony is the compelling evidence of the Folio text; and in this long great show trial of historical v. textual evidence, the text has always won. The Folio *Tragedie of Macbeth* has been defended against evidence that any historian would regard as substantial, by an almost universal assumption that Forman was an unreliable witness.

What, first of all, are the discrepancies between Forman's description and the Folio text? He recalls seeing Macbeth and Banquo riding through a wood, a sylvan (and equestrian) effect we would not expect to have been presented on the Globe stage. He records that this happened 'firste': but the play's first scene in the Folio text involves the witches alone, and is followed by the scene of the reported battle, the 'Bleeding Captain' scene. Why, given the play's imputed 'topicality', and Forman's own professional interests as a scientist, astrologer and all round 'cunning man', who did himself attempt to raise spirits – did Forman think the witches were 'feiries or Numphes' rather than what we have become accustomed to seeing them as – witches?

At times Forman seems to be recording the play's dialogue with some exactness (e.g. 'The next night beinge at supper with his noble men whom he had bid to a feaste to the which also Banco should have com, he began to speake of Noble Banco and wish the he were ther'). Yet at other times his recollections vary (e.g. in the witches' addresses to both Macbeth and Banquo) from the wording of the Folio. The notes on hand-washing have been taken to indicate that both Macbeth and Lady Macbeth attempted to cleanse their hands as a piece of stage business, which though intelligible as an account of the Folio's narrative, seems in describing specific action much more literal in its implications than the largely metaphorical language of the Folio text.

Forman's description may also be said to be as interesting for what it omits as for what it contains. His 'feiries or Numphes' do not seem to dance or sing, and are not accompanied by Hecate; in fact there is no mention (again surprising in the light of Forman's own personal and professional predilections) of Macbeth's second meeting with the Witches (the so-called 'Cavern' or 'Cauldron' scene, 4.1) at all. The drunken Porter, bearer of the most topical of *Macbeth's* contemporary allusions, does not appear in his account (2.3). The terse phrase 'contrived the death of Banko' skips quickly over that part of 3.1 in which Macbeth converses with the murderers; and there also seems to be no equivalent of 4.3, in which Malcolm and Macduff discuss the fate of Scotland.

The most readily available explanation for these discrepancies has been simply to question, on the basis of a comparison between the Folio text and his account, the accuracy of Forman's description. G.K. Hunter's[8] comments are representative:

> Simon Forman's account … diverges from the play we can read. But should we suppose that there was ever a play corresponding exactly to Forman's account?

Some of Forman's visual and verbal recollections seem closer to Holinshed's version of this story than to Shakespeare's, so it has been argued that Forman might have consulted Holinshed before or after attending the theatre and so 'contaminated' his recollections.

> It seems fairly clear from his wording that he has remembered or consulted Holinshed's chronicle of the reign; which implies uncertainty of memory and contamination from an outside source – both suspicious qualities in a witness.

The metaphor is significant. Hunter identifies himself as a prosecutor cross-examining a witness whose testimony conflicts with that of his client, the Folio text. As is customary in such circumstances everything possible is done to discredit the witness and so undermine the weight of his evidence:

> In any case Forman was not writing as a theatrical reporter; he was writing notes on matters that might be useful to remember. Can we blame him, or be surprised, if he did not write down what did not seem worth memorialising?

One wonders what kind of 'theatrical reporter' would think it useful to write down, for the convenience of subsequent scholars, a detailed account of the play's plot. It has however frequently been argued that Forman, not a theatrical reporter, recorded a very partial account of what he saw, since his interest in plays was not primarily aesthetic, and he recorded only what he found illuminating or useful. He may have omitted details that did not interest him. It is true that Forman's emphasis in other descriptions of performance included in *The Book of playes and Notes thereof per Forman, for Common Policy,* is on recording the memorable. But as it happens, that emphasis is not present in the account of *Macbeth,* which instead stresses the faculty of *observation*: 'ther was to be observed ... Observe also'. The element of the play he singles out for special emphasis is that of the doctor observing Lady Macbeth's sleepwalking, and taking notes. Prompted by this parallel it is worth recalling that Forman has been acknowledged by medical historians as a physician who 'devised exemplary ways of properly recording case histories'[9].

What of Forman's alleged use of Holinshed? Two other editors, Muir and Braunmuller:

> It is impossible to deduce very much about the characteristics of the play in 1611, as Forman probably did not write the description immediately after the performance, and his memories of the performance became mixed with his memories of Holinshed (Muir, *Macbeth,* p. xiv, n.1).

> Forman's description deviates from the Folio narrative ... and records some questionable detail – Raphael Holinshed's account of Macbeth's reign (read or remembered) apparently 'contaminates' Forman's diary entry (Braunmuller, *Macbeth,* p. 58).

Let us pursue one example of Holinshed's supposed 'contamination' of Forman's account of Macbeth. Most scholars have found the opening of Forman's description, in which he claims to have 'observed' Macbeth and Banquo riding through a wood, impossible as an account of action on the Globe stage. Instead, they have pointed to the well-known woodcut in Holinshed which shows Banquo and Macbeth on horseback as evidence of this cross-contamination: 'here Forman may be incorporating an illustration from Shakespeare's source in Holinshed's *Chronicles*'[10]. But anyone looking at this illustration will immediately recognise that it contains only one solitary single tree, which can hardly stand except in semiotic terms for a wood. The scene depicted in fact looks much more like the 'heath' on which the 'weyward sisters' plan to meet Macbeth. Nor do those figures look in the Holinshed illustration particularly like fairies or nymphs, since they are represented as three fairly ordinary women in contemporary costume (quite plausibly, then, witches).

And it just so happens that this is one play in which we can reasonably infer that some simulation of a forest was attempted on stage. As Birnam Wood has the status of a character in the drama, it may well (and it seems to me from the evidence of the text, must) have been physically represented by the use of stage properties, as here in 5.4 and 5.6.:

Syew.   What wood is this before us?
Ment.   The wood of Birnane.
Malc.   Let every Souldier hew him downe a bough,
           And bear't before him …

           … Now neere enough:
           Your leavy Skreenes throw downe
           (Rigney, *Macbeth*, pp. 97, 99).

It seems to me more likely that those 'leavy Skreenes' were also used to simulate a forest for the play's opening, than that Forman misremembered the woodcut from Holinshed to see a wood where the eye perceives only a tree. Divergences between what Forman recalls the weyward sisters saying, and what they say in the Folio, could suggest that the reporter got it wrong; or that in 1611 the wording of the play was closer to that of Holinshed than it had become by 1623.

Where Forman's notes are clearly incorrect – that is, where his details not only diverge from the Folio text, but cannot be imagined as featuring in any conceivable Macbeth play – the mistakes are auditory rather than visual. He did not get 'King of Codon' from Holinshed, but from mishearing 'Thane of Cawdor'. Anyone reading Holinshed would see that it makes no sense for Macbeth to be made Prince of Northumberland; but this can be easily understood as an error of the ear, and is far less likely as a misperception of the eye. If anything these errors place Forman, in a useful phrase from modern criminal investigation, 'at the scene'.

Forman's assumed unreliability is further explained by aspects of his character and professional status. He has not had a good press. A. R. Braunmullers' concise summary – 'Dr Simon Forman – astrologer, quack, accomplice in the poisoning of Sir Thomas Overbury' (Braunmuller, *Macbeth*, p. 57) gives a fair indication of the way in which his reputation has been routinely besmirched. True, he was an 'astrologer', as was Dr John Dee, and indeed all physicians of the sixteenth century. He was a 'quack', meaning simply one who practised medicine without appropriate qualifications, as did Shakespeare's son-in-law, Dr John Hall, and many other doctors. The evidence implicating him in the Overbury murder is hardly conclusive[11]. Militating further against Forman's reputation however is his notorious sexual promiscuity, which involved him with some prominent contemporary women, and which clearly in many cases entailed very dubious doctor-patient relations (not only was he an unqualified medical practitioner, he was also guilty of infringing those ethical principles he would, as a qualified doctor, have been bound to observe). This has resulted in some harsh criticism of his sexual mores and of his 'treatment' of women from female critics[12]; and to be defended in such a cause by A.L Rowse[13] has not helped his case.

What still remains unavoidable is the documentary evidence of Forman's record, as that of a man who went to the Globe theatre on Saturday 20 April 1611 to see a production of *Macbeth*, and may even have made some of his notes at the scene (just as the stage doctor takes notes of Lady Macbeth's sleepwalking indiscretions: '& the doctor noted her wordes'). There can be no disputing that Forman has left for us the documentation of a particular 'realisation'[14] of the text of *Macbeth*. It is at the very least a record of his experience, his 'response' to the play he saw, the 'realisation' of *Macbeth* in an eyewitness's perception and memory. Scholars and critics bent on undermining Forman's testimony tend to assert that he was in some way not a professional playgoer, but one who brought alien interests to the theatre, and carried away marginally relevant recollections from it. He viewed plays in order to pick out from them useful smatterings of advice for 'common policy'. As an astrologer and alchemist, even an amateur magician, he showed an unusual interest in magic, spells, portents and so on, and this in turn distorted his perception of the plays.

Clearly we all take our own baggage to the theatre, and bring away our own perceptions; and these plays lived in the Jacobean theatre not as authoritative scholarly editions, but as events 'observed' by artisans and apprentices, servants and soldiers, quacks and queens. There seems to be no reason why we should not conjecture that Forman's account might tell us with some degree of accuracy what was actually presented on stage as '*Macbeth*' in 1611. We know there were different textual and performance versions of *Macbeth*. Why should this not be one of them?

We may then have, via Forman's description, access to a stage version, that may in turn adumbrate a textual version of *Macbeth* as it existed in 1611. Since the bulk of Forman's account agrees with the Folio text, and the discrepancies are explicable, those very divergences could reflect genuine textual differences between the *Macbeth* of 1611 and that printed in 1623. As such the document is both valid and valuable, standing as it does by proxy for the missing Quarto text that might have given us a variant *Macbeth*. This is the text that might have represented the earliest version of the play. It is the copy that might, if we follow F.G. Fleay's[15] fanciful theory, have been destroyed in the Globe fire of 1613. It is the text that John Masefield hoped would one day be discovered in 'some old attic or cupboard'[16].

&

It is entirely feasible to attempt a reconstruction of the text of *Macbeth* as it might have existed in 1611, based on Forman's description taken as an accurate and more or less complete summary of what passed across the stage of the Globe.

The main obstacle to Macbeth and Banquo meeting the witches 'firste' as in Forman's description is 1.2, the 'Bleeding Captain' scene. Yet this scene has been universally condemned as un-Shakespearean, Middletonian, at best confused and inconsequential. It is a clumsy way of conveying to the audience certain preliminary information – about the political scene in eleventh century Scotland; about the prowess and power of great lords such as Macbeth and Banquo; about the value of their exploits to the state, and the corresponding indebtedness of the king – which is then in any case all repeated in 1.2. One should therefore cut this scene, enabling a collocation of 1.1 and 1.3, and facilitating the meeting of Macbeth and Banquo with the witches as the initial action of the play (as Forman says, 'firste'). The time-scheme which in the Folio separates 1.1 (before the battle) from 1.3 (after it) can easily be concentrated into a single continuous action. The witches would not even have needed to exit from the stage, but could have simply withdrawn ('hover') and waited for their cue to come forward and meet with Macbeth.

The Folio *Macbeth* is probably best known for those elements which work to identify the weyward sisters as sixteenth century witches, rather than the prophetic sybils ('feiries or Numphes') of both Holinshed and Forman. Yet Forman mentions none of this material, despite the fact that it would inevitably have fired his professional interest, and would surely have been worth remembering. It is reasonable to assume therefore (as indeed Kenneth Muir did assume [17]) that these elements accrued to the play, probably for court performance in 1606, as a consequence of the fashionable Jacobean interest in all things demonological, and were not present in the performance of 1611. They did not become incorporated into the Globe text, in other words, until some time between 1611 and 1623. Without the shipwrecking and wind-controlling spells, the cauldrons and incantations, the 'witches' retain much more dignity as agents of prophecy and prognostication, and resemble more closely the 'wizards' of Holinshed[18]. Similarly later for the 'Cavern Scene' where Macbeth visits the witches again, Hecate and the other three witches should simply be deleted as Middletonian interpolations[19], and the predictions attributed directly to the weyward sisters, rather than to the Folio's apparitions. This is how the event is described in Holinshed, and incidentally how it is dramatised in Davenant's subsequent adaptation.

The sequence of scenes dramatising the murder of Duncan (Folio 1.7 – 2.2) has long been held unsatisfactory in a number of ways, and scholars have suspected cutting or displacement of scenes. From Collier onwards missing scenes have been envisaged, such as one in which the murderers may have washed their hands on stage. The amount of repetition seems to me to argue the opposite, that a single continuous action has been padded out, or that an early draft, which like Q2 *Hamlet* suffered from prolixity and lack of dramatic concentration, was pared down in revision for performance. Macbeth has two separate soliloquies, but both express the same ambivalence of motive about the murder. Lady Macbeth promises to drug the grooms, and later says she has done so, both speeches couched in very similar language. The idea of smearing the grooms with blood is repeated several times.

These problems are all solved by piecing together Macbeth's two soliloquies into one (now 1.5) and running together material from 1.6, 1.7 and 2.2 into a single murder scene (this reconstruction is provided at the end of this chapter). I have assumed that this whole action (now 2.2) takes place in the chamber assigned to Duncan, with the king and the two grooms asleep within the bed-curtains. The staging is derived from the last acts of *Romeo and Juliet*, as represented in the First Quarto text of that play, which marks the onset of Juliet's drugged sleep with the stage direction '*She falls upon her bed, within the curtains*'. There she remained for the rest of the play: discovered by the Nurse at 4.4., then partially concealed again until 5.1 and 5.2.[20]. Thus Macbeth and Lady Macbeth debate their intentions with the king asleep on stage, and move behind the curtains to commit the murder and again to hide the daggers. I have further taken Forman's account of the handwashing business literally, and presented the murderers as attempting to cleanse the blood from their hands on stage; and implemented literally Lady Macbeth's many explicit promises to take a direct hand in the murder by having both husband and wife kill the king[21].

Other changes one would need to make to reconcile Shakespeare and Forman include cuts justified partly by Forman's account and partly by the Padua prompt-book: the Porter's speech, the 'portents' scene 2.4 (Forman notes these, but they are described with sufficient detail to support his account in 2.3), Macbeth's conversation with the murderer of Banquo, and the dialogue between Malcolm and Macduff. This congruence between Forman's omissions and the cuts of the Padua promptbook is striking and significant. The cuts delineated on the Folio text may reflect conventional stage practice, or might even adumbrate a text of *Macbeth* that had never contained these dramatic materials. The adapter could, in other words, have been restoring the expanded Folio text to something like its 1611 form. Such a text could have produced something very like what Forman saw, prior to being padded out, perhaps by Shakespeare himself, possibly by Middleton or another dramatist, maybe for the 1606 court performance, certainly some time before 1623.

Again it is remarkable that the Davenant version makes the same cuts. Another intriguing parallel is with the summary 'Argument' prefaced to the publication of Davenant's adaptation, which seems to have little to do with what follows, yet strikingly concurs with Forman's abstract.

> Duncan, King of the Scots, had two principal men, whom he imployed in all matters of importance, Macbeth and Banquo, those two trauelling together through a Forrest, were met by three Fairy Witches (Weirds the Scots call them) whereof the first making obeysance unto Macbeth saluted him, Thane (a Title unto which that of Earl afterwards succeeded) of Glammis, the second Thane of Cawdor, and the third King of Scotland: This is unequal dealing, saith Banquo, to give my Friend all the Honours, and none unto me: To which one of the Weirds made answer, That he indeed should not be a King, but out of his Loins should come a Race of Kings that should for ever rule the Scots.

Forman's manuscript could not have been available to the writer of this preface[22]. The shared links with Holinshed may point to a common source, and the 'Argument' could, of course, be not so much a summary of the play as a summary of the historical narrative on which it is based. But the possibility remains that both Forman and the author of the 1674 'Argument' might have been reflecting theatrical traditions in the production of *Macbeth* prior to the closure of the theatres during the Civil War; and their agreement with Forman's account adds additional weight to the argument that this text existed.

Forman's writing take us straight to that performance of the 1611 text. For him the play was 'ther ... to be observed'. If Forman's observations are our only access to the thing observed (since 1623 *Macbeth* tells us only about what was incorporated into the First Folio, not what *Macbeth* was in 1611), then this is it. Cue one (Q1) *Macbeth.*

William Shakespeare, *Macbeth* (c. 1605)

Observed by Simon Forman (1611)

Reconstructed by Graham Holderness (2001)

Actus Prima
Scena Sexta.

Hoboyes, and Torches. Enter King, Malcolme,
Donalbaine, Banquo, Lenox, Macduff,
Rosse, Angus, and Attendants.

King. This Castle hath a pleasant seat,
The ayre nimbly and sweetly recommends it selfe
Vnto our gentle sences.

Banq. This Guest of Summer,
The Temple-haunting Barlet does approue,
By his loued Mansonry, that the Heauens breath
Smells wooingly here: no Iutty frieze,
Buttrice, nor Coigne of Vantage, but this Bird
Hath made his pendant Bed, and procreant Cradle,
Where they must breed, and haunt: I haue obseru'd
The ayre is delicate.

Enter Lady.

King. Where's the Thane of Cawdor?
We courst him at the heeles, and had a purpose
To be his Purueyor: But he rides well,
And his great Loue (sharpe as his Spurre) hath holp him
To his home before vs: Faire and Noble Hostesse
We are your guest to night.

La. Your Seruants euer,
Haue theirs, themselues, and what is theirs in compt,
To make their Audit at your Highnesse pleasure,
Still to returne your owne

King. Giue me your hand:
Conduct me to mine Host we loue him highly,
And shall continue, our Graces towards him.
By your leaue Hostesse.

Exeunt.

Scena Septima.

Hoboyes. Torches.
Enter a Sewer, and diuers Seruants with Dishes and
Seruice
ouer the Stage. Then enter Macbeth.

Macb. If it were done, when 'tis done, then 'twer well,
It were done quickly: If th' Assassination
Could trammell vp the Consequence, and catch
With his surcease, Successe: that but this blow
Might be the be all, and the end all. Heere,
But heere, vpon this Banke and Schoole of time,
Wee'ld iumpe the life to come. But in these Cases,
We still haue iudgement heere, that we but teach
Bloody Instructions, which being taught, returne
To plague th' Inuenter. This euen-handed Iustice
Commends th' Ingredience of our poyson'd Challice
To our owne lips. Hee's heere in double trust;
First, as I am his Kinsman, and his Subiect,
Strong both against the Deed: Then, as his Host,
Who should against his Murtherer shut the doore,
Not beare the knife my selfe. Besides, this *Duncane*
Hath borne his Faculties so meeke; hath bin
So cleere in his great Office, that his Vertues
Will pleade like Angels, Trumpet-tongu'd against
The deepe damnation of his taking off:
And Pitty, like a naked New-borne-Babe,
Striding the blast, or Heauens Cherubin, hors'd
Vpon the sightlesse Curriors of the Ayre,
Shall blow the horrid deed in euery eye,

That teares shall drowne the winde. I haue no Spurre
To pricke the sides of my intent, but onely
Vaulting Ambition, which ore-leapes it selfe,
And falles on th' other. Soft, mine eyes deceeue.
Is this a Dagger, which I see before me,
The Handle toward my Hand? Come, let me clutch thee:
I haue thee not, and yet I see thee still.
Art thou not fatall Vision, sensible
To feeling, as to sight? or art thou but
A Dagger of the Minde, a false Creation,
Proceeding from the heat-oppressed Braine?
I see thee yet, in forme as palpable,
As this which now I draw.
Thou marshall'st me the way that I was going,
And such an Instrument I was to vse.
Mine Eyes are made the fooles o'th' other Sences,
Or else worth all the rest: I see thee still;
And on thy Blade, and Dudgeon, Gouts of Blood,
Which was not so before. There's no such thing:
It is the bloody Businesse, which informes
Thus to mine Eyes. Now o're the one halfe World
Nature seemes dead, and wicked Dreames abuse
The Curtain'd sleepe: Witchcraft celebrates
Pale *Heccats* Offrings: and wither'd Murther,
Alarum'd by his Centinell, the Wolfe,
Whose howle's his Watch, thus with his stealthy pace,
With *Tarquins* rauishing sides, towards his designe
Moues like a Ghost. Thou sowre and firme-set Earth
Heare not my steps, which they may walke, for feare
Thy very stones prate of my where-about,
And take the present horror from the time,
Which now sutes with it. Whiles I threat, he liues:
Words to the heat of deedes too cold breath giues.

A Bell rings.

I goe, and it is done: the Bell inuites me.
Heare it not, *Duncan*, for it is a Knell,
That summons thee to Heauen, or to Hell.

Actus Secundus. Scena Prima.

Enter Banquo, and Fleance, with a Torch
before him.

Banq. How goes the Night, Boy?

Fleance. The Moone is downe: I haue not heard the
Clock.

Banq. And she goes downe at Twelue.

Fleance. I take't, 'tis later, Sir.

Banq. Hold, take my Sword:
There's Husbandry in Heauen,
Their Candles are all out: take thee that too.
A heauie Summons lyes like Lead vpon me,
And yet I would not sleepe:
Mercifull Powers, restraine in me the cursed thoughts
That Nature giues way to in repose.

Enter Macbeth, and a Seruant with a Torch.

Giue me my Sword: who's there?

Macb. A Friend.

Banq. What Sir, not yet at rest? the King's a bed.
    He hath beene in vnusuall Pleasure,
And sent forth great Largesse to your Offices.
This Diamond he greetes your Wife withall,
By the name of most kind Hostesse,
And shut vp in measurelesse content.

Mac. Being vnprepar'd,
Our will became the seruant to defect,
Which else should free haue wrought.

Banq. All's well.
I dreamt last Night of the three weyward Sisters:
To you they haue shew'd some truth

Macb. I thinke not of them:
Yet when we can entreat an houre to serue,
We would spend it in some words vpon that Businesse,
If you would graunt the time.

Banq. At your kind'st leysure.

Macb. If you shall cleaue to my consent,
When 'tis, it shall make Honor for you.

Banq. So I lose none,
In seeking to augment it, but still keepe
My Bosome franchis'd, and Allegeance cleare,
I shall be counsail'd.

Macb. Good repose the while.
Banq. Thankes Sir: the like to you.

Exit Banquo.

Macb. Goe bid thy Mistresse, when my drinke is ready,
She strike vpon the Bell. Get thee to bed.

Exit

Scena Secunda.

Enter King, Lady and Attendants.

King. See, see our honor'd Hostesse:
The Loue that followes vs, sometime is our trouble,
Which still we thanke as Loue. Herein I teach you,
How you shall bid God-eyld vs for your paines,
      And thanke vs for your trouble.

Lady. All our seruice,
In euery point twice done, and then done double,
Were poore, and single Businesse, to contend

Against those Honors deepe, and broad,
Wherewith your Maiestie loades our House:
For those of old, and the late Dignities,
Heap'd vp to them, we rest your Ermites.

King. Commend me to your honor'd Husband.
I'll now to sleepe, whereto my dayes hard Iourney
Soundly inuites mee.

King and Attendants Sleepe within the Curteines.

Lady. Who's there? what hoa? My Husband?

Enter Macbeth.

Macb. Didst thou not heare a noyse?

Lady. I heard the Owle schreame, and the Crickets cry.

Macb. Hearke, who lyes i'th' second Chamber?

Lady. Donalbaine.

Mac. We will proceed no further in this Businesse:
He hath Honour'd me of late, and I haue bought
Golden Opinions from all sorts of people,
Which would be worne now in their newest glosse,
Not cast aside so soone.

La. Was the hope drunke,
Wherein you drest your selfe? Hath it slept since?
And wakes it now to looke so greene, and pale,
At what it did so freely? From this time,
Such I account thy loue. Art thou affear'd
To be the same in thine owne Act, and Valour,
As thou art in desire? Would'st thou haue that
Which thou esteem'st the Ornament of Life,
And liue a Coward in thine owne Esteeme?
Letting I dare not, wait vpon I would,
Like the poore Cat i'th' Addage.

Macb. Prythee peace:
I dare do all that may become a man,
Who dares do more, is none.

La. What Beast was't then
That made you breake this enterprize to me?
When you durst do it, then you were a man:
And to be more then what you were, you would
Be so much more the man. Nor time, nor place
Did then adhere, and yet you would make both:
They haue made themselues, and that their fitnesse now
Do's vnmake you. I haue giuen Sucke, and know
How tender 'tis to loue the Babe that milkes me,
I would, while it was smyling in my Face,
Haue pluckt my Nipple from his Bonelesse Gummes,
And dasht the Braines out, had I so sworne
As you haue done to this.

Macb. If we should faile?

Lady. We faile?
But screw your courage to the sticking place,
And wee'le not fayle. *Duncan* is asleepe,
The Doores are open, and the surfeted Groomes
Doe mock their charge with Snores. I have drugg'd their Possets
That Death and Nature do contend about them
Whether they liue, or die. Their knives unsheath'd
Do lend themselves unto our ready hands.
What cannot you and I
Performe vpon th' vnguarded *Duncan*?
What not put vpon his spungie Officers?
Then who shall beare the guilt of our great quell?
Who dares receiue it other,
As we shall make our Griefes and Clamor rore,
Vpon his Death?

Macb. I am settled, and bend vp
Each corporall Agent to this terrible Feat.
Harke! Did not you speake?

Lady. When?

Macb. Now.

La. Peace: it was the Owle that shriek'd,
The fatall Bell-man, which giues the stern'st good-night.

Macb. Me thought I heard a voyce cry, Sleep no more:
Macbeth does murther Sleepe, the innocent Sleepe,
Sleepe that knits vp the rauel'd Sleeue of Care,
The death of each dayes Life, sore Labors Bath,
Balme of hurt Mindes, great Natures second Course,
Chiefe nourisher in Life's Feast.

Lady. What doe you meane?

Macb. Still it cry'd, Sleepe no more to all the House:
Glamis hath murther'd Sleepe, and therefore Cawdor
Shall sleepe no more: Macbeth shall sleepe no more.

Lady. Who was it, that thus cry'd? why worthy Thane,
You doe vnbend your Noble strength, to thinke
So braine-sickly of things: Infirme of purpose:
Giue me a Dagger: the sleeping, and the dead,
Are but as Pictures: 'tis the Eye of Childhood,
That feares a painted Deuill. If he doe bleed,
Ile guild the Faces of the Groomes withall,
For it must seeme their Guilt.

Macb. Bring forth Men-Children onely:
For thy vndaunted Mettle should compose
Nothing but Males. Will it not be receiu'd,
When we haue mark'd with blood those sleepie two
Of his owne Chamber, and vs'd their very Daggers,
That they haue don't? Let's about it straight.

                  Macbeth and Lady stabbe king

Macb. This is a sorrie sight.

Lady. A foolish thought to say a sorrie sight.
Goe get some Water,

And wash this filthie Witnesse from our Hands.
Why did you bring these Daggers from the place?
They must lye there: goe carry them, and smeare
The sleepie Groomes with blood.

Macb. Ile goe no more:
I am afraid, to thinke what we haue done:
Looke on't againe, I dare not.

Lady. Your Constancie hath left you vnattended.

Hides daggers. Knocke within.

Macb. Heere, Ile cleane my Hands. Whence is that knocking?
How is't with me, when euery noyse appalls me?
What Hands are here? hah: they pluck out mine Eyes.
Will all great *Neptunes* Ocean wash this blood
Cleane from my Hand? no: this my Hand will rather
The multitudinous Seas incarnardine,
Making the Greene one, Red.

Enter Lady.

Lady. My Hands are of your colour: but I shame
To weare a Heart so white. Come, let me washe.
A little Water cleares vs of this deed.
Yet who'd ha' thought the olde man t'haue had so much
Of blood in him? What will these hands
Ne're be cleane? Heere's the smell of blood still.
All the perfumes of Arabia will not sweeten
This little hand.

Knocke.

I heare a knocking at the South entry:
Retyre we to our Chamber:
                              Knocke.

Hearke, more knocking.
Get on your Night-Gowne, least occasion call vs,
And shew vs to be Watchers: be not lost

So poorely in your thoughts.

Macb. To know my deed,

Knocke.

'Twere best not know my selfe.
Wake Duncan with thy knocking:
I would thou could'st.

Exeunt.

CHAPTER SEVEN

Visions and Revisions:
Hamlet

ᔑᕱ

WRITING AROUND *Hamlet* (and I include here writing for theatre and film) is almost as pervasive as writing about it. But such writing can take a number of different forms. Works that have been accurately described as '*Hamlet* spin-offs' are too numerous to detail here, and include the full range of dramatic, poetic, filmic, televisual and fictional modes (in addition to musical and visual versions and adaptations). When dealing with theatre and film, we are in the somewhat different environment of performance interpretation, where it is not always easy to draw hard and fast distinctions between a radical and innovative production of the play, a free adaptation or systematic revision, and a spin-off. It is clear for instance that a work which places *Hamlet* within a larger action, even though that macro-narrative will itself act as parallel and analogue, is different from a production in which the 'standard' (Q2/F) text, however extensively abridged, fragmented and re-assembled, is still discernible as the basis of the retextualisation. Thus the film *Last Action Hero* presents itself as a *Hamlet* for modern times, but is clearly a spin-off rather than an adaptation[1]; while the fifteen-minute performance of *Hamlet* as a school play in Tom Stoppard's *Dogg's Hamlet* is still a relatively straightforward version of the play[2]. Even the most condensed abridgements and reconstructions can remain, in some senses, 'Shakespeare's' *Hamlet*[3]. Similarly in film versions of the play, which typically fragment, adapt and transfer the text, one could distinguish between a radical reconstruction such as that of Celestino Coronado[4] and a spin-off like Akira Kurosawa's *The Bad Sleep Well*[5]. The theatrical experiments of Charles Marowitz, Peter Brook and Robert Lepage[6] seem to me to be still productions of *Hamlet* rather than reconstructions; Deborah Levy's play *Pushing the Prince into Denmark*[7] is clearly a re-writing.

In poetry and prose similar distinctions can be drawn. *Hamlet* has spawned a number of historical and romance novels and crime thrillers, some of which could be classed as re-writings, or at least absorptions of the play into another medium. Most are spin-offs. Examples of the latter would include Michael Innes' *Hamlet Revenge!*, which builds a country-house murder and espionage tale around an amateur theatricals production of *Hamlet*[8]; Damon Runyon's story 'The Melancholy Dane', where an impromptu performance of the play is staged in a bombed-out hut in Tunisia during the Second World War[9] and Carole Corbier's novel *In the Wings*, a modern action revolving around a contemporary production of *Hamlet*[10]. Poetic responses in the form of the short modern lyric tend towards modernist re-writing, often taking a cue from Brecht's famous ironic sonnet on Hamlet ('this introspective sponger in a shirt') which is in itself a versification of the short critical essay on the play Brecht included as section 67 of his 'Short Organum for the Theatre'[11]. An example of this treatment would be R. S. Gwynne's poem 'Horatio's Philosophy' which shows Horatio trying to write a tragedy out of the 'rancid stew' of what happened in *Hamlet*[12].

At least one critical book is addressed entirely to *Hamlet* rewrites, Martin Scofield's *The Ghosts of Hamlet*[13]. Scofield's essay dwells on modernist writing, showing how most of the major figures of twentieth century literature have at some point engaged with the text of *Hamlet*. But the encounters that emerge from his pages always seem to produce an unmistakably modernist *Hamlet*, and the history he traces is one of cultural repositioning, rather than one of creative reconstruction, reinterpretation, re-writing. By that stage, the end of the nineteenth century, *Hamlet* was a massive presence within the culture, an unassailable artistic monument, the great masterwork of the great master dramatist. Modernist writers were naturally prompted to position themselves *vis-à-vis* its cultural potency, to clear their own space of operations, and much twentieth century *Hamlet*-oriented writing is satirical, distanced by irony and detachment from what was perceived to be the tradition. At the same time there is, in all the writers surveyed by Scofield – Joyce, Eliot, Yeats, Lawrence, Kafka – a serious, often sustained, grappling with *Hamlet*, and most of them can be found writing about the play in discursive critical prose as well as in poetry and fictional narrative.

It is now much more generally understood, as hinted at in Chapter Four above, that *Hamlet* took its origin from a similarly open and combative cultural moment. The Jacobean *Hamlet*, with its three published texts, its mysterious relation to a lost ur-*Hamlet*, its multiple and discordant sources, seems at some distance from the cultural colossus that bestrode the later nineteenth and early twentieth centuries, and against which modernism critically and creatively reacted. In that early modern period we see *Hamlet* being continually re-written, passing through a plurality of texts; we know that more than one *Hamlet* play appeared on the stage and we can with reasonable confidence surmise that as both 'play' and 'text', *Hamlet* existed in a contested multiplicity of modes and manifestations.

Once this view of the Elizabethan and Jacobean dramatic culture is agreed, then it follows that such writing would find its natural home in an environment of free adaptation and uninhibited re-writing. However, even those who now accept this view of early modern culture balk at this obvious inference. When David Scott Kastan reviews the history of Restoration and eighteenth century Shakespeare, he is alternately dismayed and intrigued by the liberties then notoriously taken with the texts:

> On the stage ... Shakespeare was not merely modernized, but aggressively modified to satisfy the expectations of the fashionable audiences that filled the theatres ... turned ... into a contemporary playwright, at once modern and highbrow, for the theatrical environment in which he was now performed ... Shakespeare is not merely adapted on stage but diluted[14].

Yet in the same chapter Kastan acknowledges that this iterability is the essential character of the Shakespearean drama:

> Considered as theatrical scripts, Shakespeare's texts received the precise treatment they requested. They were modified – as indeed they always have been – to play successfully on the stages of the time (Kastan, *Book*, p. 88).

At one moment these adaptations are 'depredations' visited on the plays by the theatre, painfully 'endured' by the texts (Kastan, *Book*, p. 95); at another, evidence of that very 'malleability' that is a condition of cultural 'endurance':

> Shakespeare survived precisely by being accessible and pliant in the hands of his lovers (Kastan, *Book*, p. 88).

Following this pliancy to its bending extreme, the following chapter discusses a number of examples of formal re-writing of *Hamlet* in twentieth century theatre, fiction, and critical prose.

৯

Recently successful versions of Shakespeare in television and film have reinforced the potentiality of free adaptations, suggesting that a new period for creative re-writing of Shakespeare is in the offing. Baz Luhrmann's celebrated film of *Romeo and Juliet* (1996) used Shakespearean language, but reset the play in an imagined contemporary California, creating an effect closer to *West Side Story* (1961) than to the drama of the 1590s. More recently Andrew Davies brilliantly adapted *Othello* (2001) for television, re-writing both narrative and script, and turning Shakespeare's Moor into the commissioner of the Metropolitan Police. Particularly successful (at the box office if not with critics) is the film *Shakespeare in Love* (1998), written by Tom Stoppard and Mark Norman, which envisages the writing and production of *Romeo and Juliet* taking place in the context of an imagined love affair in Shakespeare's own life, and within a comically reconstructed Elizabethan theatre industry.

While we are accustomed in the theatre to seeing Shakespeare's dramas shifted into modern or historical settings, and punctuated by contemporary themes, the film adaptations mentioned above represent rather the kind of radical re-writing of Shakespeare that was widely practised in the Restoration and eighteenth century theatres, where the Shakespeare text was regarded as raw material for a wholesale reinterpretation of language, narrative and dramatic setting. It can however be argued that these free adaptations are in actuality the 'Shakespeare' of today, appropriately translated into modern idiom, just as the radical re-writings of Davenant and Dryden and Tate *were* the Shakespeare of the seventeenth and eighteenth centuries. For within this medium it is not only possible to convert Shakespeare into an intelligible modern form, as one would translate Latin into English. It is also possible for modern writers to engage with the writing of the past in a creative contention that both recuperates and reconstructs that past.

The interactions can be quite complex. It is well known for instance that Tom Stoppard was called in to co-write or revise Mark Norman's screenplay for *Shakespeare in Love*. Many viewers noticed the obvious resemblances between the film and the brilliant comic novel by Caryl Brahms and S.J. Simon, *No Bed for*

Bacon[15], which also features a Shakespeare with writer's block who can't decide how to spell his name, and a young lady Viola who wants to become an actor. Although the two works are quite different, the influence of the novel is certainly in there somewhere, as are *1066 and All That, Blackadder II*, and any number of other exercises in spoof history and theatrical in-joke humour.

But Stoppard was no stranger to the logistics of re-setting Shakespearean drama into an alternative action, as witnessed both in his masterpiece of absurdist drama *Rosencrantz and Guildenstern are Dead*[16], and in the less well-known experimental piece *Dogg's Hamlet*. *Dogg's Hamlet* is set in a traditionalist public or grammar school, and turns on a comparison between the language of Shakespeare's play, perceived as remote and unfamiliar, and an unintelligible private language developed by the dramatist for the characters from some observations of Wittgenstein. The school setting is the clue to this inventive but ultimately juvenile improvisation. The play falls naturally into two parts, the second of which is the abridged performance of *Hamlet*, which is as indicated above textually straightforward, and complicated only by the comic performance conditions that enclose and contextualise it.

The better-known example of *Rosencrantz and Guildenstern are Dead* is a much more systematic exercise in re-writing *Hamlet*. Here Stoppard constructed a play around the independent lives of the two marginal characters, Rosencrantz and Guildenstern, who are the little people, pliable instruments of the powerful, useful only 'to swell a progress', in Eliot's words, or to 'start a scene or two'[17]. Their very presence in Elsinore is a consequence of their subordination, since the King and Queen have sent for them to spy on Hamlet. This they do with little success, and Hamlet continually makes fools of them. They almost always appear together, and their characters are virtually indistinguishable. They try to manipulate Hamlet, but Hamlet manipulates them. The King sends them to take Hamlet to England, with an instruction that the Prince be executed: but Hamlet changes the letter so that Rosencrantz and Guildenstern are executed in his place.

Stoppard puts these two marginal characters into the foreground of his play: they are its 'heroes'. The same things happen to them as happen in Shakespeare's *Hamlet*: they have no autonomy, being pushed and pulled here and there by others; they have no individuality, or at least no one remembers which of them is which; and the play ends with their execution, contrived as a practical joke[18]. The difference is that in Stoppard's play, the main concern is not with the major characters of *Hamlet* but with the 'private' lives of Rosencrantz and Guildenstern, with what they do when they are not on stage, or when they are waiting in the wings for their appearances in the text of Shakespeare's play.

The main dramatic and thematic business of the Shakespeare play – the apparition of the ghost, Hamlet's task of revenge, the hero's tortured and divided personality – are all marginalised in Stoppard's play. We see Hamlet in this play in exactly the same way as Rosencrantz and Guildenstern see him, as a man who speaks an extraordinary language, behaves in ridiculous ways for no obvious reason, and fools and humiliates the helpless victims of his practical jokes. The King and Queen also talk in this mysterious fashion (one of the play's characteristics is a controlled movement from ordinary modern conversation to Elizabethan blank verse) and give Rosencrantz and Guildenstern absurd commands without explanation.

Most contemporary reviewers in 1967 saw *Rosencrantz and Guildenstern are Dead* as a 'drama of the absurd', comparable to Becket's *Waiting for Godot*. John Russell Taylor voiced this majority opinion in his book *The Second Wave*:

> We know from Beckett that Godot will not come, nothing will ever change, the two figures will remain waiting in the wings of life for the rest of their lives, never quite grasping what is happening centre-stage of life[19].

In this interpretation the action of the play is a simple parable of the 'absurd' nature of human existence, a demonstration of life's essential meaninglessness, its absence of any choice or purpose, its lack of any direction or ultimate significance. Ronald Hayman concurred with this view of the play as an absurdist metaphor for the futility of life, but simultaneously proposed a radically different approach:

> The theatrical situation is used as an image of the human condition. Birth, growth and death come to seem like the fatalistic web of text that holds the actor stuck[20].

It is one thing to be trapped by the human condition, quite another to be trapped by a *text*, which is after all a man-made construction. If we ask what it is in this play that limits and constrains human freedom, the answer is not a universal human condition but a specific cultural object, a play (*the* play) by Shakespeare. If the dramatic narrative of the play enacts not a general human condition, but the subjection of human beings to particular social and ideological forces, then it is perhaps as close to Brecht as to Beckett. *Rosencrantz and Guildenstern are Dead* can be read as a play about Shakespeare and about the powers of culture over its 'subjects'. The play *Hamlet* is shown by Stoppard to be exactly such a potent cultural token, forcing compliance with an ideological hegemony. At many points in the play Rosencrantz and Guildenstern try to act spontaneously, attempt to escape from the determining pressures of the *Hamlet* play in which they are implicated. They attempt to intervene, to change things, to acquire some control over the process they are caught in. But their actions are never free. At one point one of them shouts into the wings, 'I forbid anyone to enter' (Stoppard, *Dead*, p. 52). Immediately the entire Danish court sweeps on stage. Whenever they try to do something spontaneous, they find it fits into the predetermined pattern of the *Hamlet* play. 'If we just began to suspect', Guildenstern ominously suggests, 'that our spontaneity is part of their order, we'd be finished' (Stoppard, *Dead*, pp. 42-3). As indeed of course they are.

Rosencrantz and Guildenstern are Dead is not then wholly an absurdist play, for the force that determines and shapes the lives of the characters is not some mysterious alien power, never seen or understood. It is a text, a play, albeit the most celebrated play of the most famous of playwrights. Whatever powers the play possesses, it cannot be regarded as invincible or impervious to change. Stoppard's own play explicitly demonstrates how free adaptation of a classic text can provide the contemporary writer with an opportunity of creative intervention, the active making and remaking of culture. In both its modernity and its engagement with the past *Rosencrantz and Guildenstern are Dead* remakes Shakespeare as cultural reconstruction, revision and reassessment, rather than as continuity and stable cultural tradition.

But Stoppard was by no means the first dramatist to reconceive *Hamlet* in the light of twentieth century priorities and preoccupations. Rayner Heppenstall's 'The Hawk and the Handsaw' was written and produced for radio in the late 1940s and published together with two other scripts as *Three Tales of Hamlet* in 1950[21]. In the introductory material to the published volume mention is made both of Ernest Jones's Freudian reading of *Hamlet*, and of W.W. Greg's hypothesis on 'Hamlet's Hallucination'[22]. 'The Hawk and the Handsaw' is thus based partly on criticism and commentary, as well as on the action of *Hamlet*. In fact, the exercise could be described as an attempt to adjust the narrative of *Hamlet* to the priorities of twentieth century criticism, to 'correct' (in Pierre Macherey's terms)[23] the work by completing it and filling its silences, in this case with insights derived from modern critical interpretation. All criticism, Macherey argues, does this, but Heppenstall goes a step further by altering *Hamlet* to fit the subsequent criticism the play had already generated. Thus the text of Shakespeare's play is fragmented and re-installed into a revisionist account of the *Hamlet* story that purports (to some extent ironically) both to elucidate the play's mysteries, and to foreground the contemporary hermeneutic context of the 1940s.

Heppenstall imagines a performance of *Hamlet* put on in Elsinore by certain 'English tragedians' forty years after Hamlet's death. Fortinbras is still king, and his chief councillor is Horatio (who seems, however, from his conversational style to have mutated into Polonius). Shakespeare's play is initially overheard from outside the hall by a 'Doctor'. The doctor (who numbers among his previous patients Lady Macbeth) is prompted by the play to recollect the 'poor melancholic prince' and to listen to the reprise of his tragedy: 'let us hear these shadows' (Heppenstall, 'Hawk', p. 23). The function of memory, as Heppenstall's radio play will show, is important to this doctor, since he proves to be a proto-Freudian psychotherapist.

King Fortinbras and Horatio are watching *Hamlet*, a play in which they themselves are of course represented. The parallel with *The Murder of Gonzago* performed inside *Hamlet* and before Claudius does not escape notice, but the situation is radically changed. Echoing Hamlet's own words 'The play's the thing', Horatio suggests '*That* play's the thing', not to trap a guilty king, but to further popularise the rule of King Fortinbras in Denmark. Fortinbras is not so sure: he stops the performance as soon as his own character appears on stage.

Horatio is introduced as the custodian of Hamlet's memory, still busy writing a 'chronicle' which will tell the prince's story. His particular problem is that of filling in the gaps left by the plot of Shakespeare's *Hamlet*. 'The time in Wittenberg', he says, 'is the rub' (Heppenstall, 'Hawk', p. 35). While at the university Hamlet was evidently corresponding with aristocratic youth across

Europe, and the letters Horatio is editing appear to handle matters of dangerous speculation, even 'heresy' (Heppenstall, 'Hawk', p. 35). The memoir is, however, unlikely to be published since its contents might cause offence to some still surviving relatives of the deceased queen.

Fortinbras ask Horatio if there is a 'ghost' in his story, since there had certainly been one in the play they have just witnessed. The ghost is not, however, for Fortinbras the real 'enigma', which is that of Hamlet himself. 'What manner of man was he?' asks Fortinbras (Heppenstall, 'Hawk', p. 36). Then following classic critical debates on Hamlet's 'character', Fortinbras recapitulates some of the elements of Shakespeare's plot, assembling evidence for the existence of two incompatible Hamlets, intellectual and man of action, 'dreamer and doer' (Heppenstall, 'Hawk', p. 37).

Fortinbras and Horatio than begin to question the doctor, who admits to having been acquainted with the prince and to knowing something of his private mind. He recalls meeting Hamlet on the battlements of Elsinore (the dialogue between prince and doctor is dramatised in the radio script as a flashback, with interruptions and commentary from the listening audience of Fortinbras and Horatio), and finding Hamlet literally whetting his dagger in preparation for revenge on Claudius. Questioning Hamlet as to purpose and motive, the doctor soon convinces the prince that the key elements of his story – the ghost, the poison poured in his father's ear – must necessarily be symbolic rather than actual, products of infantile fantasy rather then evidenced observations of the real.

As a Freudian analyst the doctor hypothesises the Oedipus complex as the cause of Hamlet's vindictiveness, hatred and sexual obsession:

> … love and hate weave a tangled skein about the human heart. And every child, loving his mother – and from that so strong love comes all love of women – has on a time most passionately willed his father out of the picture (Heppenstall, 'Hawk', p. 59).

Through protracted analysis of Hamlet the doctor readily discloses that as a child the prince, infatuated with a young girl (later to
become Ophelia's mother) witnessed her in adulterous copula-
tion with his own father the king. To distract the boy the girl had
given him a book, which unfortunately happened to be *The Murder of Gonzago*. The child witnessed his father sexually possessing
a beloved mother figure, and the consequent murderous impulse
generated in him was fuelled by the old Italian tragedy of fratri-
cide. All is fantasy: ghost, poison, murder. 'Old' Hamlet was, in
fact, stung to death by a serpent in his orchard.

The mystery of the play is thus imaginatively solved. It is
inferred that through psychoanalysis, Hamlet reached an understanding of his own mental condition and narrowly avoided the
unjust murder of his uncle. Fortinbras wonders if the doctor's art
had not perhaps revealed too much: another denouement, in
which Hamlet could have killed Claudius and become king,
might have been preferable. It is possible by delving too deeply
into the psyche to 'call up yet further questionable shapes' (Heppenstall, 'Hawk', p. 69) that may serve only to discompose both
the human mind and the social order. Fortinbras will certainly
not let the doctor anywhere near *his* unconscious: 'My dreams
shall be my own, and any ghosts that haunt me private to myself'
(Heppenstall, 'Hawk', p. 73).

Nor is Horatio any better pleased with the outcome of the
analysis of prince and play, since it amounts to a revisionist
reworking of the basis of his *Hamlet*:

> If this tale be true, here are whole chapters likely to become
> unstitched, and I must to my inkhorn again (Heppenstall, 'Hawk',
> p. 52).

'Unstitched': a figure for the literal disintegration of an assembled
codex, and the metaphorical deconstruction of a fixed record, a
settled account. Of the making (and remaking) of books, there is
no end.

ↄ

John Updike's *Gertrude and Claudius* is generally understood to be a 'prequel' to Shakespeare's *Hamlet*[24]. The novel certainly ends, not by closing itself down, but by closing in on the inception of *Hamlet* (though not the opening scene with Horatio and the soldiers on the battlements of Elsinore, but rather the first scene involving Claudius and Gertrude, Act 1 scene 2). Nonetheless in terms of the span of its action, Updike's novel does not stray far beyond the parameters prescribed by Shakespeare's play. *Hamlet,* in its constant allusions and parallels, and its interweaving of past, present and future, covers a period stretching from Hamlet's birth on the day of his father's victory over 'old' Fortinbras, to an adumbrated future where 'young' Fortinbras becomes King of Denmark, and only Horatio survives to tell dead Hamlet's story. Even the first thirty pages of the novel, which narrate the courtship and marriage of Gertrude and Claudius, are woven from suggestions made from within the play, as well as details derived from the common sources (cited by Updike in his 'Preface' as primarily the twelfth century *Historiae Danicae* of Saxo Grammaticus, and the fifteenth century translation of Saxo by Francois de Belleforest in his *Histories Tragiques,* 1570)[25]. Updike reviews the cultural evidence presented in *Hamlet,* reiterating and clarifying Shakespeare's own implicit model of the historical change from a Scandinavian warrior society to the culture of the Renaissance. Like a historian reviewing and reassessing familiar evidence, he represents the *Hamlet* story as a family saga informed by modern views on history, marriage, the position of women. But the novel also self-consciously deals not just directly with Shakespeare but indirectly with critical debates about historiography, culture, masculinity.

Nonetheless, though the novel's action pivots on the same seminal event as that which drives the play – Claudius's murder of 'old' Hamlet and his subsequent marriage to his brother's widow – it interfaces directly with *Hamlet* only at the very end, where a sudden and unprecedented formal deployment of Shakespearean quotation engineers a deliberate overlap between novel and drama. For the rest Updike, like Stoppard, lets his imagination play freely in the interstices of Shakespeare's *Hamlet*, giving definition and resolution to those aspects of the story about which the play is reticent or ambiguous.

Such speculative revision is the novel's precondition, since it is a 'film noir' tale of an adulterous liaison ending in murder. That this is an inference from the text is suggested by the fact that there is nothing in the play, not even from Hamlet himself, to explicitly accuse Gertrude of betrayal prior to her husband's death; even though the identification of Geruthe as 'concubine' to Fengon (Claudius) was one of the very few changes de Belleforest made to Saxo's narrative. For Updike, who interestingly synthesises a sceptical modern view of marriage with parallels drawn from the mediaeval romance of adultery, this would be the obvious explanation for what happens in *Hamlet*. His story is above all the story of Gertrude, her youth, marriage, disenchantment with her dull husband, seduction by his worldly younger brother. Using both the sources and modern criticism, he is able to step outside Prince Hamlet's own poisoned horror of adultery and incest[26], and to reorient Gertrude's story as a sympathetic tale of a trapped and bored woman, seeking outside her arranged marriage the liberty and sexual fulfilment she is denied within it.

Naturally then, this is *Hamlet* without the Prince of Denmark, and throughout the novel Hamlet himself is an absent or shadowy presence. Even when called to be 'on stage' by the action, the narrative never enters his consciousness (except briefly at the novel's conclusion) but always holds him objectively at a distance. His birth is Gertrude's labour (pp. 33-4), his childhood her alienation from motherhood in a patriarchal society (p. 35). As a young man he is seen by Gertrude as seeking his father's company and shunning hers (pp. 53-4). By Part II he is absent in

Wittenberg, and at the opening of Part III we see Claudius demanding his return to Denmark (p. 163). By this stage a guilty and haunted Gertrude has begun to perceive her son as a threat, while Claudius hopes to win him over with courtly diplomacy. Only in the closing pages, as the action is about to dovetail with Shakespeare's play, is the figure of Hamlet granted consciousness and the power of direct speech (though naturally the words he uses are not 'his' or Updike's, but Shakespeare's):

> ... the Prince from beneath his clouded brow studied the two glowing middle-aged faces hung like lanterns before him – hateful luminaries fat with satisfaction and health and continued appetite. He tersely conceded, to shunt away the glare of their conjoined pleas, "I shall in all my best obey you" (p. 210).

The child thus remains external to his mother's emotional life and to her relationships. But Updike is not just 'saving' the Prince for his after-life in Shakespeare's play, or tactfully avoiding any indiscreet treading on Bardic toes. Through Hamlet's constitutive absence he constructs the character of the prince as his mother perceives him: attached to the father, never close to her; a reproach to her for her failure to love her husband; a source of shame compounding the guilt of her adultery; and finally a real source of danger, as she finds herself newly queened, but haunted by the presence of her dead husband, and beginning to suspect some foul play in the manner of his demise. By these means Updike shapes a character readily imaginable as Shakespeare's Hamlet (particularly, as it happens, the Hamlet of Q1); but also a character that sits easily within Ernest Jones's Freudian (and Wilson Knight's post-Freudian) analyses which are in any case slyly prefigured in the novel:

> "He blames himself, I believe, for his father's death", Claudius smoothly explained. "He feels he willed it, in desiring you".

Thus far it appears that Updike has brought Shakespeare up to date by laying alongside Hamlet another exquisitely-crafted study of suburban sexuality and the frailty of the American (or rather Danish) dream. And at one level the tale is certainly a conventional romance of adultery. Old Hamlet is a conventional hero and politician, vigorous and caring but dull and insensitive. He falls asleep before consummating the marriage (p. 25). His absorption into kingship is accompanied by a wasting of personality:

> The public self he had developed felt to her so wearisomely hollow. Kingship had gutted the private man even in a nightgown (pp. 53-4).

In middle age he becomes, at least in her eyes, fat, balding, pompous and unattractive. Like a modern woman trapped in a constraining marriage, Gertrude sees herself as incarcerated in a mediaeval castle that comes to symbolise the restrictions of patriarchy. Denmark is a prison, not to the melancholy prince, but to his mother:

> "Elsinore has been a dungeon to me ever since I watched my father die within it" (p. 94).
>
> Her life as appraised through this inward eye had been a stone passageway with many windows but not one portal leading out (p. 56).

Her *crie de coeur* is for liberation, self-fulfilment, release: 'When ... do I serve the person I carry within?' (p. 94). Into this vulnerable relationship comes Feng (Claudius), suave and courtly, a soldier of fortune rather than a pillar of the state. He is Heathcliff-dark against his brother's northern whiteness (like Othello he woos Gertrude with tales of the dangers he had passed). He appears as an eloquently seductive hedonist beside the stiffly conventional husband. A true 'new man', he listens to his sister-in-law: 'She was unused to a man she could talk to' (p. 52). Gertrude invites seduction, virtually demanding the conventional gifts and love-talk; and finally Claudius proves himself as both romance hero and courtly lover by awakening the middle-aged wife's sleeping beauty:

> In their hours of stolen intimacy, Fengon [Claudius] discovered to
> her in the white mirror of his own body, furred and pronged, a
> self laid up within her inner crevices and for forty-seven years
> merely latent, asleep (p. 129).

Their joint betrayal discovered by the husband, Claudius moves
to murder with such swift unpremeditated decision that the
assassination seems virtually a *crime passionel.*

Of course Updike is conscious of this convergence of his
imagined tale with the patterns of conventional romance. This
awareness is foregrounded by continual references to early mediaeval romance literature, especially the poetry of the French
troubadours, and by the ultimate beaching of the romance idyll
itself onto the sterile shore of a new, but distinctly *déjà vu,*
marriage. In addition however there is a careful historicising of
the narrative, which is imitated from Shakespeare, but used to
suggest vicissitude and repetition, transformation and recur-
rence, in human relationships and human destinies.

Updike draws attention to this historicity by dividing the
novel into three parts, and changing the names of the characters
with each structural transition. Thus in Part I Gertrude, Hamlet
senior and Claudius are given their names from Saxo Grammaticus: Gerutha, Horwendil and Feng. In Part II they become
Geruthe, Horvendile and Fengon, as in de Belleforest's translation. Only in Part III do they assume their Shakespearean names.
Similarly the Prince mutates from Amleth to Hamblet to Hamlet.
The shifting nomenclature provides a sense of fragmentation
proper to a story constructed (as was Shakespeare's) from diverse
narrative sources, but also neatly justifying Updike's liberty of
adaptation. It also hints at a modern sense of time as discontinu-
ity rather than smooth serial progression. This technique aptly
emulates the broad historical lines of Shakespeare's *Hamlet,*
which with characteristic concentration enacts a very rapid transition from a heroic mediaeval Denmark to a European
renaissance state. But it also reinforces the underlying sense of

characters caught in a pre-determined action over which they have no ultimate control. Whatever their aspirations or motives these are people trapped in a denouement which will produce as an inevitable outcome suspicion, discovery, murder, usurpation, haunting and revenge: in short, Shakespeare's *Hamlet*.

All this is focused in Part III where the erstwhile lover has become the husband, the prodigal younger brother the king, and begins to seem in Gertrude's eyes curiously indistinguishable from his predecessor.

> Even in their privacy he spoke as if there were others about them (p. 164).

And of a particularly sententious observation from Claudius she remarks on the similarity to her husband, "'Hamlet used to say just that'" (p. 193). Elsinore remains a prison, now haunted by the ghost of its murdered king (p. 193). Gertrude's anxiety and foreboding swell as Claudius's confidence grows. "'Something'" she confides to him "'will not rest'" (p. 196). His closing emotions are of complacent self-satisfaction: 'He had gotten away with it. All would be well' (p. 211).

The novel ends with dramatic irony in a silence already occupied by a ghost, 'some passing emanation' (p. 194). But if *plus ca change, plus c'est la meme chose*, then history is merely repetition, an endless cycle of desire and disenchantment. The novel of betrayal, adultery and murder merely prepares the way for a drama of treachery, incest and revenge.

The novel is carefully distanced from the play in point of style as well as action. The world of *Hamlet* is a wide (both temporally and spatially) historical context 'bounded in a nutshell', condensed by violent concentration into a closeted interior capable of unfolding on a Jacobean stage. Its rich dramatic language populates that confined space with a discourse capable equally of broad allusion and keen particular insight. It maps space and time, realising geography and chronicle; and at the same time penetrating depths of exultation and anxiety, desire and hate.

In the novel's modernist fictional mode the impersonal narrator engages much more intimately with the psychological and physical detail of the character's experience, unobtrusively mediating experiential consciousness, especially Gertrude's, to the reader. Typically then, there is no larger context for the drama to operate in, no equivalent of the Purgatory from which 'old' Hamlet's ghost is temporarily released. Updike's characteristically 'lacquered' style is the medium that seeks in its very artifice to allude outwards towards context and contingency, to link experience with larger dimensions of history and theology.

Christianity in the novel is associated always with privation, mortification, taboo:

> Being in the chapel frightened her, as if her young body were a sin, to be avenged some day, pierced from underneath even as she sipped the rasping wine … (p. 13).

'Old' Hamlet's Christianity is identified with emotional abstraction and Machiavellian politics. He objects strenuously to his son's studies in Wittenberg as "'learning to *doubt* – learning mockery and blasphemy when I'm trying to instil piety and order into a scheming, rebellious conglomeration of Danes'" (p. 80). Just as the prince's scholastic studies seem to foreshadow religious upheaval, Claudius's itinerant lifestyle has given him also a much broader perspective on religion, a familiarity with Constantinople and with Islam, with eighth century iconoclasm and other theological controversies of Byzantium. He prefers to adapt religion via French love poetry into a piety of courtly romance:

> "It is a possibly heretical article of my own faith," he began again, "that a creator would not engender so fierce a love in me without allowing in its object the gleam of a response" (p. 91).

He feels no religious compunction or moral scruple about killing his brother: 'his religion had become cold necessity, and the form of his worship lucky acrobatics upon the bare bones of things' (p. 191).

For all the beautifully rendered empiricist particular of aesthetic and erotic experience, ultimately Updike does not succeed in filling with his doctrines of art and love the spaces opened up by his own language. Between the particular of experience and the larger contexts that give it meaning there is literally nothing. When the ghost appears it does so only as a symptom of Gertrude's anxiety, 'a mote to trouble the mind's eye'. There is no place in the novel's universe from which a real ghost could conceivably come.

✌

That conundrum is precisely the starting point for Jacques Derrida's book *Spectres of Marx*[27]. It is clearly impossible here to do justice to this complex, difficult and beautiful book. My focus will be on the extent to which Derrida uses *Hamlet* as a platform for his explorations into the legacy of Marx, and finds himself in the process rewriting Shakespeare as a way of articulating his own contemporary reflections on the past.

The subject of the book is Marx, but Marx as a 'spectre' or a multiplicity of 'spectres', haunting twentieth century European culture and society. Derrida sketches the immediate philosophical and political influence of Marx not only on his generation of intellectuals, but on modern culture in general: 'we are all heirs of Marxism'; we '*must assume the inheritance of Marxism*' (p. 54). But his real interest is not in any continuous legacy of ideas transmitted across generations, but rather in the shocking and disruptive apparition into modern culture of Marxism as a ghost, that haunts the present and demands to be spoken with. It is here, in the idea of 'filiation' as rupture and haunting, that Derrida finds apt metaphors in Shakespeare's *Hamlet*.

The book's basic idea is that, following the collapse of Marxist communism and the advance of a post-modern enlightenment that validates global capitalism and liberal democracy, Marx is positioned as a ghost of the past, hopefully laid, but remarkably resistant to exorcism. In Derrida's view however, Marxist philosophy continues to haunt the present with its reservoir of unrealised aspiration, its fundamental commitment to 'justice':

> ... if there is a spirit of Marxism which I will never be ready to renounce, it is ... a certain emancipatory and *messianic* affirmation, a certain experience of the promise that one can try to liberate from any dogmatics and even from any metaphysico-religious determination, from any *messianism*. And a promise must promise to be kept, that is, not to remain 'spiritual' or 'abstract', but to produce events, new effective forms of action, practice, organisation, and so forth (Derrida, *Spectres*, p. 89).

It is this 'messianic' core of hope and promise, aspiration that cannot be written off because it has not yet been realised, that haunts the twentieth century. It could be argued that this is a philosophical adjustment that symptomatises only the death-throes of an utterly-discredited Marxism, whose promise of a material revolution that would liberate humanity had so signally failed. To counter this argument Derrida undertakes a sustained re-reading of certain key texts of Marx, in order to show that no-one understood better then him the compelling reality of the spectral, the immaterial (Derrida points out repeatedly, for example, that the second word and first noun of the *Communist Manifesto* is 'spectre'). Some of the implications of such neo-Marxist revisionism for literary criticism and theory have been discussed above (in Chapter 3).

It is fairly easy to see, in the light of this much-simplified abstract, what put Derrida in mind of *Hamlet*. Marx, like 'old' Hamlet, is a revered father figure of the past whose memory has been 'murdered' and traduced. He returns as a ghost with a compelling request for communication, conversation, further discussion. He imposes on his own 'sons' an injunction – to secure justice – which is both irresistible and impossible to implement in the form it is given. People attempt to explain him away, or even to exorcise him as a 'goblin damn'd'. But the perturbed spirit will not rest, like language in Eliot's poem, 'will not stay in place/Will not stay still'²⁸. The command he imposes represents a demand for the restitution of justice. But we can respond to that command not with obedience, but only by actively seeking new ways of negotiating and coming to terms with that unavoidable, irksome, non-negotiable responsibility.

But Derrida goes much further than merely adducing a literary parallel to support a philosophical argument. His engagement with *Hamlet* is of such a pervasive and intense kind that the play literally haunts the book, from the quotation that opens Chapter 1 (from *Hamlet*, 1.5), to the concluding epigraph: 'Thou art a scholar: speak to it Horatio' (Derrida, *Spectres*, p. 177). Although the most concentrated incorporations of Shakespeare lie in the early chapters (which will be the focus of my detailed analysis), *Hamlet* provides the whole essay with some of its key terms and concepts. This is particularly exemplified by repetition of Hamlet's phrase 'the time is out of joint', which serves Derrida virtually as a deconstructionist manifesto, since in deconstruction all language, all experience are by definition 'disjointed', internally divided, fissured by *différance*.

Derrida's prefatory 'Exordium' poses the problem as that of 'learning to live', knowing (to use Hamlet's words), how 'to be'. Each person lives 'alone, from oneself, by oneself'. But living can only be understood in relation with its binary opposite, death. The 'commitment' to live knowledgeably 'has no sense and cannot be *just* unless it comes to terms with death' (Derrida, *Spectres*, p. xviii). Death is life's 'other', that 'undiscover'd country' that contains the past, and with it the lives of all those who have died, and for whom the living must bear some responsibility. At the same time life has another 'other', the future, that which has not yet been lived, and to which the living should also be responsible:

'To be just: beyond the living present' (Derrida, *Spectres*, p. xx). Awareness of past and future problematises the present, creating what Derrida calls a '*non-contemporaneity with itself of the living present*' (Derrida, *Spectres*, p. xix). This is what 'unhinges' the present, makes the time perpetually 'out of joint'.

The space of Derrida's inquiry is therefore one 'between life and death'. And it is here that he uses the language of *Hamlet* to open up exactly such a space in which his paternal ghost, Marx, can appear, speak and be spoken to. First, he imagines the haunted castle of Elsinore as the 'old Europe' which Marx saw as haunted by the spectre of communism:

> It is always nightfall along the 'ramparts' on the battlements of an old Europe at war. With itself and with the other (Derrida, *Spectres*, p. 14).

For Derrida the scene is automatically Marx's 'Europe'. A more natural identification might seem to be with mediaeval Denmark or Jacobean England. But Derrida's parallel draws in part on Paul Valéry's 1919 essay 'La crise de l'esprit', which imagines a 'European Hamlet' surveying the Continent in the immediate aftermath of the First World War:

> Now, on an immense terrace of Elsinore, which stretches from Basel to Cologne, that touches on the sands of Nieuport, the lowlands of the Somme, the chalky earth of Champagne, the granite earth of Alsace – the European Hamlet looks at thousand of spectres. But he is an intellectual Hamlet. He meditates on the life and death of truths. His ghosts are all the objects of our controversies; his remorse is all the titles of our glory … If he seizes a skull, it is an illustrious skull – 'Whose was it?' – This one was *Lionardo* … and this other skull is that of *Liebnitz* who dreamed of universal peace. And this one was *Kant qui genuit Hegel, qui genuit Marx, qui genuit* … Hamlet does not know what to do with all these skulls. But if he abandons them! … Will he cease to be himself?[29].

The vista from those displaced 'battlements' is the Europe of 1919, a waste land populated by millions of ghosts, littered with innumerable skulls[30]. Valery addresses the contrast between this version of Hamlet as an intellectual, preoccupied with cultural inheritance, and the carnage and destruction that culture has created. But Derrida follows the logic of Valery's genealogy, showing that Shakespeare begat Marx just as Marx begat Derrida's own generation.

> Time is off its hinge, time is off course, beside itself, disadjusted, says Hamlet. Who thereby opened one of those breaches, often they are poetic and thinking peepholes, through which Shakespeare will have kept watch over the English language; at the same time he signed its body, with the same unprecedented stroke of some arrow. Now, when does Hamlet name in this way the disjoining of time, but also of history and of the world, the disjoining of things as they are nowadays, the disadjustment of *our* time, each time ours? And how is one to translate 'The time is out of joint'? A striking diversity disperses across the centuries the translation of a masterpiece, a work of genius, a *thing* of the *spirit* which precisely seems to *engineer itself*. Whether evil or not, a genius *operates*, it always resists and defies after the fashion of a spectral thing. The animated work becomes that thing, the Thing that, like an elusive spectre, *engineers* a habitation without proper inhabiting, call it a *haunting*, of both memory and translation. A masterpiece always moves, by definition, in the manner of a ghost (Derrida, *Spectres*, p. 18).

This prose has to be analysed as a 'literary' or 'creative' medium, rather than as (if there is any such thing) a purely philosophical exercise of reason. The time that is 'out of joint' is the Renaissance Europe of *Hamlet*, Marx's nineteenth century, and the *fin-de-siècle* of Derrida's own writing. When Hamlet spoke that truth, he opened up a 'peephole' through which the invisible could be seen, an *aporia* that enables commerce between the living and the dead. The author of this classic motto of deconstruction was (at several removes) 'Shakespeare'. Prising apart the jointed structure of the time, Shakespeare opened up a viewing-point comparable to that of the soldiers at the opening of *Hamlet,* on the ramparts of Elsinore. Poised on a frontier; exposed to visits from another world, another 'scene'; between life and death. Shakespeare is then imagined as looking through that peephole and keeping watch 'over the English language', still and always on the lookout for the coming of the spectre. In this way Shakespeare 'signed' the 'body' of language, contributing to it a classic formulation that remains perpetually applicable, showing how language can confer reality on the invisible, 'give to aery nothings/A local habitation, and a name'.

We seem at this point perilously close (for Derrida) to a simple model of writing in which the 'genius' embodies his unique insights into a permanently valuable, transhistorically intelligible record. He then moves away from that position by asking the question 'when'? When exactly in time is Hamlet's question asked? The sixth century? 1603? 1848? 1993? Or rather any time and no time, 'each time ours', whenever the question is asked in reading, criticism and performance, whenever a new fashion of disjointedness is revealed. Even the quotation itself is neither innocent nor unmediated, since it is always 'translated', formally from language to language, or actually in terms of the repetition that always alters. Later (p. 19) Derrida provides examples of the very different forms in which the metaphor has been conveyed into other languages. This dispersed 'diversity' of renderings is characteristic of a 'masterpiece', a spiritual entity that defies closure but exists only in its local manifestations, a '*thing* of the *spirit*' that is always reconstructed, interpreted and translated, yet paradoxically seems to '*engineer itself*'. Here the 'masterpiece' itself has become the ghost, 'spectral', a lifeless object that is yet 'animated', a 'habitation without proper inhabiting', an elusive yet powerful apparition that haunts its own continuance in every repetition of 'memory and haunting'.

This passage exemplifies how Derrida synthesises deconstructionist theory and the language and symbolism of *Hamlet* with a rhetoric that advances an argument by guiding the reader through an imaginative experience. The argument can be unpicked and summarised: both the play *Hamlet* and the writer Shakespeare occupy modern culture after the fashion of ghosts, dead yet strangely 'animated', historically oriented yet historically different in every manifestation. But Derrida's prose does not operate in that discursive and expository way, but rather leads the reader on a quest along those ramparts of the mind where Hamlet is always watching and waiting for the *revenant* to arrive. The experience of reading such writing is rather like the fantasy of finding oneself inside a computer game. We are listening to a scholar arguing: but we are also inside Shakespeare's play. The voice persuades: but the ghost beckons.

Clearly this is not a rewriting of *Hamlet* in the same way as the other examples discussed in this chapter. But what makes Derrida's engagement with Shakespeare more than just a critical deployment of literary reference is this saturation of his language with the language and imagery of *Hamlet*. He does not simply 'quote' Hamlet as illustration, but weaves its language in and out of his own text, so the play remains visible as a distinct strand in the colour and pattern of the finished material. Derrida's whole style of writing is, controversially, the opposite of a lucid expository prose. His style is a condensed rhetoric, running typically to the lapidary aphorism; but it is also a rhythmically-imbued poetic eloquence, based on elaborate patterning and subtle repetition of words, a vigorous creative intervention into language. As indicated earlier, commentary on a text can become incorporated as part of the text (like mediaeval glosses or footnotes in an edition of Shakespeare). Similarly, a creative reworking like John Updike's can build in critical material along with the 'primary source' of the play itself. Derrida's method is rather, self-consciously and self-reflexively, to make the activity of commentary simultaneously a critical and creative refashioning of the original text. Here we can obtain a penetrating critique of our times and reach a new understanding of *Hamlet*. But in order to achieve both objectives, Derrida has us speaking with ghosts.

৯৹

Published together with 'The Hawk and the Handsaw' in *Three Tales of 'Hamlet'* is another radio play by Rayner Heppenstall, 'The Fool's Saga'[31]. This play has less to do with Shakespeare's *Hamlet* than with the history of Saxo Grammaticus, and with the later Icelandic version of the Hamlet tale, *Ambeles Saga*. Here Heppenstall attempts to take the Hamlet story back into the heroic saga culture from which it derived: 'to try to get back to the Hamlet beyond Saxo Grammaticus' (Heppenstall and Innes, *Three Tales*, p. 93). The drama is set in sixth century Jutland and Pictish Britain, Hamlet being, as Heppenstall puts it in his Introduction, 'a contemporary of Beowulf' (Heppenstall and Innes, *Three Tales*, p. 93). The Polonius character indeed reminisces about old King Hrothgar and the legendary Swedish monster-killer. This is Saxo's story, not Shakespeare's: Hamlet successfully kills Feng, and the plot is extended to encompass Hamlet's final heroic death in battle. In order to ground the action in this ancient culture, Heppenstall inserts into his text a number of verse adaptations of Scandinavian heroic poetry (see pp.112-5).

My own novel *The Prince of Denmark*[32] also attempts to mediate between these two historical periods, the Scandinavian world historicised by Saxo, and the Renaissance Europe fiction-alised by Shakespeare. As many critics have shown, Shakespeare's play pivots on the continuities and conflicts between the pagan and heroic society of the *Historiae Danicae*, in which revenge for a father's murder is a clear and unproblematic obligation on a son, and the Christian nation-state of Hamlet's Denmark (or Shakespeare's England), where moral imperatives are far less clear cut. Between Saxo and Shakespeare lay Belleforest's translation of

1570, which deliberately set the action back into a 'Dark Ages', and distanced the writer's own Christian ethos from the Viking world of blood-feud and legitimate revenge. In Shakespeare's play the historical transition is imagined as a fault-line between two generations, and formulated in persistent contrasts: between the heroic and hard-drinking world of 'old' Hamlet, and the sophisticated Renaissance culture of his son; the combat between 'old' Hamlet and 'old' Fortinbras, compared to the Machiavellian subterfuge of the duel between Hamlet and Laertes; 'old' Hamlet's taste for single combat, and Claudius' courtly diplomacy; the simplicity of the revenge ethic as imposed on Hamlet by the Ghost's command, and the complexities it entails when translated into a new environment of Renaissance sovereignty and Christian forbearance[33].

The Prince of Denmark also seeks to explore the imaginable contiguity of these contrastive cultures by setting a sequel to the Hamlet story in an anachronistic eleventh century Denmark where the new Christian faith co-exists with older pagan loyalties, and where the old heroic ethos has been subdued in favour of new conceptions of nationalism and of a progressive European culture. In this version 'old' Hamlet (Amled) emerges from a culture of Viking violence in which conquest via single combat with 'old' Fortinbras (Fortenbrasse) is possible. But he appears as a king with a wiser and more far-sighted vision of Denmark's future, as a pacified nation capable of playing a role in the new European Christian Empire. Here the dispatching of Hamlet to university in Wittenberg is symptomatic of that progressive vision, a preparing of the young prince for rule by an education in philosophy, politics and religious study, rather than a training in warfare and generalship.

In *The Prince of Denmark* the older heroic culture is contextualised by the presence of parenthetical extracts from Anglo-Saxon and Icelandic sources, which amplify cultural and historical contrasts developed from the sources, but also from suggestions in Shakespeare's play. The heroic ethic is represented for instance by extracts from *The Battle of Maldon* and the *Volsungasaga,* and by a fictionalised heroic lay celebrating the victory of Amled over Fortenbrasse. The new cultural conditions of the later Middle Ages and Renaissance are depicted in narrative, dialogue and description; in the mental reflections of Amled and Polonius; and in the improvised relationship of Hamlet and Ofelia. But it is articulated particularly in a completion of Hamlet's Wittenberg diary (the 'tables' mentioned in the play), a personal record which traces his intellectual development from mediaeval scholasticism to a Reformation philosophy that in turn radicalises his views on sovereignty, nationhood and government (in what is perhaps the novel's longest stretch of the imagination, Hamlet is taught at the University of Wittenberg by Martin Luther)[34].

In this re-fictionalisation of the Hamlet legend, then, Amled has carefully prepared for the succession of a son who is fully equipped with the education necessary to 'carry on the work of modernising Denmark and bringing it into the new Europe not as a poor relation but as a nation of power and influence' (p.41). The murder of Amled by Claudius, who had clearly hoped for election himself in his due turn, aborts this plan, leaving Denmark under Norwegian military occupation, and Horatio charged with the responsibility of telling Hamlet's story. The novel then extrapolates the action forward by another generation, imagining the birth of a son to Hamlet and Ofelia, a child who is spirited away and hidden from the Norwegian threat among monks on the island of Lindisfarne. Horatio is informed of his existence by the dying queen and devotes his life to finding the boy.

Here the novel twists the key historical contrast of the play around into another loop, since Horatio's plan is to find the child, apprise him of the circumstances of his father's death, reunite him with the Danish army in exile and restore him to the throne by overthrowing Fortinbras. In place of Hamlet's vision of a new

Denmark, we find a repetition of the revenge ethic and a planned restoration of heroic and military values. Horatio imposes on the young prince (given the name 'Sigurd' to define his destiny by reference to Scandinavian mythology) a command to revenge and restore that is parallel to the Ghost's injunction formerly given to his father. Horatio is depicted as one whose education has not dislodged a deep imaginative commitment to pagan and heroic values, symbolised in his dream of *Ragnr Rokr*, the twilight of the gods (pp. 60-1).

But Sigurd's monastic education has developed a stage further and he is thoroughly imbued with a Christian ethos (he is seen reading the Lindisfarne Gospels). Though an attempt is made to re-educate him into heroic values via Scandinavian mythology, his imagination, active in a series of vivid dreams, remains divided between pagan violence and Christian forgiveness. The dreams give expression to the seductive romanticism of heroic chivalry but also to the deeper interpellation of a Christian vocation. The action climaxes with Sigurd meeting his father's spirit on the battlements of Elsinore, and receiving from him not an injunction to revenge, but a gospel of peace (the passage appears at the end of this chapter). The novel ends with his declining to kill Fortinbras and disappearing out to sea into a self-imposed and unexplained exile. The persistence of historical and cultural conflict is suggested by three separate eyewitnesses who respectively perceive his exit as either ignominious defeat, chivalric scorn or Christian resignation. The novel ends with an ambiguity of resolution, expressed in the language of *Beowulf*[35]:

> But nobody knew, in absolute truth – neither the crafty counsellor
> in court, nor the brave hero beneath the blue sky – who, at the
> last, unloaded that cargo (p. 228).

The Prince of Denmark is a palimpsest of texts. Initially it is parasitic on the master-text of Shakespeare's *Hamlet,* imitating its language, repeating some of its action, filling in some of its silences, extrapolating a denouement from its manifold narrative possibilities. But *Hamlet* is also, like *King Lear*, a palimpsest of sources, and the novel goes back behind the play to reinstate the story in its mediaeval and Scandinavian context. I have already mentioned the citations of heroic literature, but there are also many other parenthetical extracts from sources such as the *Nibelungenleid* and the *Laxdaela Saga*, which provide imaginative romance motifs for the story of Ofelia; Old English poems such as *The Wanderer* and *Bede's Death Song,* which adumbrate a context of exile and pilgrimage; passages from Bede's *Ecclesiastical History of the English People*, which offer historical and philosophical parallels to aspects of the novel's action.

Shakespeare's *Hamlet* also makes much use of texts – diplomatic embassies, a diary, love-letters, books, play-scripts, ballads and especially letters, some of which are mentioned (Claudius to Norway, Polonius to Laertes), others quoted (Hamlet to Ophelia, Claudius, and Horatio). Such texts are adduced in the play as evidence, yet their meaning is invariably hotly disputed. They are employed to define and resolve, but they only disrupt and confuse. Not only are such texts open to free interpretation, they are also iterable. The classic instance here is Hamlet's alteration of the letters carried by Rosencrantz and Guildenstern to England, perverted from their initial meaning, converted into a missive bearing exactly the opposite of its intended significance. Strategic recontextualising is also evident in Hamlet's adaptation of the play on the sack of Troy and strategic rewriting in *The Murder of Gonzago*. In general the written and quoted texts within the dramatic text are presented almost as models of post-structuralist instability and hermeneutic failure, as when Claudius declines to react to the dumb-show that graphically illustrates his crime. They are no more effective in securing sure communication, or in ordering the world, than are the deeply ambiguous and disruptive verbal messages of the Ghost, or the mad Ofelia's disjointed speech, or indeed Hamlet's

Saxo-based 'antic disposition'. Text destabilises and discomposes, writing disintegrates and deconstructs. But to a purpose: to disclose a truth that insists on being told and retold, modified and revised, adapted and reconstructed: 'Tell my story'.

The Prince of Denmark deploys some of these same texts, as quotation and as narrative, and invents additional documents to perform similar functions. The letters quoted in *Hamlet* are augmented and recontextualised (for example, the letters for England, the true and the forged, are presented in full); but here are new letters that did not find their way into the text of *Hamlet*: a letter from 'old' Fortenbrasse to Amled, a sequence of letters filling out the story of Ofelia, and critically a letter from Fortinbras to Laertes which throws new light on Hamlet's death. Other documents represented as interior texts include real and fictional literary works, and invented state papers (we see Horatio, for example, compiling minutes of the council meeting that elects Fortinbras king). There is a heroic poem, composed within the action by a *scop* to celebrate Amled's defeat of Fortenbrasse, and later perused by Hamlet's son as a written work, set alongside a mythological account of the funeral of the slain god Balder.

In the novel such texts serve to rebuild the archaeological layers of cultural change that lie between us and the myth and history *Hamlet* articulates and evokes. They help to complicate the legendary record, lay it open to interpretation, as in the prefatory extract from an adapted history, 'The Chronicle of Ansgar', which offers a particular and at first sight idiosyncratic view of the events of Shakespeare's play. And they permit the development of a complex and multiple consciousness within the characters themselves, as in Horatio's openness to both Christian and pagan influences, a contradiction that is reenacted and finally resolved by the young prince. At one point 'Sigurd' reads side by side the opening of St John's Gospel and the Old English elegy *The Wanderer*. Both strike at his imagination, and form the basis for the destiny he finally chooses, though his choice may be less an embracing of Christian commitment than a revulsion from the violence of the past. The dragon Fafnir, in the old legend slain by Siegmund, becomes the dragon of Revelation. But the heroic militarism employed to destroy both remains ambivalent and ethically problematical for an imaginary post-heroic generation.

$$\sim$$

Hamlet, says Martin Scofield at the opening of his book on the play's presence in modern literature, is 'a specular and ductile medium' (Scofield, *Ghosts,* p. 3). The metaphors are apt and useful. 'Specular' captures a range of implications for the possibilities of vision, from the refracting medium of a semi-transparent lens to the reflective surface of a polished mirror. In addition it suggests a complex mode of seeing that is both perceptual and creative, what we see 'in' the play and what it reflects back to us via the process of observation. Hamlet himself famously defines 'the purpose of playing' as reflexive, to 'hold, as 'twere, the mirror up to nature'. By the eighteenth century this had become a commonplace for drama as naturalistically mimetic: but Hamlet would have had in mind a perspective mirror, designed to trick the eye, or in this case 'catch' the conscience of the king. Mirrors capable of reflecting undistorted images were still a fairly new invention in the sixteenth century, so the figure of the mirror is more likely to suggest a fragmented or distorted image than an accurate reflection, as in Tyndale's translation of 1.Corinthians 13: 'Now we see in a glass even in a dark speaking'[36]. The mirror has depth as well as surface, like the lake described in Wordsworth's 'Prelude'[37], which baffles the 'perplexed' eye of the beholder, unable to distinguish 'discoveries' in the depths from reflections on the water, the 'substance' from the 'shadow'[38].

The other term 'ductile' has been my focus in this chapter. The play can be 'led', twisted, manoeuvred into many different shapes and forms. It is also 'conductive', an effective channel of communication between past and present, self and other, even (see below) between life and death. 'The play haunts us still' (Innes, *Revenge!*, p. 156). Both meanings insist on what Stephen Greenblatt, using another metallurgical figure, calls the 'malleability' of the Shakespearean text: the fact that the text is responsive to actions upon it, co-operates with adaptation, offers itself up for conversion and transformation:

> The fantastic diffusion and long life of Shakespeare's works depends on their extraordinary malleability, their protean capacity to elude definition and escape secure possession[39].

A Haunting

Then at last, at the very end of his long dream-journey, Sigurd found himself once again atop the battlements of Helsingor. It was a great relief finally to have reached his destination. On the ramparts that surmounted the overhanging crags, high above the surging and crashing of the waves, he saw a young man, dressed in black, leaning against the battlements, and staring out to sea.

When he approached him, the man turned towards him with a smile of great sweetness, with eyes soft with tenderness, and alight with understanding.

'Put up thy sword into the sheath', he said gently. 'The cup which my father hath given me, shall I not drink it?'

He put his arm around the boy's shoulder, and both looked out to sea.

'A new commandment I give unto you' he said, softly and easily: 'that you love one another. As I have loved you'.

He leaned down and kissed the boy on the forehead, and his kiss was like the touch of peace; then he faded on the crowing of the cock. (pp. 218-9).

From *The Prince of Denmark*

CHAPTER EIGHT

Writing and Fighting:
Henry V

ৡ

W E HAVE TWO TEXTS OF *Henry V*: Q1 (1600) and F1 (1623). The earlier text has always existed in the shadow of the later. Until very recently (and still to some extent) it was regarded as a 'Bad Quarto', illegitimately recorded from performance or incompetently recollected from memories of performance; a badly printed, abridged, unauthorised version of Shakespeare's 'true originall copie'. As with the other so-called 'Bad Quartos', *The Cronicle History of Henry the fift* has been interpreted in three ways: as an early draft, later revised by Shakespeare into the Folio text; as an inaccurate documentation, either from observation or memory, of a performance of the Folio text; or as an accurate record of an abridged production of that same text. The first of these, the 'early draft' opinion, initiated by scholars such as Pope and Johnson, assumes that the play existed and was produced in the form of the Quarto text, before being expanded and revised into *The Life of Henry the Fift*, F1. The second, deriving from editors such as Capell and Steevens, assumes that the Folio version represents the starting point, that the play was produced from that text, and that the Quarto represents not an abridged version, but an incomplete record of the complete text. Both assumptions accept the F text as the real thing, Shakespeare's play, and Q1 as derivative.

The view that the Quarto partially and inaccurately records a performance of the Folio text was developed and established by G.I. Duthie, along with Greg and Pollard an exponent of 'Bad Quarto' theory: 'the condition of the Q text suggests that it is a memorial reconstruction made by actors who had taken part in performance of F or of a stage version based on F'[1]. Modern scholars gravitate towards the opinion that the Quarto is an accurate record of an abridged text used in provincial performance. The editor of the Arden 2 Shakespeare text, J.H. Walter, uses both the memorial reconstruction and the abridgement theories: identifying *The Cronicle History of Henry the fift* as a memorially reconstructed 'Bad Quarto' – 'that is, a corrupt version of the play presumably concocted by one or two members of the company from memory'[2] and then placing the Quarto text by terms of limitation: 'the Q version may well be based on a cut form of the play used by the company for a reduced cast on tour in the provinces' (Walter, *Henry V*, p. xxxviii). ... 'based, cut, reduced, provinces' – in one short sentence is assembled a whole vocabulary of strategic marginalisation. The Quarto is everything that the Folio is not: 'based' (both derivative and degraded), not authentic; 'cut', not whole; 'reduced', not entire; 'provincial' rather than metropolitan.

So assuming that the starting point was an authoritative text (the Folio text) that was used for performances at the Globe, the Quarto text is characterised in both memorial reconstruction and abridgement theories as multiply second-hand. The Arden 3 edition of T.W. Craik, which prints a facsimile of the Quarto text, is notwithstanding based on the same assumptions: F was printed from Shakespeare's manuscript, where Q 'shows signs of having been memorially reconstructed from stage performances of the F text'[3]. Craik however also guards against the notion that this might make Q an accurate record of performance: 'Q's cuts and other alterations are such that it is unsafe to conclude that they reflect what was done to the play in these performances' (Craik, *Henry V*, p. 96).

Gary Taylor in the individual Oxford Shakespeare edition also follows this line of interpretation, concluding that the Quarto represents an actual performance text, but not one authorised directly by Shakespeare. The Folio text 'shows every sign of having been printed directly from "foul papers"'; while a combination of 'extraordinary features' of the Quarto text – abridgement, significant exclusions, verbal variation, a pervasive textual 'corruption' and a penchant for 'nonsense' –

> seems explicable only upon the assumption that Q is the result of a reconstruction by memory of the play as performed – as performed, moreover, in a severely abridged and adapted text, such as might have been used by a troupe of actors touring the provinces[4].

On this basis Taylor discredits the Quarto as a control text: 'certainly the bulk of the readings in which it differs from F have no claim whatsoever on our attention'; though in the same paragraph he describes the same text as 'an historical document of far more authority than the hypotheses of any twentieth century scholar' (Taylor, *Henry V*, p. 23). These assertions are not as self-contradictory as they appear, since Taylor's evaluation of the Quarto differentiates its status as a record of performance ('a transcript of the text of Shakespeare's play by two men whose living depended on their memories, and who had acted in *Henry V* within a year or so of its first performance', p. 23) from its status as an embodiment of the author's 'intentions'.

Q1 having remained always in the shadow of F1, the standard practice of modern scholarship and editing has been comparative evaluation between the two texts, concentrating therefore on the quality of the Quarto text and on the significance of its apparent omissions. The first of these concerns can be addressed relatively simply. *The Cronicle History of Henry the fift* has often been regarded as a 'bad' text on the basis of insubstantial evidence. For example, G.I. Duthie identified as 'nonsense' Flewellen's speech at the siege:

> *Flew.* There is an Ensigne
> There, I do not know how you call him, but by Jesus I think
> He is as valiant a man as *Marke Anthonie,* he doth maintain
> the bridge most gallantly: yet he is a man of no reckoning:
> But I did see him do gallant serve.
> *Gouer.* How do you call him?
> *Flew.* His name is ancient *Pistoll*[5].

Why, asks Duthie, does Flewellen contradict himself over his knowledge of Pistoll's name? The obvious answer is memorial reconstruction: 'I do not think we could comfortably attribute this ineptitude to Shakespeare even in a first draft, whereas on the other hand it may well have been brought about through memorial confusion' (Duthie, p. 111). Duthie seems to have forgotten that chronic absent-mindedness is Flewellen's key character trait, or rather one of the main running gags supporting his comic role:

> *Flew.* Captain *Gower,* what call you the place where Alexander the big was borne? … (*Cronicle History*, p. 73)

> … the Rivers name at *Monmorth,*
> *Is called Wye*
> But tis out of my braine, what is the name of the other …
> (*Cronicle History*, p. 74)

> … our King being in his ripe
> Wits and judgements, is turne away, the fat knite
> With the great belly doublet: I am forget his name. (*Cronicle History*, p. 74).

Duthie goes on to quote these same examples but only to draw the wrong conclusion. His argument is that the forgetting of Pistoll's name is not a consistency of comic role but an 'anticipation' of the subsequent scenes: 'The reporter has confused this scene with IV vii. There, in the passage from line 22 on (F numbering), Fluellen, in both Q and F, twice declares that he has forgotten a name' (Duthie, p. 112). In this way the hypothesis of memorial reconstruction makes unnecessarily heavy weather of a perfectly intelligible piece of dramatic writing, and an obvious consistency in the treatment of Flewellen's character.

৯০

Gary Taylor, who as we have seen, goes some way towards acknowledging the Quarto's authority and incorporates selective readings from it into his edition, nonetheless follows Duthie with the same charge of nonsense, inveighing with the full armoury of bibliographical rhetoric against the text's 'corruption'.

> It is difficult to deny that Q is far more frequently and seriously corrupt than F. One need not submit to the draconian metrical legislation of Pope in order to recognize that Q far more frequently and awkwardly departs from the decasyllabic five-stress line which, with certain standard variations, constitutes the norm of Shakespearean verse. That Q on occasion prints nonsense need not surprise us; but the quality of the nonsense bespeaks some extraordinary agency of corruption (Taylor, *Henry V*, p. 21).

Taylor's example is a passage from the Bishop's speech on the Salic Law:

> The Archbishop of Canterbury's disquisition on the Salic Law provides a particularly compelling example of [corruption], because the speech in F clearly derives from its counterpart in Raphael Holinshed's *Chronicles,* and F's version in turn clearly underlies the nonsense printed in Q:
>
>> Hugh Capet also, that usurped the crown,
>> To fine his title with some show of truth,
>> When in pure truth it was corrupt and naught,

> Conveyed himself as heir to the Lady Inger,
> Daughter to Charles, the foresaid Duke of Lorraine;
> So that, as clear as is the summer's sun,
> King Pepin's title and Hugh Capet's claim,
> King Charles his satisfaction all appear
> To hold in right and title of the female.

The Lady Lingard was the daughter of Charlemain, not Charles the Duke of Lorraine; 'the foresaid Duke of Lorraine' has not in fact been mentioned at all; nor has King Pepin; nor has King Charles … (Taylor, *Henry V*, p. 21).

The Folio version of this speech is as follows[6]:

> King *Pepin*, which adopted *Childerlike*,
> Did as Heire Generall, being descended
> Of *Blithild*, which was the daughter to King *Clothair*,
> Make Clayme and Title to the Crowne of France,
> *Hugh Capet* also, who vsurpt the Crowne
> Of *Charles* the Duke of Lorraine, sole Heire male
> Of the true line and stock of Charles the Great:
> To find his Title with some shewes of truth,
> Though in pure truth it was corrupt and naught,
> Conuey'd himselfe as th' Heire to th' Lady *Lingare*,
> Daughter to *Charlemaine*, who was the Sonne
> To *Lewes* the Emperor, and *Lewes* the Tenth,
> Who was sole Heire to the Vsurper *Capet*,
> Could not keepe quiet in his conscience,
> Wearing the Crowne of France, 'till satisfied,
> That faire Queene *Isabel*, his Grandmother,
> Was Lineall of the Lady *Ermengare*,
> Daughter to *Charles* the foresaid Duke of Lorraine:
> By the which Marriage, the Lyne of *Charles* the Great
> Was re-vnited to the Crowne of France.
> So that as clear as is the Summers Sunne,
> King *Pepins* Title, and *Hugh Capets* Clayme,
> King *Lewes* his satisfaction, all appeare
> To hold in Right and Title of the Femaile:
> So doe the Kings of France vnto this day.

The Folio text certainly gives more of Holinshed's narrative than the Quarto; but in point of historical accuracy, it is not without its own oddities. 'Charlemaine' and 'Charles the Great' seem to appear here as two separate people, when in fact, they were one and the same. The Lady 'Lingare' ('Inger' in Q, corrected to 'Lingard' in modern editions) was actually the daughter of Charles the Bald, not Charles the Great. Baldness and greatness are known to co-exist (as in the case of Shakespeare himself): but that is no reason for confusing these attributes. The confusion was, on the other hand, well established and of considerable authority, since it appears in Holinshed, copying from Halle: 'the Lady Lingard, daughter to King Charlemaine, son to Lewes the emperor, that was son to Charles the Great'[7].

The Folio text thus also stands accused of 'nonsense'. So too, though, to be fair, does the common source of both texts, Holinshed's *Chronicles*. 'King *Lewes* the Tenth', for example, was really King Louis IX. The error was again made by Holinshed in copying from his primary source, Edward Halle's *Union of the Two Noble and Illustre Fameliess of Lancaster and York*. Yet the Quarto's 'nonsense' is attributed to 'some extraordinary agency of corruption' (Taylor, *Henry V*, p. 21). In place of this same Louis, the Quarto substitutes the name of the current French king, Charles:

King *Charles* his satisfaction all appeare,
To hold in right and title of the female ... (*Cronicle History*, p. 38)

In both Holinshed and the Folio text, the reference is clearly to King Louis' concern with the lineage of his grandmother, about which he demands to be 'satisfied'. The Quarto text, however (whether copying from the Folio or from Holinshed) omits the passage dealing with that claim, and jumps straight from the Lady Inger to the lines which in F and Holinshed concern the Lady Ermengare. This could be an 'eyeskip' error. Or it may be that where both Holinshed and F add, to the emphasis on King Louis' claim to legitimacy, a reference to subsequent French kings

– 'So doe the Kings of France vnto this day' – Q economically
substitutes the name of the current French king, Charles, in order
to stress that the claim through the female line is all that sustains
the incumbent French monarchy.

Since, however, the Folio text could not tell the difference
between Charles the Bald and Charles the Great; and since Holinshed could not tell the difference between Louis the X and Louis
IX; it is perhaps assuming too much to expect the Quarto to distinguish between the Lady Lingare and the Lady Ermengare. One
woman's name sufficed to make the dramatic point about female
succession.

Taylor assumes that the Folio text, with its more accurate,
extensive and literal copying from Holinshed, necessarily constitutes the more authentic, more Shakespearean of the two
versions. That may be a reasonable assumption. Equally reasonable would be the contrary assumption, that in the Folio we find
a medium of slavish, unimaginative versification unexemplified
anywhere else in the play; and that in the Quarto we find the
work of a dramatist or scriptwriter who has pared down and
refined the historical trivia of Holinshed to a single, unmistakable
dramatic effect. Historical accuracy *per se* is hardly a strong point
in any of the available texts.

※

It should be possible, by putting aside the 'Bad Quarto' nomenclature, to address the text directly, in terms both of its intrinsic
characteristics and its differences from the Folio version. Before
doing so, however, it is necessary to consider another, related
argument, which is that the Quarto text represents not just a
memorially reconstructed and abridged version of F, but a *cen-
sored* version of the play. The significance of 'omissions' (i.e.
passages that appear in one text and not another) varies from one
theoretical context to another. The very concept of 'omission', of

course, presupposes that the shorter text is a reduced version of the longer. The memorial reconstruction theory tends to assume that 'omissions' derived from lapses of memory, or from the pirate-actors remembering more accurately their own parts and the scenes in which they played a substantial role. 'Abridgement' theory assumes that omissions arise simply through the process of cutting to reduce the running time: again, the effects could be fairly arbitrary, depending on who made the cuts (though if we assume, as Andrew Gurr does, that the cuts were made by members of the company going about their everyday business, then the process of abridgement takes on a new legitimacy. See below for further discussion). And, in fact, it had already been extensively argued that the differences between Q and F constitute highly significant omissions of particular types of material. Here for example is Gary Taylor:

> The text actually printed in 1600 … omits, from the play as we know it, the opening scene (with its revelation of mixed ecclesiastical motives for supporting Henry' claim to France), lines 115-35 of 1.2 (which culminate in the Archbishop's offer of church financing for the war), all reference in 2.1 to Henry's personal responsibility for Falstaff's condition, Cambridge's hint of motives other than simple bribery for the conspiracy against Henry (2.2.154-9), the bloodthirsty MacMorris and most of Henry's savage ultimatum in 3.3, all of Burgundy's description of the devastation Henry has wreaked on France (5.2.38-62). Whoever was responsible for them, the effect of the differences between this text and the one printed in all modern editions is to remove almost every difficulty in the way of an unambiguously patriotic interpretation of Henry and his war – that is, every departure from the kind of play which theatrical convention and the national mood would have led audiences of 1599 to expect (Taylor, *Henry V*, p. 12).

Taylor's suggestion is that initial performances of the play, using the Folio text, must have disappointed patriotic expectation, leading to an abridgement which carefully omitted every obstacle standing in the way of such an interpretation.

Annabel Patterson in her *Shakespeare and the Popular Voice*[8] has pursued this line of argument in more historical detail, proposing that the Quarto text displays an illuminating relationship with the political conflicts of the period 1599-1601. The 1600 text seems to Patterson a much more straightforward, unambiguously patriotic play, a drama which would seem in its ideological orthodoxy and political loyalty to answer quite readily to the patriotic interpretations of Tillyard and Lily B. Campbell. The longer version in the Folio seems by contrast a much more ambiguous text, offering a liberal and possibly even dangerous range of political commentary on the immediate historical context of its production. The Quarto seems to pull back from the incendiary political conflicts (involving especially the Earl of Essex) into which the fuller version, for whatever reason, seems to have intervened. Particularly dangerous must have been the fifth Chorus of the Folio version, with its coded reference to Essex returning in triumph from his Irish expedition.

> In 1600, then, the fifth Chorus was so ambiguous that Shakespeare's company ... could not have risked giving it the publicity of print, where its textual instabilities would be fully open to inspection. It brought down with it, presumably the rest of the Choruses, including those whose message might well have enhanced the simple patriotism of the Quarto text as a whole (Patterson, *Popular*, in Holderness, *History Plays*, pp. 176-7).

Clearly this line of interpretation brings the Quarto text into serious consideration. Annabel Patterson is interested in the variant texts as exemplifying different kinds of historical intervention into contemporary politics, rather than with value judgments discriminating one text from another in terms of literary quality. None the less, this theoretical approach could easily be seen as an extension of the 'Bad Quarto' theory, since it argues that the fuller text contains a much greater potentiality for subversion; and that the shorter text is reduced to strict conformity with the political and ideological orthodoxy of the day. The Quarto text, it could then be argued, is of 'merely' historical interest; and it is from the Folio text that modern criticism derives its interpretation of the play as a critical and subversive interrogation of monarchy, imperialism, heroism and war. It is certainly the case that those many modern readings of *The Life of Henry the Fift* that have found possibilities of subversion in the play have focused on the device of the Chorus and on some of the speeches and scenes not to be found in the 1600 Quarto text[9].

⁊⊙

The examples provided show that in most treatments of Q1, the Quarto is invariably read in relation to the Folio: either, in the 'Bad Quarto' approach, as exemplifying a quality of badness measurable by the demonstrable goodness of the more familiar text; or as constituted not by its own characteristic dramatic structure and poetic texture, but by those passages in the Folio text for which the Quarto contains no equivalent.

Let us attempt to characterise the play as an independent theatrical document. It is first necessary to identify its genre and conventions. *The Life of Henry the Fift* is remarkable particularly for its introduction of the Chorus, that distancing epic device designed both to bring the events of history into dramatic immediacy, and to estrange them into epic remoteness. In other respects it adheres to the dramatic structure developed for the historical drama in the *Henry IV* plays: with long 'serious' scenes of political and military action, intercut with shorter scenes of comic parody and travesty. One critical element in this latter relationship is the absence of Falstaff, whose participation in *The Life of Henry the Fift* was projected at the end of *The Second Part of King Henry the Fourth*, but who figures in *The Life of Henry the*

Fift only through the reporting of his death. Critical opinion has dwelt on this non-appearance of a great comic character, and read that absence as symptomatic of a movement away from comedy towards the epic and historical. It is certainly true that the Falstaffian comic function performed by the remaining tavern companions, Pistoll, Bardolfe and Nym, is substantially reduced in *The Life of Henry the Fift* by comparison with the *Henry IV* plays. It is equally apparent that this diminution applies less strongly to the Quarto text, which generally presents shorter versions of the 'serious' scenes, and thereby gives a correspondingly greater prominence – despite the absence of the Scottish and Irish captains – to the comic scenes involving Pistoll and Bardolfe, Gower and Flewellen.

That deflection of the play towards the comic mode affects both 'serious' and 'comic' passages alike. We are accustomed to thinking of the portrayal of Henry in this play as closely aligned to that aloof and fastidious figure who at the end of *The Second Part of King Henry the Fourth* formally renounces his comic heritage along with his low-life companions. The King Henry of *The Cronicle History* more closely resembled the Prince Hal of the Eastcheap scenes in those earlier plays. The genre of the Elizabethan history play was an eclectic form, containing many plays in which the new historical style, based on a close relationship with the Tudor chronicles, interacted with older modes, with the conventions of romance and the manners of comedy. In such plays the historical drama reveals itself as very much a popular genre, often acknowledging by its themes and situations an origin on the public stages of citizen London. Where tragic history plays like *Richard II* tend to restrict the dramatic action to authentic historical events and characters, the comic history maintained a freedom to invent actions and situations without precedent, or even quite unthinkable, in written history. Its sources were less the written chronicles, more materials from a still largely oral popular culture – ballads, romances, folk-tales, fairy-stories.

It represents an older kind of history, still indeed visible in the Tudor chronicles, in which the rich and varied fantasy worlds of myth and legend consort with the new positivism of historical narrative.

In historical medleys such as *James IV* and *Edward I,* historical characters mingle with citizens and figures of legend such as Robin Hood. It was this genre that produced the dominant tradition for the dramatic representation of Henry V: a comic tradition, in which the king's 'riotous youth' is used positively as a way of humanising the monarch. This king is not so much the epic hero of Agincourt as the good fellow of Eastcheap; not the mirror of all Christian kings, but the prince of carnival. In Dekker's *The Shoemaker's Holiday* (1599), a carnival play based on the London apprentices' Shrove Tuesday saturnalia, Henry V appears as a 'bully king' who associates freely with citizens and apprentices, dispenses justice and equality, resolves conflict and promotes harmony. Here the king does not need to pose as a common man, as does Henry in the *Henry V* plays on the night before Agincourt. The main source for the *Henry IV* and *Henry V* plays, the anonymous *Famous Victories of Henry the Fifth,* is distinguished by its predominantly comic mode.

Each scene in which the king or his representatives appear in *The Cronicle History of Henry the fift* is largely concerned with the enactment of some kind of game, role play, trickery, deception or practical joke. The play begins with an action already in process – 'Shall I call in Thambassadors my Liege' – and Henry holds up that action to debate the legitimacy of the war. Although certainly long for a parenthesis, that debate is essentially a pause before the action continues with the entry of the Dolphin's Ambassadors. The main business of the scene is thus the mocking gift of the tennis balls. Each scene involving Henry is in a similar way centred on a particular game: the grim practical joke on Cambridge, Masham and Gray; Exeter's returning of the Dolphin's mockery; the king's disguising himself as a common man on the night before Agincourt, his deception of the soldier Williams and the staged quarrel with Flewellen, and his wooing of the French princess. Of course, all these examples are common to the two texts: but in the Quarto the comic behaviour of the king is much more clearly and consistently in focus, unimpeded by the historicising rhetoric of the Folio's Chorus. That part of the dramatic action representing the siege of Harfleur, which in *The Life of Henry the Fift* fills most of an 'act' – beginning with the Chorus's description of the siege, followed by Henry's famous 'Once more vnto the Breach, / Deare friends' address to his troops, and ending with the long and particularly brutal speech of threatening to the citizens of Harfleur – appears in the Quarto pared down to a simple exercise in bluffing:

> *King.* How yet resolves the Governour of the Towne?
> This is the latest parley weele admit:
> Therefore to our best mercie give your selves,
> Or like to men proud of destruction, defie us to our worst,
> For as I am a souldier, a name that in my thoughts
> Becomes me best, if we begin the battery once againe,
> I will not leave the halfe atchieved Harflew,
> Till in her ashes she be buried,
> The gates of mercie are all shut up.
> What say you, will you yeeld and this avoyd,
> Or guiltie in defence be thus destroyed? (*Cronicle History*, p. 55)

The distinction between Quarto and Folio here cannot focus simply on what is there in one and absent in the other. The differences amount to a clear distinction of genre. The Folio is epic and heroic, realistic and historical – dwelling on the stirring rhetoric of battle, the documentary detail of war, the complexities of diplomacy and power. The Quarto stages the successful siege as a clever trick that happens to work. The Henry of the Quarto is presented not as an epic hero or an awe-inspiring historical character, but as a 'gentle gamester':

For when cruelty and lenitie play for a Kingdome,
The gentlest gamester is the sooner winner (*Cronicle History*, p. 60).

Thus in the Quarto there are continual interrelations and transactions of meaning between 'serious' and 'comic' scenes,
unpunctuated by any epic distancing. The dramatic structure
allows for effects of great immediacy and dramatic dislocation:
consider how a relaxed summit meeting in the French court gives
sudden place to a scene of military violence:

> *King.* Well for us, you shall returne our answer backe
> To our brother England.
>
> *Exit omnes.*
>
> *Enter* Nim, Bardolfe, Pistoll, Boy.
>
> *Nim.* Before God here is hote service
> (*Cronicle History*, pp. 53-4)

One effect of this diminution of the principle of contrast by
which 'high' and 'low' styles, epic and comedy, are juxtaposed is to
draw the figure of the king out of the removed distantiation of
history, and towards the everyday world of the popular audience.
The cultural differentiation between king and commoners is thus
reduced, and the play reconfigures a hierarchical society as a
community united in the process of festival. This 'plebeianising'
tendency of the Quartos has been noted[10]; but it is by no means
the only effect of this play's investment in the comic-romance
historical mode.

In *The Life of Henry the Fift* an epic style raises the discursive
and ideological level of monarchy's representation to such a pitch
that Henry's descent into the role of common man – as in the
scene of his disguising before Agincourt – seems distastefully
opportunistic and calculated. Yet that same epic style has the
power to redeem Henry from any critical or interrogative implications released by that juxtaposition. The Folio's Chorus
prepares the ground for Henry's conversation with the soldiers by

its passionate celebration of 'The Royall Captaine of this Ruin'd Band', greeting all his soldiers as 'Brothers, Friends and Country-men'. The king's quarrel with the soldier Williams raises a dangerous shadow of internal dissension: but one that is then redeemed, within the conventions of epic, by Henry's heart-searching soliloquy on the anxieties of kingship, and his heroic 'Crispin's Day' speech on the battlefield. In the Quarto text the debate with the soldiers is just as productive of critical questions as its counterpart in the Folio; and William's resistance to Henry's persuasions is actually intensified, since the expression of loyalty – 'I would not have the king answere for me. / Yet I intend to fight lustily for him' – assigned in the Folio to Williams, are here attrib-uted to another of the three soldiers. Henry's subsequent soliloquy ('O God of battels steele my souldiers harts', p. 67) is merely a prayer for forgiveness of his father's usurpation, and has nothing to declare about the relations between king and subject. Thus the penetrating questions posed by Williams continue to reverberate right into the battle itself; and Williams' final refusal to be humiliated by the royal jest carried all the pride and dignity of plebeian resistance to authority:

> My Liege, all offences come from the heart:
> Never came any from mine to offend your Majestie.
> You appeard to me as a common man:
> Witnesse the night, your garments, your lowlinesse,
> And whatsoever you received under that habit,
> I beseech your Majestie impute it to your owne fault
> And not mine (*Cronicle History*, p. 78).

The extraordinarily 'levelling' effect of this moment has much greater force in the Quarto than in the Folio text: since while in the latter the king consistently occupies the epic and historicist conventions appropriate to monarchy, occasionally stooping with studied calculation to the level of his subjects; in the Quar-to a plebeianising and carnivalisation of the monarch effectively sets Henry and Williams face to face, man to man, in a ritual enactment of that myth of equality that underlies the comic-romance motif of 'the king disguised'[11]. Williams' professional dignity and plebeian pride can be set against that orgiastic festival of violence, celebrated on the field of Agincourt, which in the Quarto aligns Henry very closely with Pistoll:

> *Alarum soundes*
>
> What new alarum is this?
> Bid every souldier kill his prisoner.
> *Pist.* Couple gorge.
>
> Exit *omnes.*
>
> (*Cronicle History*, p.73)

ॐ

Andrew Gurr in his New Cambridge Shakespeare edition of Q1 breaks from most of the key assumptions of the editorial tradition (especially memorial reconstruction and provincial touring), and offers a different set of arguments about the Q1 text. But there are some interesting continuities. He agrees that it was a cut version of the F text, the text that went into the Folio, and that it was probably made by two of the Lord Chamberlain's Servants. But he disputes the assumption that the process was in any way illegitimate or piratical, and he defends the text against the 'Bad Quarto' designation. His case is that such abridged texts were the only way in which plays were ever performed on the stages of Elizabethan and Jacobean London, the F text being an example of a 'maximal' ideal text, authorised by the Master of the Revels, and the Q text an example of a performance version or 'minimal' text, as derived from the F text by the company for their own professional purposes. As such Q1 is 'closer to the version of the play that Shakespeare's company first put on the stage in 1599', 'the closest we are ever likely to get to the editorial ideal (or will o' the wisp) of the Oxford edition, Shakespeare in performance at the Globe in 1599'[12].

Gurr's view then, which seems broadly compatible with the new textual criticism, is that these texts were in continuous iteration, entailing the collaboration of multiple agents, so that 'no single moment existed when a written script, a uniquely authoritative record of the "performance text", could be established' (p. 2). Between the manuscript-based playbook and the abridged copy used for performance lay 'a whole series of likely transcriptions any or all of which might have modified the original authorial intention' (p. 3). In this way Gurr reconciles New Bibliography and New Textualism, Alexandria and Pergamum. He has his ideal text, based on an authorial manuscript, reflecting the author's intentions. And he has his specific, historically contingent realisation of the text in theatrical performance, Q1. Both are referred to a point of origin: F1 to defining authorial intention, as modified by official state authorisation; Q1 to the will o' the wisp of contemporary performance. Neither is accessible; neither is a 'material entity'; neither exists except in and through the stories we choose to tell about them. The modern edition of F1 is a late twentieth century narrative, not a representation of Shakespeare's manuscript; just as an 'authentic' production of *Henry V* on the New Globe stage[13] is an invention of the modern theatre, not a replication of what happened there (or near there) in 1599. When Gurr starts to speculate on the specific conditions in which he imagines Q1 to have been copied from the F text, he is creating his own Stoppardian para-drama (Gurr, *First Quarto*, p. 9).

> It was put together for performance in London and elsewhere in late 1599 or early 1600 by several members of the company. It was undoubtedly an authoritative players' text. At least two, possibly more of the company's players who had speaking parts shared the work. Most of the manuscript was recorded by dictation, chiefly from the rough playscript, helped in places by the players' memories of their parts. On occasion there may also have been some resort to an authorial manuscript ...

One starts to see and hear all this, with faces and voices and props: the rough playscript, the authorial manuscript ... but the mini-drama being observed is more the work of Andrew Gurr than of Shakespeare.

In some ways nothing much has changed. Gurr's edition posits two texts, one the author's and the other the theatre's. He denies all imputations of impropriety and dishonesty in the process of copying and revision, since this was invariably how the players got from the maximal authoritative text to the minimal performance programme. He eschews the value judgements that have traditionally been used to discriminate sheep from goats, good from bad texts. The two texts are treated as equals (legitimate 'likely transcriptions'), though Q1 is accorded a privileged status as closer to the stage than F1. But we are still working within a New Bibliographical paradigm, since there is an ideal text and there is a derivative one (albeit the latter is not castigated on behalf of the former). One is complete, the other abridged; one directly authorial, the other mediated via the actors; and above all, one is a searching interrogation of monarchy, imperialism, war, state power; while the other is a simple patriotic play reflecting the buoyant nationalism of the 1590s. The suggestion that the F text with its ambivalent Choruses never appeared on stage in 1599 disposes of uncountable reams of commentary (including some of mine) that assumes it was, and that it functioned there as an exemplar of theatrical verse narrative. On this view the potential subversiveness of the F text remained a closely-guarded secret within the acting company until some time after the publication of the First Folio. The implications for our whole understanding of early modern culture – for the relations between high and popular cultures, for the drama's potentiality for subversive discourse – are huge. Laurence Olivier's film of *Henry V* should be banned as utterly misleading. Perhaps the 'wooden O' never did have crammed within it the words that mediate 'the very casques/ That did affright the air at Agincourt' (Craik, *Henry V,* p. 120).

I still remain agnostic about the status of these two texts. In the *Shakespearean Originals* edition of 1992 I said we should consider Q as a text 'valuable in its own right' (*Cronicle History*, p. 28). Andrew Gurr in his NCS edition is making a similar emphasis when he talks about the text being 'uniquely valuable' (p. 1). Gurr continues to honour the traditional editorial mission of establishing the relations between the two substantive texts; while my purpose was 'not to advance new or revised arguments about the relations between the two texts; but partly to dissociate Quarto from Folio so as to view the earlier text in its own right as an independent cultural object; and partly to essay comparisons between Quarto and Folio on the assumption of textual multiplicity and equivalence, as distinct from the tradition of interpretation predicated on the Quarto's self-evident inferiority' (*Cronicle History*, pp. 22-3). This still remains in my view a worthwhile activity. As Stephen Urkowitz has pointed out, the 'memorial reconstruction' hypothesis itself

> seems to have prevented close examination of the fundamental documents of our literary-dramatic tradition by its practitioners, teachers of literature and performers of plays. Labeling certain texts as 'bad' quartos has removed them from the normal discourse in which such documents would otherwise be included[14].

The various surviving printed texts of early modern drama should be accepted as the 'fundamental documents', and should be 'studied for what they are, in and of themselves, rather than solely as pernicious desecrations of Shakespeare's iconic originals' (Urkowitz, 'Good news', p. 204).

On the other hand in practice both the *Shakespearean Originals* and the *New Cambridge Shakespeare* editions spend most of their time talking about the relations between the two texts, how they originated and what their differences are. I now recognise that this is inevitable: but not because the Q text is part of a greater whole, Shakespeare's intended text, that is in turn best represented by the Folio; but rather because all these texts are copies, of themselves and of one another; copies of something we can never grasp, never obtain. All texts are copies extrapolated from 'the very origin of the destabilising moment'[15].

There is still room for a recuperation of Q1 that emphasises the singularity of the individual play text, the specific identity it reassumes when disentangled from the conflated master text and 'restored' to something more like its original shape and form. But this exercise remains subject to the universal 'law of impurity', to the 'principle of contamination'[16]. We will never be able to see Q1 other than in terms of its difference from F: the gaps, the omissions, the displacements and deferrals that define it by its insufficiency, its lack of completeness. In Q1 we encounter a gap between the Folio's 'wooden O', itself an *aporia,* and what scholars believe happened at the Globe in 1599. But like the wooden O itself, this is another version of Peter Brooke's 'empty space', a gap to be filled with language and activity, with a repetition of words and a renewal of bodily presence.

The famous opening Chorus of the Folio *Henry V*, whether or not it was ever staged, provides a brilliant exposition of the complex relations between presence and absence, representation and presentation.

> Pardon, gentles all,
> The flat unraised spirits that have dar'd
> On this unworthy scaffold to bring forth
> So great an object. Can this cockpit hold
> The vasty fields of France? or may we cram
> Within this wooden O the very casques
> That did affright the air at Agincourt! (Craik, *Henry V*, p. 120).

At one level a mere technical apology for the limitations of the contemporary theatre, the opening Chorus also expresses a defensive conviction of the present as immeasurably inferior to a vanished past, the quotidian a poor shadow of the immanent, presence approximated inadequately by an empty representation. The actors are conscious of themselves as unworthy proxies for the aristocratic subjects they are attempting to imitate. This 'diminution effect' is then applied generally to the contemporary world, in contradistinction to the past; particularly to the events and characters of history, as compared with the actors who merely simulate their vanished greatness; and specifically to the relative standings, within the social hierarchy, of modern plebeian actors and the antique aristocratic figures of historical legend.

The Globe theatre, that 'unworthy scaffold' with its flat and unadorned wooden stage, is the banal and unhistorical present, a 'wooden O' which in its very shape figures the perceived relative vacuity of the modern world. The theatre is a mere 'cockpit', a place of sport and trivial entertainment, where actors strut their feathers and fly at one another in raucous and petty squabbles. Those actors themselves are 'flat unraised spirits' in at least two senses. They are low-life, plebeian craftsmen who do not share in the lofty nobility possessed by the kings, queens and nobles whom they represent. Equally, they are compared to the spirits of the dead, 'flat', ineffective, without vitality; disembodied, they remain 'unraised', incapable of engaging with the vibrancy of corporeal existence, the concrete substantiality of real historical presence.

Yet each of these disclaimers contains the potentiality for quite other levels of meaning. The wooden 'O' of the theatre can seem a lifeless vacuum, emptiness, a mere nothing. But like the womb, such an empty space can also be the source of all vitality, all existence. The necromantic potency of 'imaginary forces' can indeed raise the dead, lift those 'flat' spirits into fully-embodied, moving or terrifying, incarnate phantoms of theatrical presentation.

All glory and greatness – the casques of Agincourt, the proud-hoofed horses – are in the past, irrevocably lost in the dark backward and abysm of time. From its level platform of contemporaneity, the present can only glance over its shoulder in nostalgic recollection of a vanished magnitude. And yet the only means by which that transient glory can be apprehended is through the 'imaginary puissance' of theatrical representation, past splendour resurrected into full daylight, a brittle glory that nonetheless gleams brightly in the mirror of the stage.

The mechanisms by which this operation is conducted are openly and unashamedly declared in metaphors derived from the modern bourgeois world of financial accounting:

> … since a crooked figure may
> Attest in little place a million...
> Let us, ciphers to this great accompt,
> On your imaginary forces work (Craik, *Henry V*, p. 120).

Although the 'crooked figure', a circular 'O', may appear to be a vacant, hollow sign, it has the semiotic capability of vastly increasing the magnitude of its referent. Like the ostensibly empty 'O' of the theatre, the numerical zero can in practice signify plenitude and totality: just as the minuscule 'ciphers' of book-keeping can represent an infinitely larger sum of wealth, so the actors can stand in for the greatness of history, the presence of the real.

So by emphasising the distance between reality and representation, the Chorus is claiming, rather than disclaiming, cultural power. Those modern technical and artisanal processes of acting, book-keeping, writing for the stage, seem from the aristocratic standpoint of the past to be trivial and hollow processes, mere gaps in the substance of a culture that ought to consist uniformly of great men and their deeds. But it is for precisely that reason that they are capable of opening up a space for active and positive intervention on the part of the drama. The theatre may be a wooden 'O' but it can still fill that empty space with grand narratives of English history. The book-keeper's tiny clerical inscription seems a mere squiggle but it has the power to augment number and increase scale. The dramatic writer, granted at best an ambiguous status by the traditional codes of his society, can nonetheless, in this arena, make kings his subjects. The popular audience, a collective of unhistorical characters constituted into the passivity of spectatorship, can by its thoughts collaborate in the production of the real.

Together these cultural forces conspire to create a collective imagination that has enormous and varied powers of freedom and control:

> Jumping o'er times,
> Turning th'accomplishment of many years
> Into an hour-glass ... (Craik, *Henry V*, p. 120).

The dramatic imagination, through the lively physical exertions of the actors, can exercise a virtually acrobatic liberty over chronology, 'Jumping o'er times'; but at the same time condensing the passage of many years into two-hour's traffic of the stage, confining the scope and scale of history into a strictly delimited space measurable by chronometer. Within the hour-glass the dust of vanished existence is contained, pent fast, shaped into a form both fixed and fluid, compact and evanescent; as in Hopkins' metaphor: 'soft sift/In an hour-glass – at the wall/Fast, but mined with a motion, a drift'[17]. Every grain of sand stands for a man, or an event, or a historical reality. In measured flow the dust is channeled into a tiny aperture (another *aporia,* an 'O' or empty space) and thereby mimics the process of time, dust to dust, the present flowing imperceptibly but inevitably into past.

The hour-glass is a metaphor for the passage of time. But it is also a tool of measurement, an instrument of demonstration, a practical and utilitarian technology for controlling as well as acknowledging time. Time is measured by the empty space that appears after the sand that filled it has gone, so in one sense time is the absence of presence. But the sand has not disappeared, it has merely flowed into another space. By simple inversion of the hour-glass, the whole process can begin again, the dust of time recycled to initiate another passage: another hour, another play, another ritual enactment of that endless process of making and re-making, losing and finding; earth to earth, ashes to ashes, dust to dust.

Far from appearing here as a trite emblem of an abstraction 'Time', in the context of this Chorus the hour-glass is a packed and potent symbol of the way in which drama can simultaneously acknowledge the loss of the past, admit the inaccessibility of presence, and yet by a simple trick of 'turning' formally re-enact history, reconstruct presence. A skilled craftsman's flick of the wrist, or a mountebank conjurer's sleight of hand, are the apparently trivial preconditions for a reinstatement of the real. Just as the Chorus is as much concerned with the material conditions of production as with what is produced, the emphasis of this metaphor is only partly on the process signified by the hour-glass's operation. It is also on the hour-glass as a tool, and on the bold artisanal skill that can 'turn' a history of aristocratic achievement into a modern and popular cultural process.

Dust and Dreams

(From *The Ruin*)

... When it was built, bright was the building,
Gorgeously gabled. Masses of men
Milled in the mead-hall; the row of rioters
Rang through the roof. Thickly they thronged,
Proud in their pleasure, choice in their cheer.
But Destiny doomed them,
Dealt them a double blow: pillaged by plague,
Battered by battle, the flower of the folk
Fell. This fort fragmented, and fell to waste,
To rack and ruin. The masons melted away,
The valiant men vanished. Hence are these halls
Desolate and dreary: tiles are torn
From the red roof. Decay's destroyed,
Reduced to rubble, this peerless pile:
Where once, in old days, a host of heroes
Happy in heart, glittering with gold,
Fair and wine-flushed, fed on the sight
Of shimmering silver, and joyed in gems.
Ravished by riches, gladdened by gold,
They gazed on the splendour of this bright burg,
This celestial city and its circling domains.

PART THREE

Textual Conclusions

Writing in the Dust

ᴥ

T HE TITLE OF THIS concluding chapter is appropriated not directly from *Henry V's* hour-glass, but from a pamphlet reflecting on the events of 11 September 2001 (when Islamic terrorists piloted two planes into New York's famous 'Twin Towers', demolishing the buildings and killing almost 3,000 people), published by Dr Rowan Williams (now Archbishop of Canterbury, but then Archbishop of Wales). Being in New York, and close to the World Trade Centre, on 11 September, Rowan Williams found himself subsequently trying to write, as he puts it, on, and in, the dust of destruction[1]:

> When we finally escaped from our building, it was quite hard to breathe normally in the street: dense fumes; thick, thick dust; a sort of sandstorm or snowstorm of dust and debris; large flakes of soft grey burned stuff falling steadily ... It can't have been silent ... But I remember it as quiet; the very few words spoken to each other, the ghostliness of it all.

Through this vivid description of the atrocity itself, Williams expresses the sheer difficulty of finding a language adequate to the situation: 'one person's attempt to find words for the grief and shock and loss of one moment' (Williams, *Writing*, p. 80).

He tries to construct a writing that will hold together, and in place, both the experience, and some approximately appropriate response; writing that will stick to the swirling atoms of dust, without hardening into dogma or hatred: 'all that is written here begins in the dust of the streets that morning' (Williams, *Writing*, p. 79).

Rowan Williams is preoccupied with this fundamental distinction between writing as a fixed, immanent meaning, compelling assent to a master-narrative; and writing that is open and ephemeral, local and particular, even anecdotal in its context-specific fragmentariness. One of the examples he provides to illustrate this contrast is a distinction between the written instructions provided to the terrorists[2], and the messages sent by passengers on the planes to their loved ones. On the one hand, a Koran-based religious discourse of substantial weight and gravity; on the other, trite and conventional expressions of affection. But also, on the one hand, a religious language of great antiquity, its dignity hopelessly compromised by its dishonesty, its attempt to 'make a martyr's drama out of a crime' (Williams, *Writing*, p. 2); and on the other a secular language of 'pointless, gratuitous love' (Williams, *Writing*, p. 2), which is everything that religious language ought to be – words of a 'terrible simplicity' (Williams, *Writing*, p. 11) that can create a 'breathing space' in the midst of choking dust, uncontrollable violence (Williams, *Writing*, p. 2).

But the metaphor of writing in the dust finally comes home in what Williams calls the 'stray story' of the woman taken in adultery in St John's Gospel (Chapter 8). The story (like the woman) is astray because it is omitted by almost all the oldest manuscripts, and by the earliest versions (Syriac, Coptic and some Old Latin). Neither is it mentioned by the earliest church fathers. Where it does appear its location is itinerant: it appears in several places in John, and even in Luke (21.38). St John's Gospel is in any case generally, though not universally, held to be a copy, dating from the late first century, a recapitulation of the earlier 'synoptic' gospels. The story of the woman taken in adultery is most probably an interpolation or later addition[3]; a 'supplementation' that seems to complete the text, seems utterly right and natural in its place, but at the same time by its uncertainty of origin opens the text up to further hermeneutic transaction[4].

Rowan Williams's interest in the story is that it shows Jesus 'writing in the dust':

> But Jesus stooped down, and with *his* finger wrote on the ground[5].

But what kind of writing is going on here? Commentators have variously assumed either that Jesus is drawing invisible lines on a hard surface ('the ground'), or inscribing actual signs into dust or sand. The Greek gospel gives 'γη', earth; and the Latin Vulgate follows this with '*terra*'. Neither word spells out whether the surface is to be imagined as hard or soft, baked earth or fluid sand[6].

Behind the story there is a much more familiar and defining image of writing: that of the Jewish Law directly inscribed onto stone by 'the finger of God' (Exodus, 31.18):

> The tables *were* the work of God, and the writing *was* the writing of God, graven upon the tables (Exodus, 32.16, from *The Bible*, eds. Carroll and Prickett, OT p. 106).

No image could convey more effectively the notion of an authoritative text: traced by the divine authorial hand, executed by God's power: indelibly inscribed, unmediated meaning[7]. It is the fixity of these inflexible writings that is invoked by the Scribes and Pharisees when they bring the guilty woman before Jesus ('Moses in the law commanded us, that such should be stoned'). What Jesus says revises the law, leaving the prohibition in place ('go, and sin no more'), but basing it in a new covenant of forgiveness and mercy (John 8.5, 8.11. *The Bible*, eds. Carroll and Prickett, NT p. 126). But what if anything, did he write on the ground?

The parallel with the earlier engraving of the Law can be

taken literally, as in the painting by Pieter Breughel the Elder (1565, Courtauld Gallery), where Jesus is shown cutting words with his finger into the stone floor of the Temple. Again God writes in stone but writes out a new covenant. More persuasive however is the view that Jesus writes something that is to be erased: that he scribbles, and then rubs out, words in the dust. Words engraved on stone express the inflexible compulsion of the Law. The new Law emphasises the possibility of redemption, regeneration, a fresh start. Sin can be absolved, writing erased or over-written as in a palimpsest ('hath no man condemned thee?... Neither do I condemne thee'. John 8.10-11. *The Bible*, eds. Carroll and Prickett, NT p. 126). Not death by stone; but new life, written in the dust.

Modern bibliography proposes that all writing is writing in the dust: 'writing that won't last, something exposed to dissolution' (Williams, *Writing*, p. 79). This is either because the material foundation of writing easily disintegrates, so it survives only in altered copy, or not at all; or because in its elusively iterable nature, writing more closely resembles a continually dispersing dustcloud than an indelible inscription on a tablet of stone.

⚜

11 September 2001 tested our language of tragedy[8], and Jennifer Wallace has written on the disaster as a modern example of an ancient genre. She describes two 'public projects for retrieving and mourning the dead' from the World Trade Centre:

> One was the grim excavation of the rubble at Ground Zero and the search for traces of the 2,823 people who died there. The other was the daily publication in the *New York Times* of a brief biography of each victim, a 200-word profile accompanied by a photograph which soon became well know collectively as the 'Portraits of Grief'[9].

The portraits are themselves 'powerful works of tragedy bringing a human dimension to an inhuman disaster'; tragic because they 'give shape to the disaster by transforming ordinary lives into significant narratives' (Wallace, 'Tragedy', p. 16). Wallace then compares the search for traces of the 2,823 people who died with examples from classical tragedy: the literal and figurative disintegration of the body, and the human effort to reassemble or reconstruct what has been dispersed and fragmented, to be found in *Hamlet* and *The Bacchae*. The archaeological excavation of Ground Zero was a search for certainty in the recovery of remains, a work of mourning like Agave's desire to have the limbs of her dismembered son 'joined decently together'; or like Hamlet's mission to 'set ... right' a disjointed time[10].

As the excavation progressed, it became increasingly obvious that nowhere near all the victims would be accounted for. Wallace quotes a fire fighter, faced with a dwindling pile of rubble and a list of 1,800 people still untraced:

> 'You've got a great number of people that you want to find, and you've got a certain amount of dirt that's left. And there's a gap. That gap is going to be a sorrowful one' (Wallace, 'Tragedy', p. 17).

The 'gap' is literally, as Wallace observes, between 'statistics and physical dust'. But as a 'gap' of sorrow, it also represents the space of tragedy, the lacuna between hope and despair, between 'consolation and disillusion' (Wallace, 'Tragedy', p. 17). Such gaps are the enduring legacy of a disaster like 11 September: the hole in the Manhattan skyline where the Twin Towers used to be; the rips in the insular complacency of a nation unaccustomed to enemy action on its own soil. An architect's design for replacing the towers showed one of the buildings constructed as an open rectangle, embodying the unfilled space of its original destruction. But a gap to be bridged, as Wallace observes; a hole to be filled with memory and mourning; a space in which to 'write stories'.

જ઼

11 September did not however create such a gap, but only revealed its existence. The attack did not bring violence into the world; it only brought a new level of international violence to America. In doing so it burst a seam, broke a coupling, ripped open a suture and let daylight in through the self-evident fault-lines that separate east from west, rich from poor, strong from weak, America from her many demonised 'others'.

But all human experience, all language and all culture are built over such fissures in the fabric of existence. For Derrida, speech is the illusion of presence; writing potentially a means of demonstrating absence. The sign is always a 'deferred presence'[11]. Language attempts to overcome this deferral of meaning, but in doing so only reinscribes it. As Graham Ward puts it:

> Derrida suggests the openness of textuality to an indefinite future, a deferred eschaton – an openness that cannot be closed. We are always *in medias res* – moving between an origin which can never be recovered or single and a conclusion which can never be determined. We occupy a place, as such, in the shifting sands of semiotic systems, haunted by the possibility of presence and stable identity, but forever unable to produce it (Ward, *Theology*, p. 15).

Once again we are back to writing in the dust, drawing signs in the shifting sand, signs no sooner inscribed than erased[12]. Writing is, in Derrida's terms, an elegy for lost presence, an act of mourning for that which lies already in the past. But the very signs employed to represent that lost presence announce the absence of the presence they signify. Presence is again postponed, pushed into the future, a 'deferred eschaton' (Ward, *Theology*, p. 16). Words dissolve in the sand, the dust blows over them. Hence there is always, in Ward's terms, 'a gap between event and consciousness'; but also between reality and experience, between signifier and signified, between now and then. If a text is 'no longer a finished corpus of writing, some content enclosed in a book or its margins, but a differential network, a fabric of traces referring endlessly to something other than itself'[13], then the text itself is also a 'gap'. A hole, an empty space, an *aporia* through which we can glimpse a place beyond borders, 'the limits' (Derrida), 'an unlimited place' (Cixous), the indefinable[14].

In this study we have encountered a similar range of ways in which the Shakespearean text is received and understood. In New Bibliography we have seen a search for the writing on the tablets of stone, written by the finger of the God-like author, eternal and immanent meaning indestructibly inscribed onto a medium (the manuscript that remains reconstructible, even though it has long since joined the broken tablets of Exodus, and mingled with the sands of the desert). In the past I have remonstrated, together with many other scholars and critics, against this 'idealism'. Now I see the error of New Bibliography as residing not in its hope of finding what was lost, an aspiration that lies at the heart of all writing, but in its belief that scholarship can fight its way back through centuries of textual change to a point of recovery, to finding the original again. And this is a natural desire. There *was* a point of origin for Shakespeare's plays and we will always be fascinated by it, mourn for its passing, long for its rediscovery. In Henry James's words, 'where shall you find a *presence* equally diffused, uncontested and undisturbed?'[15]. But the prelapsarian perfection of the manuscript is not to be recovered in the past by archaeological excavation, but rather extrapolated towards that final deferred 'eschaton' that lies at the other end of time. What we are doing when we remake Shakespeare's texts (or those of any other writer) is more a matter of building towards an unrealisable future than recapturing an irrevocably vanished past. In that process our mourning for the lost past is projected forwards into mourning for the endlessly deferred future. As such it embraces bereavement, and with all the powers of the imagination invests in what Derrida calls 'the work of mourning'[16]. Even the London *Times* has caught up with some of these speculations:

> Readers are never quite as enthusiastic about an author's available works as they are about that which might have gone missing. A poem in the hand is not worth a few lines hidden in a bush. The demi-epic grandeur of Spenser's *Faerie Queene* does not stop enthusiasts from hankering after a further five books. The lavishness of the Shakespearean oeuvre does not prevent a phalanx of scholars ferreting away in the world's libraries for forgotten folios. The quest for the vanished text has all the compulsion of classic suspense fiction: mystery, the thrill of the chase, and the long dreamt-of moment when all that was hidden is revealed[17].

It follows that we should finally be as dissatisfied with the 'materialist' reaction to New Bibliography as we have become with New Bibliography's idealism. Historical determinism will not capture the nature of writing any better than an abstract essentialism. In practice however, as I showed in the early chapters of this book, materialist approaches have converged with poststructuralism and deconstruction, and thus avoided any relapse into 'mechanical materialism' or mere positivism. The attempt to fix the text in history is now recognised as a simultaneous unfixing of its location in both past and present. In search of identity, we find relationship; in search of individuality, we find otherness; in search of a firmly-grasped historical context, we find ourselves engaging with the text in an invisible space of historical difference. Derrida's work on Marx demonstrates conclusively (if I may use the word) that the materialist cultural analysis we used to trust is no longer an option, and that all cultural work opens up our minds to the spectre of the invisible. As Marx himself said, 'All that is solid melts into air'; or in Prospero's words, into 'thin Ayre'[18]. Once we have understood this inalienable condition of alienation, we are free to exercise the imagination in exploring the infinite possibilities of cultural revision and textual reconstruction.

Shakespeare now exists in an environment of textual multiplicity. Virtually all the new approaches, whether critical, theoretical or bibliographical, agree on this. The text is multiple, iterable, subject to an inevitable law of change. It is never original, always copied. The grounds on which *a priori* assumptions could be made about the automatic superiority of one text over another have disappeared: so texts remain to us as plural, relative to one another, not severed into separation by some absolute judgement, but embedded in network of differences. The text gives us no direct access to any pure space of authorial intention, for someone has always already got there before us. It follows that all texts are collaboratively authored and textual editing is no less a collaborative activity.

All this can point towards a post-modern nihilism and a view of culture as some impersonal giant photocopier. None of this however disposes of the general considerations with which I began: above all the fact that any text is inseparable from an act of making. Modern bibliography concentrates on the 'technological' aspects of cultural production, where New Bibliography, for all its focus on the concrete, ultimately deferred to the original manuscript, always taking the essential 'text' as its lodestar. But as both my arguments and my illustrations have shown, these features are aspects of the same process. Writing, publication and theatrical performance are practical crafts that take place in a restlessly changing environment of productive technologies. But none of them would be necessary were there not some point of origin, some act of creation which brings into being a piece of organised language considered worth preserving and circulating. And the genesis of such works is inseparable from creativity and imagination. Hence we inevitably search the technological 'text' for the 'text' that lies within it, the originating idea. The text is changeable, multiple, unfixed and unstable. Yet it has an origin in the indefinable, the invisible, the limitless. As Thomas Hardy put it, we follow 'tracks unchosen and unchecked' that only lead away from a writing that remains 'at heart unread eternally'[19]. In both these respects the text obeys the fundamental laws of our existence, moving and operating just as we do, between flesh and spirit, mortality and immortality, life and death.

I think it was Raymond Williams who initiated the convention of inserting the critic as a person into his/her own discourse as a physical presence, a character in the action. One of the best-known examples is that of Terence Hawkes opening his book on Shakespeare by depicting himself, eating fish-and-chips by the river at Stratford-upon-Avon[20]. The device is an act of critical self-consciousness, impossibly representing the author as a speaker who is both producer of, and a subject within, his own writing. There is more to this then mere disarming self-reflexiveness, like Alfred Hitchcock edging himself into his own films. For the author is being dramatised within the critical discourse, constructed as a specification of the author-function. Paradoxically an element of fiction enters the medium with the insertion of the real writer. Person or persona? Language is doubled, producing two voices: the one who writes and the one who speaks within the writing. I am eating fish and chips; I am the one who says he is eating fish-and-chips ... The net effect is one of displacement rather than presentation, the production of a ghost writer. As Mallarme said of Hamlet, 'il se promene, lisant au livre de lui-meme'[21].

I have just given a lecture at the New Globe Theatre in Southwark, and am traversing the river over the Millennium Bridge.

Walking from south to north, from Bankside to the City, over this newest of all London's bridges, spanning the gap between those binary oppositions. Surely in its lyrical, elegant lines one of the most graceful structures ever fashioned from concrete and steel, the Millennium Bridge by its name links two centuries, the twentieth that saw my induction into this world, and the twenty-first that will most assuredly witness my departure from it. It is not the bridge in E.M. Forster's vision that connects prose and poetry, beast and monk, and 'spans [our] lives with beauty'[22]; nor is it the rainbow bridge that Froh throws over the abyss to Walhalla in *Das Rheingold* (though on the water below float oily slicks of iridescence, a fractured spectrum that continually breaks and re-forms).

The Millennium Bridge is already world-famous, but less for its beauty and utility than for the history of its construction. When initially opened, its structure proved to be so unstable that it was closed for almost a year for rectifying repairs. But not before its instability had entered legend, such that it may well remain forever the 'Wobbling Bridge'. Now it stands, stiff and stark, firmly fixed in its proper place: perhaps a disappointment to those who come in search of difference, the eccentric, the unusual. How many people would flock to visit the Erect Tower of Pisa?

Crossing the Thames by means of this conduit, I am also conscious of a transit from past to present that is more than the clock's ticking. Behind me is the past: the site of Shakespeare's Globe; the once-pulsing heart of the Elizabethan theatre industry. Directly ahead of me, neat and severe in its perfect proportions, is St Paul's, neo-classical phoenix arising from the conflagration that destroyed Tudor London. But glancing back, I'm struck again by the obvious fact that the replica Globe is just about the newest building on the Southwark skyline, as bright and clean as a shopping mall. Its antique costume is even more oddly displayed beside the much older power station now distinguished as

London's premier space for contemporary art, Tate Modern. By contrast with both, St Paul's is old. And old it looks, rising from the dust, shouldering aside much newer buildings, levitating on the mist of a fine October rain. The fact that its architecture is shamelessly imitative of the great cathedrals of Europe, in no way for me detracts from its authenticity; since it was in those churches of Venice and Florence and Rome that I myself became again aware of just how full empty space can be.

Back to the future then; face towards the past. Behind me the New Globe, emulating a vanished and inaccessible original, a supplementation that fails to complete, a brightly painted sign that cheerfully announces the irrecoverable absence of its original. Yet now a modern space, a theatre that never was until now; a new wooden O that echoes resoundingly with the cacophony of many voices. Ahead of me St Paul's, its exquisite dome packed with the plenitude of absent being.

From words to the Word. The bridge wobbles.

Pilgrimage

(From *The Seafarer*)

And so my heart heaves to wander the waves,
The unplumbed oceans, and taste of the tang
Of the salt-sea's spray; to seek the deep streams
And their restless rolling. There I might seek
Friendship in foreign lands, there I might find
Homeless, a home on an alien shore.
Again and again an impulse invites me,
A peregrine urge to fare far forth;
A mood of migration irks me to travel
The pilgrim's passage, the wanderer's way.

Postscript

❧

I WROTE THE CLOSING PAGES of this book in an Oxford pub named after the hero of Thomas Hardy's novel *Jude the Obscure*[1]. There was nothing deliberate about it: I accepted an invitation to an Oxford University Press book launch; I was half an hour early; I had almost finished the book. And the pub stands next door to OUP's magnificent building in the suburb of Oxford known as Jericho, Hardy's thinly disguised proletarian quarter 'Beersheba'. But the circumstance demands to be read as, at least, mildly symbolic.

I must have been about thirteen when I first looked with Jude Fawley's eyes across the flat brown land of Hardy's novel and saw, on the horizon, the gleam of a celestial city. In pursuit of that dream Jude came to 'Christminster' and settled in 'Beersheba' among the 'struggling men and women' who make up the real city, 'town' as opposed to 'gown'; a living text, a compendious 'book of humanity' (Hardy, *Jude*, p. 168). At night Jude walks the deserted, lamp-lit streets, sensing behind those impermeable college walls the ghostly presences of Oxford's illuminati, Arnold and Newman, Browning and Swinburne. I managed to make my way across the walls (frequently, as I remember: they seemed to me there to keep 'gentlemen' in, rather than to shut strangers out) and found myself in privileged communication with Jude's ghosts, as an undergraduate avidly reading Arnold and Newman, Browning and Swinburne. But I too had my ghosts, the spectres of men like Jude, who I could feel standing outside, hands in pockets, watching me at what I could hardly bring myself to describe as 'work'. I saw nothing but pleasure and pride in their pale features: but I could never expunge an aching of self-reproach from my own heart.

Jude's life, though tragic, is also exemplary: as he lies dead, 'a smile of some sort on his marble features', a corresponding pallor illuminates his books, 'roughened with stone-dust where he had been in the habit of catching them up for a few minutes between his labours' (Hardy, *Jude*, p. 490). Jude never finally succeeds, of course, in reconciling learning and labour, but at least he tried; and the aspiration embodied in his story should not be written off just because it has not been achieved. By going to university I broke with my predecessor generation of men who made things with their hands: men like my father, who laboured manually all his life, who shot-blasted metal and scraped hides in foundries and tanneries[2].

Jude read Greek, but he also built and carved in brick and stone, an 'effort as worthy as that dignified by the name of schol-arly study' (Hardy, *Jude*, p. 131). I can make nothing with my hands; nor can I integrate literature and labour, books and work. But at least I can attempt to show the extent to which books have labour in them, and how their meanings are produced by the practical craft of their construction, as well as by the imaginative and intellectual work that creates them. I can also try to demon-strate, by revising the relations between 'authorship' and 'collaboration', the canonical books of our culture and Hardy's 'book of humanity' are much more closely inter-related than his distinction suggest. My own books are not roughened with stone dust; but I know something now of how they were formed, as we ourselves are: neither by pure thought and feeling, nor by some impersonal mechanism of construction but by labour, from the dust of the ground. The dust that we are, and to which we shall return.

I cannot deny that I found in Oxford something of Jude's 'city of light and learning'[3]. But what has long compelled my imagination is rather his vision of Christminster, the city on the horizon; clear then ambiguous, distinct then fading:

> Points of light like the topaz gleamed. The air increased in transparency with the lapse of minutes, till the topaz points showed themselves to be the vanes, windows, wet roof slates, and other shining spots upon the spires, domes, freestone work, and varied outlines that were faintly revealed.

> ...the windows and vanes lost their shine ... the vague city became veiled in mist (Hardy, *Jude*, p. 61)

Before I was born Evelyn Waugh spoke of the Oxford of Arnold and Newman (and, though he does not mention him, of Jude the Obscure), as 'submerged now and obliterated, irrecoverable as Lyonesse'[4]. Elsewhere in the same novel Waugh defines nostalgia as a response to irreparable loss: 'When the waterholes were dry people sought to drink at the mirage' (Waugh, *Brideshead*, p. 794).

Back in Oxford, writing in a corner of the Jude the Obscure heritage theme-pub, in a Jericho now as gentrified as Notting Hill, the dream seems ever further away, perpetually receding. What I sought here, and never found, is after all closer to the young Jude's natural identification of his visionary city, not with any real place, but with a city set on a hill, 'the heavenly Jerusalem' (Hardy, *Jude*, p. 60). Still it hints and beckons, drawing ever closer and closer; inaccessible, though fleetingly visible, as in Hardy's 'outlines' and 'shining spots', the 'points of light', the dark wetness on roof and dome. Even here, in those spaces between the spires, one still can feel it, the presence of a dream: Jude's vision of Christminster; Wordsworth's 'something evermore about to be'; or Tennyson's 'gleam'[5], which slips over the horizon, flutters in the corner of the eye, or flickers invisibly outside the borders of the page I am writing, the words you are reading. Like the past itself, we can only glimpse it, "ere it vanishes/Over the margin…'. Like the Ghost in *Hamlet*[6],

> *Barn.* 'Tis heere.
>
> *Hor.* 'Tis heere.
>
> *Mar.* 'Tis gone.

Notes

ॐ

Preface and acknowledgements

1. 'There is no "straight" Shakespeare; we are all "translators"'. Graham Bradshaw and Kairo Ashizo, 'Reading *Hamlet* in Japan', in *Shakespeare in the Twentieth Century,* edited by Jonathan Bate, Jill L. Levenson and Dieter Mehl (Newark: University of Delaware Press, 1998), p. 350.

2. This is hitherto much more evident in secondary than in tertiary education; but interest is growing. See for example Rex Gibson, 'Narrative Approaches to Shakespeare: Active Storytelling in Schools', *Shakespeare Survey 53: Shakespeare and Narrative* (Cambridge: Cambridge University Press, 2000).

3. As suggested by a note on the manuscript copy of Middleton's *A Game at Chess*: 'This, which nor Stage nor Stationer's Stall can showe, / The Common Eye may wish for, but ne're knowe'. Quoted in Julie Stone Peters, *Theatre of the Book, 1480-1880: print, text and performance* (Oxford: Oxford University Press, 2000), p. 32.

One: Text

1. Compare Henri-Jean Martin: 'Au commencement était le signe'. See *The History and Power of Writing*, translated by Lydia G. Cochrane (Chicago: University of Chicago Press, 1994).

2. See D.F. McKenzie, *Bibliography and the Sociology of Texts* (London:

British Library, 1986), p. 5; Jerome McGann, *The Textual Condition* (Princeton, N.J.: Princeton University Press, 1991), p. 177; and especially D.C. Greetham, *Theories of the Text* (Oxford: Clarendon Press, 1999), pp. 26–7. See also D.F. McKenzie, *Making Meaning: 'Printers of the Mind' and Other Essays*, edited by Peter D. McDonald and Michael F. Suarez, S.J. (Massachusetts: Massachusetts University Press, 2002), and *The Book History Reader*, edited by David Finkelstein and Alistair McCleery (London: Routledge, 2001).

3.   From the Dylan Thomas poem. See his *Collected Poems 1934–1953*, edited by Walford Davies and Ralph Maude (London: Dent, 1988), p. 106.

4.   Genesis, 1.2–4. Quoted from *The Bible: Authorized King James Version*, edited by Robert Carroll and Stephen Prickett (Oxford: Oxford University Press, 1997), OT p. 1.

5.   James Joyce, *A Portrait of the Artist as a Young Man* (London: Jonathan Cape, 1916, 1956), p. 218.

6.   Joseph Grigely derives a similar tripartite structure from Jacques Derrida's 'moment of inscription' by arguing that this can be construed either as a 'moment of writing', a 'moment of publishing' or a 'moment of reading', each in turn representing a 'moment of stasis' in Derrida's process of continuous iterability. The three moments correspond roughly to τεκτων/*texere*, τεχνη and text. See 'The Textual Event', in *Devils and Angels: textual editing and literary theory*, edited by Philip Cohen (Charlottsville: University Press of Virginia, 1964), p. 172.

7.   William Blake, 'The Marriage of Heaven and Hell', *Blake's Poems and Prophecies*, edited by Max Plowman (London: Dent, 1927, 1965), p. 45.

8.   David Scott Kastan is saying something very similar, though from a different perspective, when he writes: 'the work of the imagination is unable to constitute itself'. See his *Shakespeare and the Book* (Cambridge: Cambridge University Press, 2001), p. 4.

9.   See Ted Hughes. 'The Thought-fox', *The Hawk in the Rain* (London: Faber and Faber, 1957, 1968), p. 14.

10. '[N]ot texts, not ideas or states of mind, not semiotic systems or social relations, not even the Book; but books – assemblies of paper and ink and thread and glue and cloth and leather …'. Hugh

Amory, 'Physical Bibliography, Cultural History, and the Disappearance of the Book', *Papers of the Bibliographical Society of America* 78 (1984), p. 344. John Updike revels in the physicality of the book in a similar way, speaking of 'the charming little clothy box of the thing, the smell of the glue, even the print, which has its own beauty' (quoted in Kastan, *Book*, p. 155). This bibliographical aestheticism is frequently mocked by proponents of the electronic media, as in William J. Mitchell's sardonic description of the book as 'tree-flakes encased in dead cow'. See his *City of Bits: space, place and the Infobahn* (Cambridge, Mass.: MIT Press, 1995), p. 56.

11. G. M. Hopkins, 'To R.B.', *Selected Poetry*, edited by Catherine Phillips (Oxford: Oxford University Press, 1996), p. 166.

12. Paul de Man, 'The Rhetoric of Blindness', in *Blindness and Insight: essays in the rhetoric of contemporary criticism* (Minneapolis: University of Minnesota Press, 1983), p. 107.

13. See Hélène Cixous: 'there is a manner of reading comparable to the act of writing'. *Three Steps on the Ladder of Writing*, translated by Sarah Cornell and Susan Sellers (New York: Columbia University Press, 1993), p. 19. Reading aloud was clearly a norm before the advent of silent reading. St Augustine found the reading habits of Ambrose strangely idiosyncratic: 'But when he was reading, his eyes glided over the pages, and his heart searched out the sense, but his voice and tongue were at rest'. This method was so unusual that Augustine speculated on its possible causes, for example, that Ambrose might have feared interruption or was being careful to conserve his voice. *The Confessions of St Augustine*, translated by E.B. Pusey (London: Dent, 1907, 1946), p. 98.

14. Jacques Derrida, *Limited, Inc.*, translated by Samuel Weber and Jeffrey Mehlman (Evanston: Northwestern University Press, 1988), p. 40.

15. See Alberto Manguel, *A History of Reading* (London: Harper Collins, 1996), p. 182.

16. See *Rewriting Old English in the Twelfth Century*, edited by Mary Swan and Elaine M. Treharne (Cambridge: Cambridge University Press, 2000).

17. Graham D. Caie, 'Hypertext and Multiplicity: the mediaeval example', in *The Renaissance Text: theory, editing, textuality*, edited by

Andrew Murphy (Manchester: Manchester University Press, 2000), pp. 30–1. A parallel instance is found in H.J. Jackson's study *Marginalia: readers writing in books* (New Haven: Yale University Press, 2001), which considers interpolated marginalia as an integrated element of the text.

18. Greetham gives the comparable example of Origen's *Hexapla*: 'His text was its own context: a six-column display of the original Hebrew, the Hebrew transliterated into Greek, the two Greek versions of Aquilla and Symmachus, the Septuagint, and the Septuagint version by Theodotion. Where was Origen in all this? Only in the insight that the reader be invited into these multiple texts and that the editor make the provisions. It is an insight that, in these post-structuralist and electronic days, we might do well to emulate' (see Greetham, *Theories*, p. 244). 'Paratext' is taken from Gerard Genette and Jane E. Lewin, *Paratext: thresholds of interpretation* (Cambridge: Cambridge University Press, 1997). See also Gerard Genette, *Palimpsests: literature in the second degree*, translated by Channa Newman and Claude Doubinsky (Lincoln: University of Nebraska Press, 1997); and Douglas Bruster, *Quoting Shakespeare: form and culture in early modern drama* (Lincoln: University of Nebraska Press, 2000).

19. McGann cites David V. Erdman's editing of a plate from *Jerusalem*, but the point would apply to any standard edition of Blake which is not facsimile, and which therefore elects to privilege the 'linguistic' over the 'bibliographic' codes.

20. 'Thou callest us then to understand the *Word*, *God*, with Thee *God*, Which is spoken eternally, and by It are all things spoken eternally. For what was spoken was not spoken successively, one thing concluded that the next might be spoken, but all things together and eternally'. Augustine, *Confessions*, p. 257.

21. Francis P. Magoun, Jr., 'The Oral-Formulaic Character of Anglo-Saxon Narrative Poetry' (1953), quoted from *An Anthology of 'Beowulf' Criticism*, edited by Lewis E. Nicholson (Notre Dame, Ind.: Notre Dame University Press, 1963), p. 189. Post-structuralist approaches to language would challenge this distinction, arguing that all speech and writing draw on linguistic 'formulae'.

22. *Beowulf*, ll. 867–74. Translation, slightly revised, from my *Anglo-*

Saxon Verse (London: Northcote House, 2000), p. 7.

23. See, for example, the description of book-making in Riddle 26 of the *Exeter Book* (translated here as 'Bibliotech' at the end of Chapter Two). Anglo-Saxon version with literal translation in *Old and Middle English: an anthology*, edited by Elaine Treharne (Oxford: Blackwell, 2000), pp. 69–70. The heroic poem *The Battle of Maldon* celebrates the courage of ealdorman Byrhtnoth in an epic medium that links straight back to values described in Tacitus's *Germania*. Byrhtnoth's wife Aelfled left a different kind of celebration, in the form of a tapestry recording her husband's deeds of philanthropy and his generosity to the church. Thus Byrhtnoth's legacy was documented via different ways of 'weaving'. See my *Anglo-Saxon Verse*, p. 60. See also Graham Ward: 'A text is the composition and arrangements of signs, any signs: words, colours, fabrics, details in a photograph'. *Theology and Contemporary Critical Theory* (London: Macmillan, 1996, 2nd edition 2000), p. xviii.

24. See my 'The Sign of the Cross: culture and belief in *The Dream of the Rood*', *Literature and Theology* 11:4 (Autumn 1997), pp. 347–75.

25. Jesse M. Gellrich, *The Idea of the Book in the Middle Ages: language theory, mythology and fiction* (Ithaca: Cornell University Press, 1985). See also Hélène Cixous, who says that reading/writing allows us to 'look straight at God' (*Three Steps*, p. 61); and Graham Ward, 'Reading ... is a religious act' (*Theology*, p. 122).

26. Jacques Derrida, *Of Grammatology*, translated by Gayatri C. Spivak (Baltimore: Johns Hopkins University Press, 1976), p. 18.

27. See Rudolph Pfeiffer, *History of Classical Scholarship from the Beginnings to the End of the Hellenistic Age* (Oxford: Oxford University Press, 1968), pp. 210–50; and J.E.W. Sandys, *A History of Classical Scholarship* (Cambridge: Cambridge University Press, 1906–8, New York: Hafner, 2nd edition 1964), vol. 1, p. 129–30. Marcus Walsh similarly studies variations between Catholic and Protestant approaches to the editing of Shakespeare in *Shakespeare, Milton and Eighteenth Century Literary Editing* (Cambridge: Cambridge University Press, 1997).

28. Pierre Bersuire, *Reportorium Morale* (quoted in Gellrich, *Idea*, p. 17). See also Graham Ward: 'All creation bears the watermark of Christ'. 'The Displaced Body of Jesus Christ', in *Radical Orthodoxy*,

edited by John Milbank, Catherine Pickstock and Graham Ward (London: Routledge, 1999), p. 165. The original metaphor is probably St Paul's: 'Ye are our epistle written in our hearts, known and read of all men'. 2 Corinthians, 3.2. *The Bible: Authorized King James Version,* edited by Robert Carroll and Stephen Prickett (Oxford: Oxford University Press, 1997), NT p. 224.

29. See Greetham, *Theories,* pp. 370–1, and also p. 406: 'McGann, like Marx, determines that "conceiving" and "thinking… appear as the direct efflux of [the] material". That is we can read back into spirit and thought the primary evidence to be obtained from materiality, which is, for McGann, text's "only condition"'.

30. P.B. Shelley, 'A Defence of Poetry', in *Shelley's Poetry and Prose,* edited by Donald H. Reiman and Sharon P. Bowers (New York: Norton, 1977), p. 337. A favourite image in modern textual debate: see McGann, *Textual Condition,* p. 5; Greetham, *Theories,* p. 169 and p. 337.

31. George P. Landow, *Hypertext: the convergence of contemporary critical theory and technology* (Baltimore: Johns Hopkins University Press, 1992), pp. 17–18. See also Jerome McGann, *Radiant Textualities: literary studies after the world wide web* (London: Palgrave, 2001).

32. Warren Cherniak and Marilyn Deegan, 'Introduction' to their edited volume *The Politics of the Electronic Text* (London: Office for Humanities Communication Publications, University of London, 1993).

33. Michael Joyce, 'A Feel for Prose: Interstitial Links and the Contours of Hypertext', *Writing on the Edge* 4.1 (1992), p. 87.

34. Jay David Bolter, 'Topographic Writing: hypertext and the electronic writing space', in *Hypermedia and Literary Studies,* edited by George P. Landow and Paul Delaney (Cambridge, Mass.: MIT Press, 1991), p. 116.

35. The current Frankenstein monster is biotechnology. For a positive spin see Francis Fukayama, *Our Posthuman Future: consequences of the biotechnology revolution* (New York: Farrar Strauss and Giroux, 2002).

36. Peter Donaldson, 'The Shakespeare Interactive Archive: new directions in electronic scholarship on text and performance', in

Contextual Media, edited by Edward Barrett and Marie Redmond (Cambridge, Mass.: MIT Press, 1995), p. 125.

37. Jay David Bolter, *Writing Space: the computer, hypertext and the history of writing* (Hillsdale, N.J.: Lawrence Erlbaum Associates, 1991), p. 4.

38. Peter Holland, 'Authorship and Collaboration: the Problem of Editing Shakespeare', in Deegan and Cherniak, *Politics*, p. 21.

39. Tom Stoppard, *The Invention of Love* (London: Faber and Faber, 1997).

40. *Horace: the Odes*, edited by Philip Francis (London: Unit Library, 1902), Book III, xxx, p. 173.

41. A. E.Housman, 'The Application of Thought to Textual Criticism' (1921), in *A. E Housman: Selected Prose*, edited by John Carter (Cambridge: Cambridge University Press, 1961), p. 132.

42. '*Infernis neque enim tenebris Diana pudicum/Liberat Hippolytum/Nec lethea valet Theseus abrumpere caro/Vincula Pirithoo*'. Horace, *Odes,* Book IV, xii, p. 195. See A.E. Housman, *More Poems* (London: Jonathan Cape, 1936), pp. 21–2. My translation ('*Thou'lt come no more*') appears here at the end of Chapter Five.

43. Jorge Luis Borges talks of Shakespeare's mind as such an emptiness: 'There was no one inside him, nothing but a trace of chill ... and the abundant, whimsical, impassioned words'. From 'Everything and Nothing' (1960), quoted in *After Shakespeare: an anthology*, edited by John Gross (Oxford: Oxford University Press, 2002), p. 5.

Two: Shakespeare

1. From the title-page of the 1608 Quarto text of *King Lear*. See my edition *M. William Shake-speare: his True Chronicle Historie of the Life and Death of King Lear and his Three Daughters* (Hemel Hempstead: Prentice-Hall, 1995).

2. David Scott Kastan, *Shakespeare After Theory* (London: Routledge, 1999), p. 15.

3. See Roger Stoddard, 'Morphology and the Book from an American Perspective', *Printing History* 17 (1987), p. 2.

4. *The Works of Mr. William Shakespeare*, edited by Nicholas Rowe (London: J. Tonson, 1709), vol. 1, A2-Av. See also N.W. Black and

Matthias Shaaber, *Shakespeare's Seventeenth Century Editors, 1632-1685* (New York: Modern Language Association, 1937).

5. McGann observes that 'All texts are subject to change and, ultimately, to final destruction. We do not have the texts of Homer, we have only texts which recollect his (if he *was* a single person) original (*oral*) performances, and those scriptural texts are separated from Homer and his world by vast stretches of time, place and circumstance. Our received Homeric texts are, at best, Alexandrian residues. The bible itself, the word of God, comes to us in vessels we know to be corrupt and broken' (McGann, *Textual Condition*, p. 182). Another good example would be the Anglo-Saxon epic *The Battle of Maldon*, which survives only in a transcription of a manuscript destroyed in the Cotton Library fire.

6. W.W. Greg, *The Editorial Problem in Shakespeare: a survey of the foundations of the text* (Oxford: Oxford University Press, 1967), p. 2.

7. Fredson Bowers, 'Textual Criticism', in *A Shakespeare Encyclopaedia*, edited by Oscar James Campbell and Edward G. Quinn (London: Methuen, 1966), p. 869. In practice not all the scholars involved were quite so categorical on these principles as Bowers. Greg was much more cautious as to whether textual problems could be solved permanently and decisively. R.B. McKerrow (a trained engineer) was sceptical about the very idea of bibliography as a science: 'Nothing can be gained, and much may be lost, by a pretence of deriving results of scientific accuracy from data which are admittedly uncertain and incomplete'. *Prolegomena for the Oxford Shakespeare: a study in editorial method* (Oxford: Clarendon Press, 1939), p. vii.

8. *The Norton Facsimile: the First Folio of Shakespeare*, edited by Charlton Hinman (New York: W.W. Norton/Hamlyn Publishing Group, 1968), p. xi. See Paul Werstine, 'Plays in Manuscript', in *A New History of Early English Drama*, edited by John D. Cox and David Scott Kastan (New York: Columbia University Press, 1997).

9. G. Thomas Tanselle, *A Rationale of Textual Criticism* (Philadelphia: University of Pennsylvania Press, 1989), pp. 14–15. D.C. Greetham points out that Tanselle uses the terms 'text' and 'work' in a manner exactly opposite to the way the terms are deployed by Roland Barthes. Barthes sees 'work' as 'Newtonian', the object that is 'seen in

bookshops, in catalogues, in exam syllabuses ... held in the hand';
whereas 'text' is 'held in language', as an *activity of production*'. See
D.C. Greetham, *Theories of the Text* (Oxford: Clarendon Press,
1999), p. 48; and Roland Barthes, 'From Work to Text', in *Image,
Music, Text*, translated by Stephen Heath (New York: Hill and
Wang, 1977), p. 157.

10. Barbara Mowatt, 'The Problem of Shakespeare's Texts', in *Textual
Formations and Reformations*, edited by Laurie E. Maguire and
Thomas L. Berger (London: Associated University Presses, 1998),
p. 132.

11. Stanley Wells, 'Theatricalizing Shakespeare's Texts', *New Theatre
Quarterly*, 26 (1991), p. 186. Margreta de Grazia calls the Oxford
Shakespeare's editorial method 'document-based' rather than
'work-based'. See her 'What is a Work? What is a Document?', in
*New Ways of Looking at Old Texts: papers of the Renaissance English
Text Society, 1985–1991*, edited by W. Speed Hill (Binghamton:
Renaissance English Text Society, 1993).

12. A current edition is Lucien Febvre and Henri-Jean Martin, *The
Coming of the Book: the impact of printing 1450–1800* (1976, London:
Verso, 1997).

13. Roland Barthes, 'The Death of the Author', in *Image Music Text*,
p. 147.

14. Michel Foucault, 'What is an Author?' in *The Foucault Reader*, edited by Paul Rabinow (New York: Pantheon, 1984), p. 119.

15. Hugh Grady, 'Disintegration and its Reverberations', in *The Appropriation of Shakespeare; post-Renaissance reconstructions of the works
and the myth*, edited by Jean I. Marsden (Hemel Hempstead: Harvester Wheatsheaf, 1991).

16. Jonathan Goldberg, 'Textual Properties', *Shakespeare Quarterly* 37:2
(1986), p. 213.

17. The following texts were all available in paperback in a Bloomsbury
bookshop in 2002: *Applause First Folio: Hamlet*, edited by Neil Freeman (Folio Scripts: Vancouver, Canada, 1998); *The First Quarto of
King Lear*, edited by Jay L. Halio (Cambridge: Cambridge University
Press, 1994); *The Tragicall Historie of Hamlet Prince of Denmarke*,
edited by Graham Holderness and Bryan Loughrey (Hemel Hempstead: Harvester Wheatsheaf, 1992); *M. William Shake-speare HIS*

true chronicle historie of the life and death of King Lear and his three daughters, edited by Graham Holderness (Hemel Hempstead: Prentice-Hall, 1995); *The First Quarto of Hamlet*, edited by Kathleen O. Irace (Cambridge: Cambridge University Press, 1998); *The Tragoedie of Othello, The Moore of Venice*, edited by Andrew Murphy (Hemel Hempstead: Prentice-Hall, 1995); *The Shakespeare Folios: Hamlet*, edited by Nick de Somogyi (London: Nick Hern Books, 2000); *King Lear: a Parallel-Text Edition*, edited by Rene Weis (London: Longman, 1993).

18. See Margreta de Grazia and Peter Stallybrass. 'The materiality of the Shakespearean Text', *Shakespeare Quarterly* 44 (1993), pp. 278–9. This essay is discussed in detail in Chapter Three.

19. Randall McLeod, 'From Tranceformations in the Text of *Orlando Fvrioso*'. *Library Chronicle of the University of Texas at Austin* 20:1–2, (1990), p. 76. See also Leah Marcus, 'Confessions of a Reformed Uneditor' in *The Renaissance Text: theory, editing, textuality*, edited by Andrew Murphy (Manchester: Manchester University Press, 2000), pp. 211–16.

20. See Ann Thompson, 'Editing Shakespeare for the Next Millennium', *The European English Messenger* 8:2 (1999), pp. 15–19.

21. See Terence Hawkes, *That Shakespeherian Rag* (London: Routledge, 1986), p. 75.

22. Stephen Orgel, 'The Authentic Shakespeare', *Representations* 21 (1988), p. 14. See also his essays collected in *The Authentic Shakespeare* (London: Routledge, 2002).

23. John Drakakis reinstates the category of 'error' in his edition of the Quarto text *The Tragedy of Richard III* (Hemel Hempstead: Prentice-Hall, 1996), pp. 17–18. But some errors may, as Dr Johnson observed, arise from our ignorance or prejudice rather than compositorial carelessness. Othello's 'base Iudean' (Judean) becomes a 'base Indean' ('Indian') in most modern texts (e.g. *Othello*, edited by Norman Sanders [Cambridge: Cambridge University Press, 1984], p. 185). Either is possible, but he remains a Judean in *The Tragoedie of Othello, the Moore of Venice*, edited by Andrew Murphy (Hemel Hempstead: Prentice-Hall, 1995). But see D.J. Enright's satire on political correctness: 'If it wasn't a base Judean he displayed/As criminally careless with pearls, then/It was an equally

base Indian'. 'All's Well that Ends, or Shakespeare Unmasked', in *Collected Poems* (Manchester: Carcanet Press, 1973).

24. F. W. Bateson, 'Modern Bibliography and the Literary Artefact', in *English Studies Today*, edited by Georges A. Bonnard (Bern, 2nd edition 1961,), p. 74. Bateson's question was actually 'If the *Mona Lisa* is in the Louvre, where then are *Hamlet* and *Lycidas*?' See Greetham, *Theories*, pp. 37–8. McGann also cites the question (*Textual Condition*, p. 9), but attributes it to James McLaverty as 'If the *Mona Lisa* is in the Louvre in Paris, where is *Hamlet*?' ('The Mode of Existence of Literary Works of Art: the case of *The Dunciad* Variorum', *Studies in Bibliography* 37 [1984], pp. 82–105). The dates would suggest that Bateson probably asked the question first (though see Chapter Seven, note 36, for an exception to this rule).

25. See Darian Leader, *Stealing the Mona Lisa* (London: Faber and Faber, 2002).

26. A classic locus of this conception is the film *Shakespeare in Love*, in which the camera dwells on the playwright's inky fingers. Kastan uses this detail as an instance of unrealisable nostalgia for presence (Kastan, *Book*, p. 121). The film shows Shakespeare filling sheet after sheet with his own name, spelt differently and repeatedly crossed out. Drawing attention to the notorious variability of Shakespeare's signature, the example discloses instability rather than presence. For the Shakespearean name as an iterable sign see Simon Shepherd, 'Shakespeare's Private Drawer: Shakespeare and Homosexuality', in *The Shakespeare Myth*, edited by Graham Holderness (Manchester: Manchester University Press, 1988).

27. Richard Bentley on the other hand used Milton's blindness as a pretext for rewriting the poems. See Marcus Walsh, 'Bentley Our Contemporary: or, editors, ancient and modern', in *The Theory and Practice of Text-editing*, edited by Ian Small and Marcus Walsh (Cambridge: Cambridge University Press, 1991). Interestingly Stanley Fish attributes to Milton a kind of ontological blindness in *How Milton Works* (Harvard University Press, 2002), arguing that Milton works from the inside out, from faith, embracing an inner truth against the evidence.

28. A notorious case in this respect is the cleaning of Michelangelo's frescos in the Sistine Chapel, which either restored the paintings to

their original brightness, or defaced accretions that had been anticipated as integral to the work. See Kathleen Brandt, 'The Grime of
the Centuries is a Pigment of the Imagination: Michelangelo's
Sistine Ceiling', in *Palimpsest: editorial theory in the humanities*,
edited by George Bornstein and Ralph Williams (Ann Arbor: University of Michigan Press, 1993). Stephen Greenblatt notes that the
evidence of artistic contracts from the Italian Renaissance both privi-
leges the work of the master craftsman, and also acknowledges the
validity of ancillary contributions. Stephen Greenblatt, 'General
Introduction', *The Norton Shakespeare: based on the Oxford edition*,
edited by Stephen Greenblatt, Walter Cohen, Jean E. Howard, Katherine Eisaman Maus (New York: W.W. Norton and Co, 1997), p. 68.

29. Robert Rauschenberg rubbed out a copy of a drawing by Willem de
Kooning and exhibited it as 'Erased de Kooning'. Darian Leader
observes that the man who stole the Leonardo gave the world 'Missing Mona Lisa'.

30. *Guys and Dolls: a musical fable of Broadway*, Music and Lyrics by
Frank Loesser, Book by Jo Swerling and Abe Burrows (London:
Josef Weinberger, 1951), 2–3–15.

31. Emily Dickinson (c. 1863), quoted in *After Shakespeare: an anthology*, edited by John Gross (Oxford: Oxford University Press, 2002),
p. 53.

32. Jacques Derrida, *Aporias*, translated by Thomas Dutoit (Stanford:
Stanford University Press, 1993), p. 65.

33. Jacques Derrida, *Limited, Inc.*, translated by Samuel Weber
(Evanston, Illinois: Northwestern University Press, 1988). p. 153.

Three: Matter

1. Margreta de Grazia, 'The essential Shakespeare and the material
book', *Textual Practice* 2 (1988), pp. 69–86. See also her *Shakespeare
Verbatim: the reproduction of authenticity and the 1790 Apparatus*
(Oxford: Oxford University Press, 1991).

2. W.W. Greg, *The Editorial Problem in Shakespeare: A survey of the
foundations of the text* (Oxford: Oxford University Press, 1967), p. 2.

3. Fredson Bowers, 'Textual Criticism', in *A Shakespeare Encyclopaedia*,
edited by Oscar James Campbell and Edward G. Quinn (London:

Methuen, 1966), p. 865. See also R.B. McKerrow, *Prolegomena for the Oxford Shakespeare: a study in editorial method* (Oxford: Clarendon Press, 1939). For an incisive commentary see Andrew Murphy, '"Came errour here by mysse of man": editing and the metaphysics of presence', *Yearbook of English Studies* 29 (1999).

4. Margreta de Grazia and Peter Stallybrass, 'The materiality of the Shakespearean text', in *Shakespeare Quarterly* 44 (Fall 1993), pp. 255–83.

5. Despite the presence within it of some distinguished female scholars such as Alice Walker, the school of New Bibliography, and its subsequent editorial tradition, was overwhelmingly male. The obvious fact that female critics now play a much bigger role in both textual theory and editing accounts in part for this implicit link between approaches to the text and a modern politics of resistance.

6. Jacques Derrida, *Spectres of Marx: the state of the debt, the work of mourning and the new international,* translated by Peggy Kamuf (New York and London: Routledge, 1994), p. 54. See also Graham Holderness, *Cultural Shakespeare: essays in the Shakespeare myth* (Hatfield: University of Hertfordshire Press, 2001), pp. 23–34; and Stephen Greenblatt, *Learning to Curse: essays in early modern culture* (New York: Routledge, 1990).

7. From *Das Kapital,* in *Marx on Economics,* edited by Robert Freeman (London: Penguin Books, 1968), p. 51.

8. *Sotheby's Catalogue,* sale of 21–22 July 1992.

9. *The Complete 'King Lear' 1608-1623,* edited by Michael Warren (Berkeley: University of California Press, 1989). Other symptomatic instances cited are Stephen Booth's edition of *Shakespeare's Sonnets* (New Haven: Yale University Press, 1977), which sets a facsimile original against a modern edition; and Paul Bertram and Bernice Kliman's *The Three-Text 'Hamlet': Parallel Texts of the First and Second Quartos and First Folio (Studies in the Renaissance,* no. 30; New York: AMS Press, 1991). See Chapter Five below for further discussion of Warren's text.

10. For the most elaborated statement of this position, see Grace Ioppolo, *Revising Shakespeare* (Cambridge, Mass.: Harvard University Press, 1991).

11. Stanley Wells, 'Theatricalizing Shakespeare's Text', in *New Theatre*

Quarterly 26 (May 1991), p. 186. See also Edward Ragg, 'The Oxford Shakespeare Revisited: an interview with Professor Stanley Wells', *Analytical and Enumerative Bibliography* (N.S.) 12:2 (2001).

12. I use this phrase advisedly. The 'onlie begetter' of Shakespeare's *Sonnets* was not, of course, the author.

13. Gary Taylor, 'Introduction' to Stanley Wells and Gary Taylor with John Jowett and William Montgomery, *William Shakespeare: A Textual Companion* (Oxford: Clarendon Press, 1987), p. 69. See also Taylor's 'The Renaissance and the End of Editing', in *Palimpsest: editorial theory in the humanities,* edited by George Bornstein and Ralph G. Williams (Ann Arbor: University of Michigan Press, 1993).

14. Michael Foucault, 'What is an author?', in *The Foucault Reader*, edited by Paul Rabinow (New York: Pantheon, 1984), p. 119.

15. Brian Parker, 'Bowers of Bliss: deconflation in the Shakespeare canon', in *New Theatre Quarterly* 24 (1990), p. 361.

16. Harold Pinter, *The Homecoming* (London: Methuen, 1966), p. 31.

17. The one possible exception to this generalisation is is the 'Hand D' contribution to the manuscript of *The Book of Sir Thomas More.* But even this is not beyond question – see Scott McMillin, *The Elizabethan Theatre and 'The Book of Sir Thomas More'* (Ithaca: Cornell University Press, 1987), esp. pp. 135–59.

18. A. E. Housman, 'The Application of Thought to Textual Criticism' (1921), in *A. E Housman: Selected Prose*, edited by John Carter (Cambridge: Cambridge University Press, 1961), p. 145.

19. Tom Stoppard, *The Invention of Love* (London: Faber and Faber, 1997), p. 24.

20. D.C. Greetham, *Theories of the Text* (Oxford: Clarendon Press, 1999), pp. 63.

21. Gustave Flaubert, 'La Legende de St Julien L'Hospitalier', *Trois Contes* (1877). See *Three Tales*, translated by Robert Baldick (London: Penguin Books, 1961).

Four: Confluence

1. The first three titles published were *The Taming of A Shrew, The True Cronicle Historie of Henry the Fift,* and Q1 *Hamlet* (see note 3 below), edited by Graham Holderness and Bryan Loughrey (Hemel

Hempstead: Harvester Wheatsheaf, 1992–3). Other titles followed in 1995 and 1996: *M. William Shak-speare, his true chronicle Historie of the life and death of King Lear and His Three Daughters*, edited by Graham Holderness; *Twelfe Night, or, What You Will*, edited by Laurie Osborne; *The Tragedie of Anthonie, and Cleopatra*, edited by John Turner; *An Excellent Conceited Tragedie of Romeo and Juliet*, edited by Cedric Watts; *The Most Excellent Historie of The Merchant of Venice*, edited by Annabel Patterson; *The Tragoedie of Othello, the Moore of Venice*, edited by Andrew Murphy; *A Midsommer Nights Dreame*, edited by T.O. Treadwell and *The Tragedy of Richard III*, edited by John Drakakis .

2. As there is frequently some inconsistency between the use of these titles, for example between volume and running titles, or between the Folio contents page and the head-title of the play, the decision to use any one is to some extent arbitrary. But all are quite different from the titles to which we have become accustomed.

3. *The Tragicall Historie of Hamlet Prince of Denmarke*, edited by Graham Holderness and Bryan Loughrey (Hemel Hempstead: Harvester Wheatsheaf, 1992), pp. 9–10.

4. Eric Sams, *Notes and Queries* 41 (March 1994); Christine Dymkowski, *New Theatre Quarterly* 35 (1993); David Bevington, *Shakespeare Quarterly* 47:3 (Fall, 1996).

5. D. C. Greetham, 'Textual Forensics', *PMLA* 3 (1996), p. 34; Janet Dillon, 'Is There a Performance in this Text?', *Shakespeare Quarterly* 45 (1994), p. 75; Jonathan Sawday, 'Beam me up too, Scotty!', *London Quarterly* 8 (1995), p. 23; Lois Potter, review of Eric Sams, *The Real Shakespeare*, *Times Literary Supplement*, 21 April 1995; Rosalind King and Nigel Alexander, letter in *TLS*, 11 February 1994; A.R. Braunmuller, quoted in *Conference Report* of the International Shakespeare Association Conference, Stratford-upon-Avon, 1992. For responses from myself and Bryan Loughrey, see letters in *TLS*, 11 February 1994; 4 March 1994; 5 May 1995; and Graham Holderness, 'Illogical, Captain!', *London Quarterly* 9 (1996).

6. Sian Griffiths, 'Well Versed in the Art of Make-up', *Times Higher Education Supplement* (19 June 1992).

7. Graham Holderness and Bryan Loughrey, letter in *THES*, 26 June 1992.

8. Michael Barron, 'Miscellany', *English* 43 (Autumn 1994), p. 177. I have a copy of an advertisement for the *Oxford Shakespeare*, which claims that it contains 'every single word Shakespeare ever wrote'. A leaflet promoting the Folio Society edition of the Oxford Shakespeare goes further: 'the most authentic edition of Shakespeare's plays that has ever been published ... an edition which reproduces the plays as Shakespeare intended them to be performed'. The leaflet cites commendations from 'the most distinguished writers and academics in the country': Anthony Burgess ('admirably edited'), John Carey ('the most interesting edition of Shakespeare since the First Folio'), and Peter Ackroyd ('there can be little doubt that this edition is closer to the original texts than any previous one'.)

9. Brian Vickers, '*Hamlet* by Dogberry: a perverse reading of the Bad Quarto', *Times Literary Supplement,* 24 December 1993, pp. 24–25. See also Vickers' letters in *TLS*, 4 March 1994 and 15 April 1994. The early texts of the series did contain errors, as we later admitted: see Graham Holderness and Bryan Loughrey, 'Shakespeare Misconstrued: the True Chronicle Historie of *Shakespearean Originals*', *Textus* 9 (1996), p. 395.

10. See especially Random Cloud (Randall McLeod), 'The marriage of good and bad Quartos', *Shakespeare Quarterly* 33 (1982), pp. 421–31; Steven Urkowitz, 'Good News about "Bad" Quartos', in *Shakespeare Study Today: the Horace Howard Furness Memorial Lectures,* edited by Georgianna Ziegler (New York: AMS Press, 1986); Paul Werstine, 'Narratives about Printed Shakespearean Texts: "Foul Papers" and "Bad" Quartos', *Shakespeare Quarterly* 41 (1990); and Peter Blayney, 'The Publication of Playbooks', in *A New History of Early English Drama,* edited by John D. Cox and David Scott Kastan (New York: Columbia University Press, 1997). Much more work on Q1 has been published since 1990, including new editions such as those of Kathleen O. Irace (*The First Quarto of Hamlet* [Cambridge: Cambridge University Press, 1998]), and Paul Bertram and Bernice Kliman (*The Three-Text 'Hamlet': Parallel Texts of the First and Second Quartos and First Folio* [*Studies in the Renaissance*, no. 30: AMS Press, 1991]). Other critical studies include Laurie E. Maguire, *Shakespearean Suspect Texts: the 'Bad Quartos' and their contexts*

(Cambridge: Cambridge University Press, 1996); Steven Urkowitz, 'Back to basics: thinking about the *Hamlet* First Quarto' in *The 'Hamlet' First Published: origins, form, intertextualities*, edited by Thomas Clayton (Newark: University of Delaware Press, 1992); Maxwell E. Foster, *The Play Behind the Play: 'Hamlet' and Quarto One* (London: Heinemann, 1991); and Eric Sams, *The Real Shakespeare* (New Haven: Yale University Press, 1995), pp. 125–35.

11. Brian Vickers, letter to *TLS*, 4 March 1994.

12. Howard Mills, *Working with Shakespeare* (Hemel Hempstead: Harvester Wheatsheaf, 1992), p. 62; quoting Holderness and Loughrey, *Tragicall Historie*, p. 27.

13. The suggestion is not as far fetched as it sounds. The 'Klingon Shakespeare Restoration Project', which can be found documented on the Internet, exists precisely to restore Shakespeare to the original Klingon language. A recent initiative is *The Klingon Hamlet*, also published as a book. 'taH pagh, taHbe't' ('To be, or not to be') gives a representative flavour. A similar exercise is attempted in *Guillaume Chequespierre and the Oise Salon*, edited by John Hulme (London: Angus and Robertson, 1985), which converts Shakespeare into a nineteenth century French poet who writes in a peculiarly inventive and polyglossial medium:

    Toute pille or, note, toute pille, date hisse de caisse tiens!
    'He fears that his gold is being pillaged and tells his wife to "hoist" the date on the till'.

14. A remarkable analogy. See John Drakakis, 'Shakespeare and the Roadsweepers', in *The Shakespeare Myth*, edited by Graham Holderness (Manchester: Manchester University Press, 1998); Graham Holderness, 'A Spear Carrier's Charter', *THES*, 29 April 1988, p. 13; Graham Holderness, 'Shakespeare and Heritage', *Textual Practice* 6 (1992), pp. 247–263; and Graham Holderness and Andrew Murphy, 'Shakespeare Country', *Critical Survey* 7 (1995), pp. 110–116.

15. See also Alan Posener, 'Materialism, Dialectics and Editing Shakespeare', *New Theatre Quarterly* 39 (1994) (which was a response to Graham Holderness and Bryan Loughrey, 'Text and Stage: Shakespeare, Bibliography and Performance Studies', *New Theatre Quarterly* 34 [1993]); Andrew Spong, 'Bad Habits, "Bad Quartos" and Myths of Origin in the Editing of Shakespeare', *New Theatre*

Quarterly 45 (1995); and Grace Tiffany, 'Calling a Spadeful a Spadeful', *Shakespeare Newsletter* (Fall, 1995).

16. The point is made by Peter Holland in *Theory in Practice: Hamlet,* edited by Nigel Wood and Peter Smith (Milton Keynes: Open University Press, 1996), p. 100.

17. Interestingly Chris Hopkins in *Thinking About Texts* (London: Palgrave, 2001), explicitly deploys the *Shakespearean Originals* text of Q1 in a comparative exercise, arguing that such critical judgements can still be made, on grounds other than moral discrimination, between texts accepted as equally 'authentic' (pp. 86–9, especially p. 85, n.3).

18. Nicholas Shrimpton, *Shakespeare Survey* 39 (1987), p. 197.

19. A point well made in *William Shakespeare: the Complete Works,* edited by Stanley Wells and Gary Taylor with John Jowett and William Montgomery (Oxford: Oxford University Press, 1988), pp. xxvii. See also Stanley Wells, 'Multiple Texts and the Oxford Shakespeare', *Textus* 9 (1996), p. 2. Irace in *The First Quarto* lists other specifically theatrical features (pp. 4–5, 8–20), and discusses modern performances of Q1, pp. 23–7, including a staged reading of the *Shakespearean Originals* edition.

20. For examples of these arguments more fully developed and illustrated, see Graham Holderness, J. Turner and N. Potter, *Shakespeare: the play of history* (London: Macmillan, 1987) and Graham Holderness, *Shakespeare in Performance: 'The Taming of the Shrew'* (Manchester: Manchester University Press, 1988).

21. 'The opponents of emendation fetishize the printed text as an object in itself, and in doing so they occlude both the process whereby it came into being and the very reason why it came into being'. John Jowett, 'After Oxford: Recent Developments in Textual Studies', in *The Shakespearean International Yearbook* 1 (1999), p. 71. See also Gabriel Egan, 'Myths and Enabling Fictions of "Origin" in the Editing of Shakespeare', *New Theatre Quarterly* 49 (1997), pp. 41–7.

22. Jacques Derrida, 'The Law of Genres', *Critical Inquiry* 7:1 (Autumn 1980), p. 55. Commenting on the *Shakespearean Originals* edition of *The Tragicall Historie of Hamlet Prince of Denmarke*, Patricia Parker notes 'how difficult it is to stay within the "material" text or to

guard its discrete textual boundaries'. An annotation that cross-references between texts represents a 'crossing of textual boundaries' and 'undoes the notion of the discrete text itself'. 'Murder in Guyana', *Shakespeare Studies* 28 (2000), pp. 170–1.

23. Dante Gabriel Rossetti, 'The Love-letter', Sonnet XX of 'The House of Life', *Rossetti's Poems*, edited by Oswald Doughty (London: Dent, 1912, 1961), p. 109.

24. See A. C. Benson, *Rossetti* (London: Macmillan, 1904), pp. 50–5. The manuscript was obviously not entirely destroyed, since several leaves of it survive and are extant in the British Library, the Houghton Library, Harvard University and the Beinecke Library, Yale. The leaves (containing the poems 'Another Love', 'Praise and Prayer' and 'Wellington's Funeral') display rough edged holes where the paper has rotted away. Rossetti described the recovered manuscript to Ford Madox Brown as pierced with 'a great hole right through all the leaves' (*Letters of Dante Gabriel Rossetti 1828-82*, edited by Oswald Doughty and John Robert Wahl [Oxford: Clarendon Press, 1965–7], vol. 2, p. 753). It should be noted that 'The Love-letter' was not one of the poems contained in this manuscript: it was written in 1870 and is thought to concern Jane Morris. This story is clearly in the background of A.S. Byatt's *Possession: a Romance* (London: Chatto and Windus, 1990) which includes an exhumation in search of lost writing. Shakespeare himself is dug up in Ian Wilson's *Black Jenny* (London: Paladin, 1992) but here in search of a different text: the DNA code that will conclusively demonstrate Shakespeare's death from tertiary syphilis.

25. Jorge Luis Borges explores the same paradox at the level of the individual soul. Shakespeare meets God and says 'I who have been so many men in vain want to be one man only, myself'. God replies: 'Neither am I what I am ... like me, you are everything and nothing'. From 'Everything and Nothing' (1960), quoted in *After Shakespeare: An anthology*, edited by John Gross (Oxford: Oxford University Press, 2002), p. 6.

26. 'The Boke of Sir Thomas More' is British Library MS. Harleian 7368. Quotation from Stephen Greenblatt, 'General Introduction', *The Norton Shakespeare: based on the Oxford edition,* edited by

Stephen Greenblatt, Walter Cohen, Jean E. Howard, Katherine Eisaman Maus (New York: W.W. Norton and Co, 1997), p. 71.

Five: Texts and Contexts – King Lear

1. Texts of the Quarto and Folio are available in 'The History of King Lear', in *William Shakespeare: The Complete Works*, edited by Stanley Wells and Gary Taylor, with John Jowett and William Montgomery (Oxford: Oxford University Press, 1986); *The Complete 'King Lear' 1608–1623*, edited by Michael Warren (Berkeley: University of California Press, 1989); *'King Lear': A Parallel-Text Edition*, edited by René Weis (London: Longman, 1993); and the Quarto alone in *The First Quarto of King Lear*, edited by Jay L. Halio (Cambridge: Cambridge University Press, 1994). Weis and Halio both use the title coined by Wells and Taylor, *The History of King Lear*. Stanley Wells's individual-text Oxford edition is an edition of the Quarto. The full title and sub-title of the 1608 publication was *M. William Shak-speare: his true chronicle historie of the life and death of King Lear and his three daughters. With the unfortunate life of Edgar, sonne and heire to the earle of Gloster, and his sullen and assumed humor of Tom of Bedlam.*

2. Conflated editions can be found in *King Lear*, edited by Kenneth Muir (London: Methuen, 1952, 1989); *King Lear*, edited by G.K. Hunter (Harmondsworth: Penguin, 1972); *The Riverside Shakespeare*, edited by J.J.M. Tobin and G. Blakemore Evans (2nd edition, Boston, Mass.: Houghton Mifflin, 1997) and *King Lear*, edited by R.A. Foakes (London: Thomas Nelson, 1997). The revised Arden edition (Foakes), draws attention to the differential provenance of texts by marking with superior characters (F and Q) those passages found in only one of the two texts. Otherwise the standard New Bibliographic copy-text methodology is employed, with a distinct preference for the Folio reading. Foakes explicitly states his objective as to present 'an idea of the work' (p. 119). For classic formulations of the relations between the two texts see A.W. Pollard, *Shakespeare Folios and Quartos* (London: Methuen, 1909) and *Shakespeare's Fight with the Pirates* (Cambridge: Cambridge University Press, 2nd edition 1920); W.W. Greg 'The Function of

Bibliography in Literary Criticism Illustrated in a Study of the Text of *King Lear*', in *The Collected Papers of Sir Walter W. Greg*, edited by J.C. Maxwell (Oxford: Clarendon Press, 1966); G.I. Duthie, *Elizabethan Shorthand and the First Quarto of 'King Lear'* (Oxford: Blackwell, 1949) and *Shakespeare's 'King Lear': a Critical Edition*, edited by G.I. Duthie (Oxford: Clarendon Press, 1949); Alice Walker, *Textual Problems of the First Folio* (Cambridge: Cambridge University Press, 1953); MacDonald P. Jackson, 'Fluctuating Variation – Author, Annotator or Actor?', in *The Division of the Kingdoms: Shakespeare's two versions of 'King Lear'*, edited by Gary Taylor and Michael Warren (Oxford: Clarendon Press, 1983).

3. Michael Warren, 'Quarto and Folio *King Lear*: the interpretation of Albany and Edgar', in *Shakespeare: Pattern of Excelling Nature*, edited by David Bevington and Jay L. Halio (Newark: University of Delaware Press, 1978); Steven Urkowitz, *Shakespeare's Revision of 'King Lear'* (Princeton: Princeton University Press, 1980); Peter Blayney, *The Texts of 'King Lear' and their Origins* (Cambridge: Cambridge University Press, 1982); and Taylor and Warren, *The Division of the Kingdoms*. The latter volume features essays by key revisionists Stanley Wells, Steven Urkowitz, Michael Warren, Paul Werstine and Gary Taylor.

4. Stanley Wells, 'Theatricalizing Shakespeare's Texts', in *New Theatre Quarterly* 26 (1991), p. 186. Wells indicates how much further he would have wished to go in Edward Ragg, 'The Oxford Shakespeare Revisited: an interview with Professor Stanley Wells', *Analytical and Enumerative Bibliography* (N.S.) 12:2 (2001).

5. See David Bevington's critical review 'Determining the Indeterminate: The Oxford Shakespeare', *Shakespeare Quarterly* 20 (1968–70), pp. 501, 502.

6. Weis, '*King Lear*', p. 5.

7. See Paul Werstine, review of Warren's *Complete 'King Lear'*, in *Shakespeare Quarterly* 44 (Summer 1993), pp. 236–7.

8. Halio, *First Quarto 'Lear'*, p. v. Brian Gibbons's note appears opposite the imprint page.

9. See *M. William Shak-speare: his true chronicle historie of the life and death of King Lear and his three daughters*, edited by Graham Holderness (Hemel Hempstead: Prentice-Hall, 1995), p. 72.

10. Quoted here from Kenneth Muir's Arden edition of *King Lear*, V.iii
    323–6, which follows the 1623 text from *Mr William Shakespeares
    Comedies, Histories, & Tragedies:*

    > *Edg.* The waight of this sad time we must obey,
    > Speake what we feele, not what we ought to say:
    > The oldest hath borne most, we that are yong,
    > Shall never see so much, nor liue so long.

11. Nahum Tate, *The History of King Lear*, edited by James Black
    (Lincoln: University of Nebraska Press, 1975, London: Edward
    Arnold, 1976), p. 95. In the text 'Vertue' is mistranscribed as 'viture'.

12. Nahum Tate, 'To my Esteemed Friend Thomas Boteler, Esq.'. Origi-
    nal-spelling version from an HTML transcript, based on a copy in
    the Furness Collection, University of Pennsylvania, and published
    on the Internet by Jack Lynch.

13. Maynard Mack, from *'King Lear' in Our Time* (1969), quoted from
    Shakespeare: 'King Lear', A Casebook, edited by Frank Kermode
    (London: Macmillan, 1969), p. 55.

14. From Raphael Holinshed's *Chronicles of England, Scotland and
    Ireland* (1587), vol. 2, quoted from Muir, *King Lear*, p. 236. See also
    The True Chronicle History of King LEIR and his three daughters
    (London, 1605).

15. *The Faerie Queene*, Book Two, Canto X, stanzas 31–2; *The Poetical
    Works of Edmund Spenser*, edited by J.C. Smith and E. De Selincourt
    (Oxford: Oxford University Press, 1912), p. 121.

16. John Higgins, *The Mirror for Magistrates* (1574), quoted from Muir,
    King Lear, p. 239.

17. Spenser, *The Faerie Queene*, Book Two, Canto X, stanza 32; Smith
    and De Selincourt, *Poetical Works*, p.121.

18. Classic critical studies like that of J.F. Danby, which reads *King Lear*
    via a Marxist understanding of early modern economic and politi-
    cal philosophies, and modern performance interpretations like the
    1970 film version directed by Grigori Kozintsev, which explores the
    Lear narrative as a grand historical epic of feudalism, have been
    able to present convincing renderings of the Lear story as history.
    See J.F. Danby, *Shakespeare's Doctrine of Nature: a study of 'King
    Lear'* (London: Faber, 1961). R.A. Foakes on the other hand
    describes *King Lear* as 'disconnected from chronicled time' (Foakes,

King Lear, p. 12). Studies that explore the generic diversity of *King Lear* include John D. Cox, *Shakespeare and the Dramaturgy of Power* (Princeton: Princeton University Press, 1989), and David Scott Kastan, *Shakespeare and the Shapes of Time* (Hanover: University Press of New England, 1982).

19. John Turner discusses the significance of such 'mythical charters' to the *King Lear* plays in Graham Holderness, Nick Potter and John Turner, *Shakespeare: The Play of History* (London: Macmillan, 1987), pp. 91–4.

20. From the *Tragedie of King Lear*, in *Mr William Shakespeares Comedies, Histories, & Tragedies* (1623). Quoted from *The Norton Facsimile: The First Folio of Shakespeare*, edited by Charlton Hinman (New York: W.W. Norton/Hamlyn Publishing Group, 1968), p. 804.

21. W.W. Greg, 'Time, Place and Politics in *King Lear*', in *The Collected Papers of Sir Walter W. Greg*, edited by J.C. Maxwell; and Madeleine Doran, *The Text of 'King Lear'* (Stanford: Stanford University Press, 1931).

22. Gary Taylor, 'Monopolies, Show Trials, Disaster, and Invasion: *King Lear* and Censorship', in Taylor and Warren, *Division*, p. 80.

23. Grace Ioppolo, *Revising Shakespeare* (Cambridge, Mass.: Harvard University Press, 1991).

24. See Wilson Knight, *The Wheel of Fire* (London: Chatto and Windus, 1930); and Jan Kott, *Shakespeare our Contemporary*, translated by Boleslaw Taborski (London: Methuen, 1965, 2nd edition 1967).

25. Gary Taylor, '*King Lear*: The Date and Authorship of the Folio Version', in Taylor and Warren, *Division*, p. 422.

26. Luce Irigiray, *This Sex which is not One*, translated by Catherine Porter and Carolyn Burke (Ithaca: Cornell University Press, 1985), p. 25.

27. A.C. Bradley, *Shakespearean Tragedy* (London: Macmillan, 1904, 2nd edition 1905), p. 291.

28. John Keats, 'On Sitting Down to Read *King Lear* Once Again', *Keats: The Complete Poems*, edited by Miriam Allott (London: Longman, 1970), p. 295.

29. Howard Felperin, *Shakespearean Representation: mimesis and modernity in Elizabethan tragedy* (1977); quoted from '*King Lear*':

contemporary critical essays, edited by Kiernan Ryan (London: Palgrave, 1993), p. 44.

30. Stephen Booth, *'King Lear', 'Macbeth', Indefinition and Tragedy* (New Haven: Yale University Press, 1983), p. 56.

31. T.S. Eliot, 'Gerontion', *Selected Poems 1909–1962* (London: Faber and Faber, 1963), p. 40.

32. Jacques Derrida, *Margins of Philosophy,* translated by Alan Bass (Chicago: University of Chicago Press, 1981), p. 65.

33. F, for example, inserts into Lear's dying speech an 'O,o,o,o' similar to that found in the Folio text of Hamlet's final soliloquy. Both could well be actors' additions. I am very grateful to Professor Foakes for giving his approval to the closing paragraphs of this chapter.

34. Stephen Greenblatt, *Shakespearean Negotiations: the circulation of social energy in Renaissance England* (Oxford: Clarendon Press, 1988), p. 1. The dialogue is continued in Greenblatt's masterly *Hamlet in Purgatory* (Princeton: Princeton University Press, 2001).

35. 'God in his time/Or out of time will correct this'. 'The Country Clergy', in R.S. Thomas, *Collected Poems 1945–1990* (London: Dent, 1993, London: Phoenix, 1996, 1999), p. 82.

Six: Notes and Queries – Macbeth

1. On 'disintegration' see Hugh Grady, 'Disintegration and its Reverberations', in *The Appropriation of Shakespeare; post-Renaissance reconstructions of the works and the myth,* edited by Jean I. Marsden (Hemel Hempstead: Harvester Wheatsheaf, 1991).

2. *Macbeth,* edited by J. Dover Wilson (Cambridge: Cambridge University Press, 1947), p. xxii. In the discussion that follows I have no intention of discrediting Dover Wilson, for whose work I have reconceived a profound respect. His work is self-contradictory, but he wanted what we all want: his three *Macbeths* and his one; three-in-one, one-in-three. He wanted the flux and the fixity; the bright star, and the gentle rise and fall; the legacy to be respectfully received and the freedom to spend it as the legatee desires.

3. Wilson, *Macbeth,* pp. xxii–xxiii, quoting W. J. Lawrence, 'The

Mystery of *Macbeth*' (1928), and Mark van Doren, *Shakespeare*
(1939).

4. *Macbeth*, edited by A. R. Braunmuller (Cambridge: Cambridge University Press, 1997), p. 6.

5. G. Blakemore Evans, *Shakespearean Prompt-books of the Seventeenth Century*, vol. 1, Part ii, 'Text of the Padua *Macbeth*' (Charlottesville, Virginia: Bibliographical Society of the University of Virginia, 1960).

6. Sir William Davenant, *Macbeth (1674)* (Cornmarket Shakespeare Series, London: Cornmarket Press, 1969); and William Shakespeare, *Macbeth (1673)* (Cornmarket Shakespeare Series, London: Cornmarket Press, 1969). See also Christopher Spencer, *Davenant's 'Macbeth' from the Yale Manuscript: an edition, with a discussion of the relation of Davenant's text to Shakespeare's* (New Haven: Yale University Press, 1961).

7. Original of Forman's manuscript is in the Bodleian Library, Oxford, manuscript Ashmole 208. Transcript quoted from Samuel Schoenbaum, *William Shakespeare: Records and Images* (London: Scolar Press, 1969) pp. 7–8. 20 April 1610 was not a Saturday but 20 April 1611 was; so scholars have assumed Forman made a common mistake in getting the new year wrong. See also Barbara Traister, *The Notorious Astrological Physician of London: Works and Days of Simon Forman* (Chicago: University of Chicago Press, 2001).

8. *Macbeth*, edited by G. K. Hunter (London: Penguin, 1967), p. 40. Forman's notes were even at one time taken to be a Collier forgery (see *Macbeth*, edited by Kenneth Muir, [London: Methuen, 1951, 1979], p. xiv).

9. Judith Cook, *Dr Simon Forman: a most notorious physician* (London: Chatto and Windus, 2001), p. 206. John D. Cox points out to me that no eyewitness record of Shakespeare's plays provides what we would now recognise as a 'literary-critical' response.

10. *The Tragedie of Macbeth*, edited by James Rigney, (Hemel Hempstead: Harvester Wheatsheaf, 1996), p. 16.

11. See Anne Somerset, *Unnatural Murder: poison at the court of James I* (London: Weidenfeld and Nicolson, 1997), pp. 76–83.

12. See, for example, Susanne Woods, *Lanyer: a Renaissance Woman Poet* (Oxford: Oxford University Press, 1999).

13. See A.L. Rowse, *Simon Forman: Sex and Society in Shakespeare's Age* (London: Weidenfeld and Nicolson, 1974) and his edition, *The Poems of Shakespeare's Dark Lady: 'Salve Deus Rex Judaeorum' by Emilia Lanyer* (London: Jonathan Cape, 1978).

14. A term used by Jonathan Goldberg, 'Textual Properties', *Shakespeare Quarterly* 37:2 (1986), p. 213.

15. F.G. Fleay, 'Davenant's *Macbeth* and Shakespeare's Witches', *Anglia* 7 (1884). Fleay was a pioneer 'disintegrationist'. See also Daniel A. Amneus, 'A Missing Scene in *Macbeth*', *Journal of English and Germanic Philology* 61 (1961) and 'The Cawdor Episode in *Macbeth*', *Journal of English and Germanic Philology* 63 (1964).

16. John Masefield, *A 'Macbeth' Production* (London: Heinemann, 1945), p. 7.

17. Notwithstanding his scepticism about Forman (he even suggests that the doctor topped himself in order to fulfil the prophecy of his own death) Muir uses his account as evidence that Hecate and the 'witches' songs' were later interpolations – 'I am inclined to think that the play was contaminated after the performance witnessed by Forman'. Muir, *King Lear*, p. xxx.

18. John Turner, reversing convention, uses Forman as evidence that Shakespeare's wierds were closer to the sybils of Holinshed than the witches of subsequent tradition. See his *Macbeth* (Milton Keynes: Open University Press, 1992), p. 20.

19. This is not in any way to invalidate the 'contaminated' *Macbeth*, only to attempt a recovery of the pre-contaminated *Macbeth* of 1611.

20. See *An Excellent Conceited Tragedie of Romeo and Juliet*, edited by Cedric Watts; and Graham Holderness, *Romeo and Juliet* (London: Penguin, 1990), pp. 60–5.

21. George Bernard Shaw wrote an engaging fantasy in which Shakespeare reveals that Lady Macbeth was more or less a portrait of his wife.'If you notice, Lady Macbeth has only one consistent characteristic, which is, that she thinks everything her husband does is wrong and she can do it better. If I'd ever murdered anybody she'd [Anne Hathaway] have bullied me for making a mess of it and gone upstairs to improve on it herself'. Quoted in *After Shakespeare: An anthology*, edited by John Gross (Oxford: Oxford University Press, 2002), p. 322. See also Michael D. Bristol, 'Vernacular Criticism and

the Scenes Shakespeare Never Wrote', *Shakespeare Survey* 53: *Shakespeare and Narrative* (Cambridge: Cambridge University Press, 2000).

22. See J.M. Nosworthy, '*Macbeth* at the Globe', *The Library*, 5th series, vol. 2 (1948), pp. 108–18.

Seven: Visions and Revisions – Hamlet

1. For a discussion of *Last Action Hero* (1993), see *Shakespeare on Film*, edited by Robert Shaughnessy (London: Macmillan 1998), pp. 1–3.

2. Tom Stoppard, *Dogg's Hamlet, Cahoot's Macbeth* (London: Faber and Faber, 1980).

3. These would include the work of the Reduced Shakespeare Company, who in *The Complete Works of William Shakespeare (Abridged)* stage *Hamlet* first as a drama workshop, secondly as a three-minute condensation, and then in thirty seconds backwards; and also Richard Curtis's *Skinhead Hamlet*, which pares down scenes to exchanges such as the following (Act 1 scene 3):

    Laertes: I'm fucking off now. Watch Hamlet doesn't slip you one while I'm away.

    Ophelia: I'll be fucked if he does.

    Act 3 scene 2 becomes:

    Player: Full thirty times hath Phoebus' cart ...

    Claudius: I'll be fucked if I watch any more of this crap.

    And so on. See *The Faber Book of Parodies*, edited by Simon Brett (London: Faber and Faber, 1984).

4. See Graham Holderness on Coronado's *Hamlet* in *Visual Shakespeare: essays in film and television* (Hatfield: University of Hertfordshire Press, 2001), pp. 78–80.

5. *In the Bleak Midwinter*, directed by Kenneth Branagh (1995). The plot is built around a production of *Hamlet*.

6. Charles Marowitz, *The Marowitz 'Hamlet'* (London: Allen Lane, 1968). See also Alan Sinfield, 'Making Space: appropriation and confrontation in recent British plays' in *The Shakespeare Myth*, edited by Graham Holderness (Manchester: Manchester University Press, 1988); and Peter Brook, Robert Lepage and Robert Wilson, *Hamlet in Pieces* (London: Nick Hern Books, 2001).

7. Deborah Levy, *Pushing the Prince into Denmark*, in *Levy Plays 1* (London: Methuen, 2000).

8. Michael Innes, *Hamlet, Revenge!* (London: Victor Gollancz, 1937).

9. Damon Runyon, 'The Melancholy Dane', in *Runyon à la Carte* (London: Constable, 1946).

10. Carole Corbier, *In the Wings* (Toronto: Stoddart, 1997).

11. See John Willett, *The Theatre of Bertolt Brecht* (London: Eyre Methuen, 1960, 3rd edition 1967), pp. 120–1; and *Brecht on Theatre*, edited by John Willett (London: Methuen, 1964, 2nd edition 1974), p. 201.

12. See R.S. Gwynne, 'Horatio's Philosophy', from *No Word of Farewell: Selected Poems 1970–2000* (Ashland, Oregon: Story Line Press, 2001). Some of these examples are represented, albeit largely fragmented into 'gobbets', in *After Shakespeare: an anthology*, edited by John Gross (Oxford: Oxford University Press, 2002). But a useful grouping of *Hamlet* poems by C.P. Cavafy, Marina Tsetayava, Brecht, Miroslav Holub and Zbigniew Herbert is featured on pp. 205–11. For Horatio as the writer who mediates between *Hamlet* and the reader, see Alathea Hayter, *Horatio's Version* (London: Faber and Faber, 1972); and below note 32.

13. Martin Scofield, *The Ghosts of 'Hamlet': the play and modern writers* (Cambridge: Cambridge University Press, 1980), p. 3. See also Alexander Welsh, *Hamlet in his Modern Guises* (Princeton: Princeton University Press, 2001).

14. David Scott Kastan, *Shakespeare and the Book* (Cambridge: Cambridge University Press, 2001), pp. 84, 90, 95.

15. Caryl Brahms and S.J. Simon, *No Bed for Bacon* (London: Michael Joseph, 1941).

16. Tom Stoppard, *Rosencrantz and Guildenstern are Dead* (London: Faber and Faber, 1968). See also Michael Scott, *Shakespeare and the Modern Dramatist* (London: Macmillan, 1989).

17. T.S. Eliot, 'The Love Song of J. Alfred Prufrock', *Selected Poems 1909–1962* (London: Faber and Faber, 1963), p. 17.

18. The practical joke goes right back to Shakespeare and beyond to Saxo. In *Der Bestrafte Brudermord*, two pirates stand on either side of Hamlet to shoot him, he ducks, and they shoot one another.

19. John Russell Taylor, *The Second Wave: British drama for the 70s* (London: Methuen, 1971), p. 100.

20. Ronald Hayman, *Tom Stoppard* (London: Heinemann, 1977, 4th edition 1982), p. 34. Compare Boris Pasternak's poem 'Hamlet' (1946): 'the play being acted is not mine'. Translated by Peter France and Jon Stallworthy; quoted in Gross, *After Shakespeare*, p. 80.

21. Rayner Heppenstall, 'The Hawk and the Handsaw', in Rayner Heppenstall and Michael Innes, *Three Tales of Hamlet* (London: Victor Gollancz, 1950). First broadcast by BBC, 27 June, 1949.

22. Ernest Jones, *Hamlet and Oedipus* (London: Victor Gollancz, 1949); and W.W. Greg, 'Hamlet's Hallucination', *Modern Language Review*, 12:4 (1917).

23. Pierre Macherey, *A Theory of Literary Production*, translated by Geoffrey Wall (London: Routledge and Kegan Paul, 1978), p. 17.

24. John Updike, *Gertrude and Claudius* (New York: Alfred A. Knopf, 2000). Quotations from London: Penguin Books edition (2001).

25. Belleforest's account was translated into English and published as *The Hystorie of Hamblet* in 1601. Updike provides two brief notes at the beginning and end of the novel, which illustrate the way in which he combines direct 'translation' with informed cultural reinterpretation. The 'Foreword' identifies the sources and analogues of *Hamlet*, from Saxo Grammaticus to *Der Bestrafte Brudermord*, indicating his attempt to re-enter the historical record and to revise Shakespeare's historical account. But the 'Afterword' strikes quite a different note, citing various old and new critical interpretations, particularly G. Wilson Knight's *The Wheel of Fire* (London: Chatto and Windus, 1930), and acknowledging Kenneth Branagh's film version of *Hamlet* as a partial source for the novel.

26. Wilson Knight's essays on *Hamlet* locate the source of the play's problem firmly in Hamlet himself, who is a victim of 'soul-sickness', an ambassador of evil, a diseased melancholic whose malaise infects the whole world around him. Knight revises Claudius as a wise and gentle king, Gertrude a noble queen, and so on. Like the Freudian interpretation, this view of the play provides a basis from which to reinterpret the other characters of the play – Claudius, Gertrude, Polonius, Laertes, Ophelia – not as Hamlet sees them but as they

can be conceived to have existed independent of Hamlet's corrosive and infectious hatred and suspicion.

27. Jacques Derrida, *Spectres of Marx: the state of the debt, the work of mourning and the new international*, translated by Peggy Kamuf (New York and London: Routledge, 1994). See also Peter Stallybrass, "'Well grubbed, old mole'": Marx, *Hamlet*, and the (un)fixing of representation', and Richard Halpern, 'An Impure History of Ghosts', in *Marxist Shakespeares*, edited by Jean E. Howard and Scott Cutler Shershow (London: Routledge, 2001). For some parallel arguments see A.D. Nuttall, '*Hamlet*: conversations with the dead', in *The Stoic in Love: selected essays on literature and ideas* (Brighton: Harvester Wheatsheaf, 1989); Francis Barker, *The Culture of Violence: essays on tragedy and history* (Manchester: Manchester University Press, 1993) and Graham Holderness, *Shakespeare: the Histories* (London: Macmillan, 2000).

28. T.S. Eliot, 'Burnt Norton', *Selected Poems*, p. 194.

29. Derrida, *Spectres*, p. 5. 'La Crise de l'esprit' in Paul Valery, *Oeuvres*, vol. 1 (Paris: Gallimard, 1957), pp. 988–1014.

30. It is also, of course, the landscape of T. S. Eliot's *The Waste Land*, published in 1922. Later in *Little Gidding* (London: Faber and Faber, 1942, p. 10) Eliot met his own 'familiar compound ghost'.

31. Rayner Heppenstall, 'The Fool's Saga', in Heppenstall and Innes, *Three Tales*, pp. 91–192. First broadcast BBC, 21 November, 1948. Gross in *After Shakespeare* wrongly attributes the play to Michael Innes (p. 332).

32. Graham Holderness, *The Prince of Denmark* (Hatfield: University of Hertfordshire Press, 2002). It is perhaps unusual for a critical book to include an analytical account of the author's own work of fiction. I hope this is an unusual critical book. It should also be pointed out that despite the evidence of publication dates, *The Prince of Denmark* was completed (and indeed in press) long before John Updike's book was published.

33. See John Turner's excellent discussion in Graham Holderness, Nick Potter and John Turner, *Shakespeare: The Play of History* (London: Macmillan, 1987).

34. Compare Vladimir Nabokov, who imagines Hamlet in Wittenberg 'always late for Giordano Bruno's lectures'. *Bend Sinister* (1947),

quoted in Gross, *After Shakespeare*, p. 192.

35. *Beowulf*, ll. 50–2. 'Men ne cunnon/secgan to sothe, seleraedenda /haeleth under heofonum, hwa tham hlaeste onfeng'. My translation is quoted from *Craeft: poems from the Anglo-Saxon* (Nottingham: Shoestring Press, 2002).

36. 1 Corinthians, 13.12. *The New Testament*, translated by William Tyndale (Worms, 1526), edited by W.R. Cooper (London: British Library, 2000), p. 370. For a modern-spelling version see *Tyndale's New Testament*, edited by David Daniell (New Haven: Yale University Press, 1989, 1995), p. 256.

37. William Wordsworth, *The Prelude: a Parallel Text*, edited by J.C. Maxwell (London: Penguin, 1971), p. 153.

38. See my *Shakespeare: the Histories*, pp. 16–18.

39. Stephen Greenblatt, 'General Introduction', *The Norton Shakespeare: based on the Oxford edition*, edited by Stephen Greenblatt, Walter Cohen, Jean E. Howard and Katherine Eisaman Maus (New York: W.W. Norton and Co, 1997), p. 1.

Eight: Writing and fighting – Henry V

1. G.I. Duthie, 'The quarto of Shakespeare's *Henry V*', in *Papers Mainly Shakespearian* (Edinburgh: Oliver & Boyd, 1964), p. 117.

2. *King Henry V*, edited by J.H. Walter (London Methuen, 1954), p. xxxviii.

3. *King Henry V*, edited by T.W. Craik (London: Routledge, 1995), p. 96.

4. *Henry V*, edited by Gary Taylor (Oxford: Oxford University Press, 1984), p. 23.

5. Quoted from *The Cronicle History of Henry the fift*, edited by Graham Holderness and Bryan Loughrey (Hemel Hempstead: Harvester Wheatsheaf, 1993), p. 57.

6. *The Norton Facsimile: The First Folio of Shakespeare*, edited by Charlton Hinman (New York: W.W. Norton/Hamlyn Publishing Group, 1968), pp. 424–5.

7. Raphael Holinshed, *Chronicles of England, Scotlande and Irelande* (London, 2nd edition 1577), vol. 3, pp. 545–6.

8. Annabel Patterson, *Shakespeare and the Popular Voice* (Oxford:

Blackwell, 1989); quoted from *Shakespeare's History Plays: 'Richard II' to 'Henry V*, edited by Graham Holderness (London: Macmillan, 1992), pp. 176–7.

9. See, for example, Graham Holderness, *Shakespeare: The Play of History* (London: Macmillan, 1987), pp. 62–84; and *Shakespeare Recycled* (Hemel Hempstead: Harvester Wheatsheaf, 1992), pp. 178–210.

10. See Leah Marcus, *Puzzling Shakespeare: local reading and its discontents* (Berkeley: University of California Press, 1992).

11. See Anne Barton, 'The king disguised: Shakespeare's *Henry V* and the comic history', in *The Triple Bond*, edited by Joseph G. Price (University Park, PA: Pennsylvania State University Press, 1975).

12. *The First Quarto of King Henry V*, edited by Andrew Gurr (Cambridge: Cambridge University Press, 2000), p. 2.

13. See Pauline Kiernan, *Staging Shakespeare at the New Globe* (London: Routledge, 2002), which includes a detailed account of the Globe's 'authentic' production of *Henry V.*

14. Stephen Urkowitz, 'Good news about bad quartos', in *Bad Shakespeare: revaluations of the Shakespeare canon*, edited by Maurice Charney (London and Toronto: Associated University Presses, 1988), p. 204.

15. Jacques Derrida, *Aporias*, translated by Thomas Dutoit (Stanford: Stanford University Press, 1993), p. 65.

16. Jacques Derrida, 'The Law of Genres', *Critical Inquiry* 7:1 (Autumn 1980), pp. 55–81.

17. Gerard Manley Hopkins, *Selected Poetry*, edited by Catherine Phillips (Oxford: Oxford University Press, 1996). p. 99.

Conclusion

1. Rowan Williams, *Writing in the Dust: reflections on 11 September and its aftermath* (London: Hodder and Stoughton, 2002), pp. 9–10.

2. These are reproduced in Stefan Aust, Cordt Schnibben, *et alii, Inside 9–11: What Really Happened* (New York: St. Martin's Press, 2002), pp. 262–313, especially pp. 307–13.

3. Biblical studies tend to resolve such problems by invoking an authentic 'tradition' which can be assumed to have held the story in suspension, releasing it into the canonical gospels at a later stage. Thus the anecdote can be assumed as traceable back to a point of origin (an event that really happened, was witnessed and reported), and to contiguity with the very incarnate body of Jesus himself (as imagined in the beautiful painting by Lucas Cranach the Younger, which shows the woman clinging to Jesus' side and he holding her hand. The Hermitage, St Petersburg). It would seem far more probable that the story is the invention of a writer who could imagine, as well as copy down, divine truth. In biblical analysis 'tradition' often performs a function similar to that of the 'author's manuscript' in traditional textual practice.

4. See Graham Ward on Derrida's concept of 'supplementation': 'Discourse is inseparable from a continual movement of displacement and dissemination (what Derrida calls "supplementation"). However each supplement, in trying to complete the meaning of that which went before it, also reproduces the inadequacy, with the result that communications, while generating further texts, require still further qualifications'. *Theology and Contemporary Critical Theory* (London: Macmillan, 1996, 2nd edition 2000), p. 15.

5. John 8.6. Quoted from *The Bible: Authorized King James Version*, edited by Robert Carroll and Stephen Prickett (Oxford: Oxford University Press, 1997), NT p. 126.

6. Oscar Wilde saw this gesture as expressive of 'poetical justice', 'the very keynote of romantic art'. *De Profundis* (London: Methuen, 1905), pp. 106–7.

7. These 'originals', like Shakespeare's manuscripts, were in fact lost, destroyed by Moses in his anger over the Golden Calf. The Law was written out again, also in colloquy with God, possibly by Moses himself, and on new tablets. Exodus, 34.28.

8. And found it in many cases (especially among Western politicians, who for their own purposes turned too readily to a language of demonisation and revenge) seriously deficient.

9. Jennifer Wallace, 'Tragedy grapples with gap between human meaningfulness and despair', *Times Higher Education Supplement*, 6

September 2002, p. 16. Published also as '"We can't make more dirt": Tragedy and the Excavated Body', *Cambridge Quarterly* 32, June 2003

10. Laurie E. Maguire compares the act of editing to that of 'laying out', giving the example of Heminge and Condell who in the First Folio 'not only remember Shakespeare', but 're-member him'. The language of their Preface ('perfect of their limbs') Maguire calls 'the language of embalment'. See her 'Shakespeare and the Death of the Author', in *The Renaissance Text: theory, editing, textuality*, edited by Andrew Murphy (Manchester: Manchester University Press, 2000), p. 142.

11. Jacques Derrida, *Spectres of Marx: the state of the debt, the work of mourning and the new international*, translated by Peggy Kamuf (New York and London: Routledge, 1994), p. 138.

12. Michel Foucault defines the notion 'man' as 'an invention of recent date' that one day will be 'erased, like a face drawn in sand at the edge of the sea'. *The Order of Things: an Archaeology of the Human Sciences* (New York: Random House, 1970), p. 387.

13. Jacques Derrida, 'Living On: Border Lines', translated by James Hulbert in *The Derrida Reader: Between the Blinds*, edited by Peggy Kamuf (Hemel Hempstead: Harvester Wheatsheaf, 1991), pp. 256–7.

14. Jacques Derrida, *Aporias*, translated by Thomas Dutoit (Stanford: Stanford University Press, 1993), p. 65. Hélène Cixous, *Coming to Writing and Other Essays*, edited by Deborah Jensen, translated by Sarah Cornell *et alii* (Cambridge, Mass.: Harvard University Press, 1991), p. 1.

15. Henry James, 'The Birthplace' (1903). Quoted in *After Shakespeare: An anthology*, edited by John Gross (Oxford: Oxford University Press, 2002), p. 21.

16. The phrase is the sub-title of Derrida's *Spectres of Marx* but the sentiment is generally held. See, for example, Gary Taylor, 'culture is always the gift of the survivor. It is always bereaved' (*Cultural Selection* [New York: Basic Books, 1996], p. 5); and Geoffrey Hartman, 'inscribing, naming and writing are types of a commemorative and inherently elegiac act' (*Beyond Formalism* [New Haven: Yale University Press, 1970], p. 223). Andrew Murphy applies this problematic to editing: 'every vision of textual presence ... is doomed to failure'.

'"Came errour here by mysse of man": editing and the metaphysics of presence', *Yearbook of English Studies* 29 (1999), p. 136.

17. *The Times*, 23 October 2002, p. 23. The closing language sounds less like the denouement of a thriller, more like the language of the New Testament: 'For there is nothing covered, that shall not be revealed; neither hid, that shall not be known'. Luke, 12:2. *The Bible*, eds. Carroll and Prickett, NT p. 92.

18. The phrase is Marx's, from *The Communist Manifesto* (1848) but it has become a post-modernist slogan: see Marshall Berman, *All That is Solid Melts into Air: the experience of modernity* (New York: Simon and Schuster, 1982). My analogy is with Prospero's speech in *The Tempest*, quoted from *William Shakespeare: the Complete Works, Original-spelling Edition*, edited by Stanley Wells and Gary Taylor (Oxford: Clarendon Press, 1986), p. 1359:

> Our Reuels now are ended: These our actors,
> (As I foretold you) were all Spirits, and
> Are melted into Ayre, *into thin Ayre*,
> And, like the baselesse fabricke of this vision
> The Clowd-capt Towres, the gorgeous Pallaces,
> The solemne Temples, the great Globe it selfe,
> Yea, all which it inherit, shall dissolue
> And, like this insubstantiall Pageant faded
> Leaue not a racke behinde: we are such stuffe
> As dreames are made on; and our little life
> Is rounded with a sleepe (my italics).

19. Thomas Hardy, 'Shakespeare After Three Hundred Years' (1916), quoted in Gross, *After Shakespeare*, pp. 343–4.

20. Terence Hawkes, *That Shakespeherian Rag* (London: Methuen, 1986).

21. 'He walks around, reading a book about himself'. Stephane Mallarme, 'Hamlet et Fortinbras', quoted in Martin Scofield, *The Ghosts of 'Hamlet': the play and modern writers* (Cambridge: Cambridge University Press, 1980), p. 30.

22. E.M. Forster, *Howard's End* (London: Edward Arnold, 1910, London: Penguin, 1941, 1979), p. 188.

Postcript

1.   Thomas Hardy, *Jude the Obscure* (1896, London: Penguin, 1987).

2.   The contribution of women to such close-knit working-class families was equally creative, but different. They made life, rather than things.

3.   I could never have felt anything other than a stranger in Oxford: divorced from my own class, alienated from the university's social ethos. On the other hand, I now recognise that there was something exaggerated in assuming the pose of a Jude the Obscure, chalking the remonstrance of Job on college gates that had after all already opened to admit me, and others like me (see letter in *Times Higher Education Supplement*, 4 March 1994).

4.   Evelyn Waugh, *Brideshead Revisited* (1945, London: Heinemann/ Secker and Warburg, 1977), p. 678.

5.   'Merlin and the Gleam', *Tennyson's Poems*, edited by Mildred M. Bozman (London: Dent, 1949, 1965), vol. 2, p. 424. William Wordsworth, *The Prelude 1799, 1805, 1850*, edited by J. Wordsworth, M.H. Abrams and S. Gill (New York: Norton, 1979), p. 608.

6.   *The Norton Facsimile: the First Folio of Shakespeare*, edited by Charlton Hinman (New York: W.W. Norton/Hamlyn Publishing Group, 1968), TLN 139–41, p. 761.

Bibliography

Allott, Miriam (ed.). *Keats: The Complete Poems*, London: Longman, 1970

Amneus, Daniel A. 'A Missing Scene in *Macbeth*', *Journal of English and Germanic Philology* 61, 1961

Amneus, Daniel A. 'The Cawdor Episode in *Macbeth*', *Journal of English and Germanic Philology* 63, 1964

Amory, Hugh. 'Physical Bibliography, Cultural History, and the Disappearance of the Book', *Papers of the Bibliographical Society of America* 78, 1984

Aust, Stefan, Cordt Schnibben, *et alii. Inside 9-11: What Really Happened*, New York: St Martin's Press, 2002

Barker, Francis. *The Culture of Violence: essays on tragedy and history*, Manchester: Manchester University Press, 1993

Barthes, Roland. 'From Work to Text', and 'The Death of the Author' in *Image, Music, Text*, translated by Stephen Heath, New York: Hill and Wang, 1977

Barton, Anne. 'The king disguised: Shakespeare's *Henry V* and the comic history', in *The Triple Bond*, edited by Joseph G. Price, University Park, PA: Pennsylvania State University Press, 1975

Bateson, F. W. 'Modern Bibliography and the Literary Artefact', in *English Studies Today*, edited by Georges A. Bonnard, Bern: 2nd edition 1961

Benson, A. C. *Rossetti*, London: Macmillan, 1904

Berman, Marshall. *All That is Solid Melts into Air: the experience of modernity*, New York: Simon and Schuster, 1982

Bertram, Paul, and Bernice Kliman (eds.). *The Three–Text 'Hamlet': Parallel Texts of the First and Second Quartos and First Folio, Studies in the Renaissance,* no. 30; New York: AMS Press, 1991

Bevington, David. 'Determining the Indeterminate: The Oxford Shakespeare', *Shakespeare Quarterly* 20, 1968–70

Black, N.W. and Matthias Shaaber. *Shakespeare's Seventeenth Century Editors, 1632 –1685,* New York: Modern Language Association, 1973

Blake, William. 'The Marriage of Heaven and Hell', *Blake's Poems and Prophecies,* edited by Max Plowman, London: Dent, 1927, 1965

Blayney, Peter. *The Texts of 'King Lear' and their Origins,* Cambridge: Cambridge University Press, 1982

Blayney, Peter. 'The Publication of Playbooks', in *A New History of Early English Drama,* edited by John D. Cox and David Scott Kastan, New York: Columbia University Press, 1997

Bolter, Jay David. 'Topographic Writing: hypertext and the electronic writing space', in *Hypermedia and Literary Studies,* edited by George P. Landow and Paul Delaney, Cambridge, Mass.: MIT Press, 1991

Bolter, Jay David. *Writing Space: the computer, hypertext and the history of writing,* Hillsdale, N.J.: Lawrence Erlbaum Associates, 1991

Booth, Stephen (ed.). *Shakespeare's Sonnets,* New Haven: Yale University Press, 1977

Booth, Stephen. *'King Lear', 'Macbeth', Indefinition and Tragedy,* New Haven: Yale University Press, 1983

Bowers, Fredson. 'Textual Criticism', in *A Shakespeare Encyclopaedia,* edited by Oscar James Campbell and Edward G. Quinn, London: Methuen, 1966

Bozman, Mildred M. (ed.). *Tennyson's Poems,* London: Dent, 1949, 1965

Bradley, A.C. *Shakespearean Tragedy,* London: Macmillan, 1904, 2nd edition 1905

Bradshaw, Graham, and Kairo Ashizo. 'Reading *Hamlet* in Japan', in *Shakespeare in the Twentieth Century,* edited by Jonathan Bate, Jill L. Levenson and Dieter Mehl, Newark: University of Delaware Press, 1998

Brahms, Caryl, and S.J. Simon. *No Bed for Bacon,* London: Michael Joseph, 1941

Brandt, Kathleen. 'The Grime of the Centuries is a Pigment of the Imagination: Michelangelo's Sistine Ceiling', in *Palimpsest: editorial theory in the humanities*, edited by George Bornstein and Ralph Williams, Ann Arbor: University of Michigan Press, 1993

Braunmuller, A. R. (ed.). *Macbeth*, Cambridge: Cambridge University Press, 1997

Brett, Simon (ed.). *The Faber Book of Parodies*, London: Faber and Faber, 1984

Bristol, Michael D. 'Vernacular Criticism and the Scenes Shakespeare Never Wrote', *Shakespeare Survey* 53: *Shakespeare and Narrative*, Cambridge: Cambridge University Press, 2000

Brook, Peter, Robert Lepage and Robert Wilson. *Hamlet in Pieces*, London: Nick Hern Books, 2001

Bruster, Douglas. *Quoting Shakespeare: form and culture in early modern drama*, Lincoln: University of Nebraska Press, 2000

Byatt, A.S. *Possession: a Romance*, London: Chatto and Windus, 1990

Caie, Graham D. 'Hypertext and Multiplicity: the mediaeval example', in *The Renaissance Text: theory, editing, textuality*, edited by Andrew Murphy, Manchester: Manchester University Press, 2000

Carroll, Robert, and Stephen Prickett. *The Bible: Authorized King James Version*, Oxford: Oxford University Press, 1997

Cherniak, Warren, and Marilyn Deegan (eds.). *The Politics of the Electronic Text*, London: Office for Humanities Communication Publications, University of London, 1993

Cixous, Héléne. *Coming to Writing and Other Essays*, edited by Deborah Jensen, translated by Sarah Cornell *et alii*, Cambridge, Mass.: Harvard University Press, 1991

Cixous, Helene. *Three Steps on the Ladder of Writing*, translated by Sarah Cornell and Susan Sellers, New York: Columbia University Press, 1993

Cloud, Random (Randall McLeod). 'The marriage of good and bad Quartos', *Shakespeare Quarterly* 33, 1982

Cook, Judith. *Dr Simon Forman: a most notorious physician*, London: Chatto and Windus, 2001

Corbier, Carole. *In the Wings*, Toronto: Stoddart, 1997

Cox, John D. *Shakespeare and the Dramaturgy of Power*, Princeton: Princeton University Press, 1989

Craik, T.W. (ed.). *King Henry V*, London: Routledge, 1995

Danby, J.F. *Shakespeare's Doctrine of Nature: a study of 'King Lear'* London: Faber, 1961

Daniell, David (ed.). *Tyndale's New Testament,* New Haven: Yale University Press, 1989, 1995

Davenant, Sir William. *Macbeth (1674),* Cornmarket Shakespeare Series, London: Cornmarket Press, 1969

Derrida, Jacques. *Of Grammatology,* translated by Gayatri C. Spivak, Baltimore: Johns Hopkins University Press, 1976

Derrida, Jacques. 'The Law of Genres', *Critical Inquiry* 7:1, Autumn 1980

Derrida, Jacques. *Margins of Philosophy,* translated by Alan Bass, Chicago: University of Chicago Press, 1981

Derrida, Jacques. *Limited, Inc.* translated by Samuel Weber and Jeffrey Mehlman, Evanston: Northwestern University Press, 1988

Derrida, Jacques. 'Living On: Border Lines', translated by James Hulbert in *The Derrida Reader: Between the Blinds,* edited by Peggy Kamuf, Hemel Hempstead: Harvester Wheatsheaf, 1991

Derrida, Jacques. *Aporias,* translated by Thomas Dutoit, Stanford: Stanford University Press, 1993

Derrida, Jacques. *Spectres of Marx: the state of the debt, the work of mourning and the new international,* translated by Peggy Kamuf, New York and London: Routledge, 1994

Dillon, Janet. 'Is There a Performance in this Text?', *Shakespeare Quarterly* 45, 1994

Donaldson, Peter. 'The Shakespeare Interactive Archive: new directions in electronic scholarship on text and performance', in *Contextual Media,* edited by Edward Barrett and Marie Redmond, Cambridge, Mass.: MIT Press, 1995

Doran, Madeleine. *The Text of King Lear,* Stanford: Stanford University Press, 1931

Doughty, Oswald (ed.). *Rossetti's Poems,* London: Dent, 1961

Doughty, Oswald and John Robert Wahl (eds.). *Letters of Dante Gabriel Rossetti 1828–1882,* Oxford: Clarendon Press, 1965–7

Dover Wilson, J. (ed.). *Macbeth,* Cambridge: Cambridge University Press, 1947

Drakakis, John (ed.). *The Tragedy of Richard III,* Hemel Hempstead: Prentice-Hall, 1996

Drakakis, John. 'Shakespeare and the Roadsweepers', in *The Shakespeare Myth,* edited by Graham Holderness, Manchester: Manchester University Press, 1998

Duthie, G.I. (ed.). *Shakespeare's 'King Lear': a Critical Edition*, Oxford: Clarendon Press, 1949

Duthie, G.I. *Elizabethan Shorthand and the First Quarto of 'King Lear'*, Oxford: Blackwell, 1949

Duthie, G.I. 'The quarto of Shakespeare's *Henry V*', in *Papers Mainly Shakespearian*, Edinburgh: Oliver & Boyd, 1964

Egan, Gabriel. 'Myths and Enabling Fictions of "Origin" in the Editing of Shakespeare', *New Theatre Quarterly* 49, 1997

Eliot, T. S. *Little Gidding*, London: Faber and Faber, 1942

Eliot, T.S. *Selected Poems 1909–1962*, London: Faber and Faber, 1963

Enright, D.J. *Collected Poems*, Manchester: Carcanet Press, 1973

Evans, G. Blakemore. *Shakespearean Prompt-books of the Seventeenth Century*, vol. 1, Part ii, 'Text of the Padua *Macbeth*', Charlottesville, Virginia: Bibliographical Society of the University of Virginia, 1960

Febvre, Lucien, and Henri-Jean Martin. *The Coming of the Book: the impact of printing 1450–1800*, 1976, London: Verso, 1997

Finkelstein, David, and Alistair McCleery (eds.). *The Book History Reader*, London: Routledge, 2001

Fish, Stanley. *How Milton Works*, Harvard University Press, 2002

Flaubert, Gustave. 'La Legende de St Julien L'Hospitalier', *Trois Contes* (1877), *Three Tales*, translated by Robert Baldick, London: Penguin Books, 1961

Fleay, F.G. 'Davenant's *Macbeth* and Shakespeare's Witches', *Anglia* 7, 1884

Foakes, R.A. (ed.). *King Lear*, London: Thomas Nelson, 1997

Forster, E.M. *Howard's End*, London: Edward Arnold, 1910, London: Penguin, 1941, 1979

Foster, Maxwell E. *The Play Behind the Play: 'Hamlet' and Quarto One*, London: Heinemann, 1991

Foucault, Michel. *The Order of Things: an Archaeology of the Human Sciences*, New York: Random House, 1970

Foucault, Michel. 'What is an Author?' in The *Foucault Reader*, edited by Paul Rabinow, New York: Pantheon, 1984

Freeman, Neil (ed.). *Applause First Folio: Hamlet*, Folio Scripts: Vancouver, Canada, 1998

Freeman, Robert (ed.). *Marx on Economics*, London: Penguin Books, 1968

Fukayama, Francis. *Our Posthuman Future: consequences of the biotechnology revolution*, New York: Farrar Strauss and Giroux, 2002

Gellrich, Jesse M. *The Idea of the Book in the Middle Ages: language theory, mythology and fiction*, Ithaca: Cornell University Press, 1985

Genette, Gerard, and Jane E. Lewin. *Paratext: thresholds of interpretation*, Cambridge: Cambridge University Press, 1997

Genette, Gerard. *Palimpsests: literature in the second degree*, translated by Channa Newman and Claude Doubinsky, Lincoln: University of Nebraska Press, 1997

Gibson, Rex. 'Narrative Approaches to Shakespeare: Active Storytelling in Schools', *Shakespeare Survey* 53: *Shakespeare and Narrative*, Cambridge: Cambridge University Press, 2000

Goldberg, Jonathan. 'Textual Properties', *Shakespeare Quarterly* 37:2, 1986

Grady, Hugh. 'Disintegration and its Reverberations', in *The Appropriation of Shakespeare; post-Renaissance reconstructions of the works and the myth*, edited by Jean I. Marsden, Hemel Hempstead: Harvester Wheatsheaf, 1991

Grazia, Margreta de. 'The essential Shakespeare and the material book', *Textual Practice* 2, 1988

Grazia, Margreta de. *Shakespeare Verbatim: the reproduction of authenticity and the 1790 Apparatus*, Oxford: Oxford University Press, 1991

Grazia, Margreta de. 'What is a Work? What is a Document?', in *New Ways of Looking at Old Texts: papers of the Renaissance English Text Society, 1985–1991*, edited by W. Speed Hill, Binghamton: Renaissance English Text Society, 1993

Grazia, Margreta de., and Peter Stallybrass. 'The materiality of the Shakespearean text', in *Shakespeare Quarterly* 44, Fall 1993

Greenblatt, Stephen. *Shakespearean Negotiations: the circulation of social energy in Renaissance England*, Oxford: Clarendon Press, 1988

Greenblatt, Stephen. *Learning to Curse: essays in Early Modern culture*, New York: Routledge, 1990

Greenblatt, Stephen. 'General Introduction', *The Norton Shakespeare: based on the Oxford edition*, edited by Stephen Greenblatt, Walter Cohen, Jean E. Howard and Katherine Eisaman Maus, New York: W.W. Norton 1997

Greenblatt, Stephen. *Hamlet in Purgatory*, Princeton: Princeton University Press, 2001

Greetham, D. C. 'Textual Forensics', *PMLA* 3, 1996

Greetham, D.C. *Theories of the Text,* Oxford: Clarendon Press, 1999

Greg, W.W. 'Hamlet's Hallucination', *Modern Language Review,* 12:4, 1917

Greg, W.W. 'The Function of Bibliography in Literary Criticism Illustrated in a Study of the Text of *King Lear',* and 'Time, Place and Politics in *King Lear'* in *The Collected Papers of Sir Walter W. Greg,* edited by J.C. Maxwell, Oxford: Clarendon Press, 1966

Greg, W.W. *The Editorial Problem in Shakespeare: a survey of the foundations of the text,* Oxford: Oxford University Press, 1967

Griffiths, Sian. 'Well Versed in the Art of Make-up', *Times Higher Education Supplement,* 19 June 1992

Grigely, Joseph. 'The Textual Event', in *Devils and Angels: textual editing and literary theory,* edited by Philip Cohen, Charlottsville: University Press of Virginia, 1964

Gross, John (ed.). *After Shakespeare: an Anthology,* Oxford: Oxford University Press, 2002

Gurr, Andrew (ed.). *The First Quarto of King Henry V,* Cambridge: Cambridge University Press, 2000

Gwynne, R.S. *No Word of Farewell: Selected Poems 1970–2000,* Ashland, Oregon: Story Line Press, 2001

Halio, Jay L. (ed.). *The First Quarto of King Lear,* Cambridge: Cambridge University Press, 1994

Halpern, Richard. 'An Impure History of Ghosts', in *Marxist Shakespeares,* edited by Jean E. Howard and Scott Cutler Shershow, London: Routledge, 2001

Hardy, Thomas. *Jude the Obscure,* 1896, London: Penguin, 1987

Hartman, Geoffrey. *Beyond Formalism,* New Haven: Yale University Press, 1970

Hawkes, Terence. *That Shakespeherian Rag,* London: Methuen, 1986

Hayman, Ronald. *Tom Stoppard,* London: Heinemann, 1977, 4th edition 1982

Hayter, Alathea. *Horatio's Version,* London: Faber and Faber, 1972

Heppenstall, Rayner, and Michael Innes. *Three Tales of Hamlet,* London: Victor Gollancz, 1950

Hinman, Charlton (ed.). *The Norton Facsimile: the First Folio of Shakespeare,* New York: W.W. Norton/Hamlyn Publishing Group, 1968

Holderness, Graham, J. Turner and N. Potter. *Shakespeare: the Play of History,* London: Macmillan, 1987

Holderness, Graham. 'A Spear Carrier's Charter', *THES,* 29 April 1988.

Holderness, Graham. *Shakespeare in Performance: 'The Taming of the Shrew',* Manchester: Manchester University Press, 1988

Holderness, Graham. *Romeo and Juliet,* London: Penguin, 1991

Holderness, Graham (ed.). *Shakespeare's History Plays: 'Richard II' to 'Henry V',* London: Macmillan, 1992

Holderness, Graham and Bryan Loughrey (eds.). *The Taming of A Shrew,* Hemel Hempstead: Harvester Wheatsheaf, 1992

Holderness, Graham and Bryan Loughrey (eds.). *The Tragicall Historie of Hamlet Prince of Denmarke,* Hemel Hempstead: Harvester Wheatsheaf, 1992

Holderness, Graham. 'Shakespeare and Heritage', *Textual Practice* 6, 1992

Holderness, Graham. *Shakespeare Recycled,* Hemel Hempstead: Harvester Wheatsheaf, 1992

Holderness, Graham, and Bryan Loughrey. 'Text and Stage: Shakespeare, Bibliography and Performance Studies', *New Theatre Quarterly* 34, 1993

Holderness, Graham and Bryan Loughrey (eds.). *The True Cronicle Historie of Henry the Fift,* Hemel Hempstead: Harvester Wheatsheaf, 1993

Holderness, Graham, and Andrew Murphy. 'Shakespeare Country', *Critical Survey* 7, 1995

Holderness, Graham (ed.). *M. William Shak-speare: his true chronicle historie of the life and death of King Lear and his three daughters,* Hemel Hempstead: Prentice-Hall, 1995

Holderness, Graham. 'Illogical, Captain!', *London Quarterly* 9, 1996

Holderness, Graham, and Bryan Loughrey. 'Shakespeare Misconstrued: the True Chronicle Historie of *Shakespearean Originals*', *Textus* 9, 1996

Holderness, Graham. 'The Sign of the Cross: culture and belief in *The Dream of the Rood*', *Literature and Theology* 11:4, Autumn 1997

Holderness, Graham. *Anglo-Saxon Verse,* London: Northcote House, 2000

Holderness, Graham. *Shakespeare: the Histories,* London: Macmillan, 2000

Holderness, Graham. *Cultural Shakespeare: essays in the Shakespeare Myth*, Hatfield: University of Hertfordshire Press, 2001

Holderness, Graham. *Visual Shakespeare: essays in film and television*, Hatfield: University of Hertfordshire Press, 2002

Holderness, Graham. *The Prince of Denmark*, Hatfield: University of Hertfordshire Press, 2002

Holderness, Graham. *Craeft: poems from the Anglo-Saxon*, Nottingham: Shoestring Press, 2002

Holland, Peter. 'Authorship and Collaboration: the Problem of Editing Shakespeare', in *The Politics of the Electronic Text*, edited by Warren Cherniak and Marilyn Deegan, London: Office for Humanities Communication Publications, University of London, 1993

Hopkins, Chris. *Thinking About Texts*, London: Palgrave, 2001

Hopkins, G. M. *Selected Poetry*, edited by Catherine Phillips, Oxford: Oxford University Press, 1996

Horace: the Odes, edited by Philip Francis. London: Unit Library, 1902

Housman, A. E. 'The Application of Thought to Textual Criticism' (1921), in *A. E Housman: Selected Prose*, edited by John Carter, Cambridge: Cambridge University Press, 1961

Housman, A.E. *More Poems*, London: Jonathan Cape, 1936

Hughes, Ted. *The Hawk in the Rain*, 1957, London: Faber and Faber, 1968

Hulme, John (ed.). *Guillaume Chequespierre and the Oise Salon*, London: Angus and Robertson, 1985

Hunter, G. K. (ed.). *Macbeth*, London: Penguin, 1967

Hunter, G.K. (ed.). *King Lear*, Harmondsworth: Penguin, 1972

Innes, Michael. *Hamlet, Revenge!*, London: Victor Gollancz, 1937

Ioppolo, Grace. *Revising Shakespeare*, Cambridge, Mass.: Harvard University Press, 1991

Irace, Kathleen O. (ed.). *The First Quarto of Hamlet*, Cambridge: Cambridge University Press, 1998

Irigiray, Luce. *This Sex which is not One*, translated by Catherine Porter and Carolyn Burke, Ithaca: Cornell University Press, 1985

Jackson, H.J. *Marginalia: readers writing in books*, New Haven: Yale University Press, 2001

Jackson, MacDonald P. 'Fluctuating Variation – Author, Annotator or Actor?', in *The Division of the Kingdoms: Shakespeare's two versions* of 'King Lear', edited by Gary Taylor and Michael Warren, Oxford: Clarendon Press, 1983

Jones, Ernest. *Hamlet and Oedipus,* London: Victor Gollancz, 1949

Jowett, John. 'After Oxford: Recent Developments in Textual Studies', in *The Shakespearean International Yearbook* 1, 1999

Joyce, James. *A Portrait of the Artist as a Young Man,* 1916, London: Jonathan Cape, 1956

Joyce, Michael. 'A Feel for Prose: Interstitial Links and the Contours of Hypertext', *Writing on the Edge* 4.1, 1992

Kastan, David Scott. *Shakespeare and the Shapes of Time,* Hanover: University Press of New England, 1982

Kastan, David Scott. *Shakespeare After Theory,* London: Routledge, 1999

Kastan, David Scott. *Shakespeare and the Book,* Cambridge: Cambridge University Press, 2001

Kermode, Frank (ed.). *Shakespeare: King Lear, A Casebook,* London: Macmillan, 1969

Kiernan, Pauline. *Staging Shakespeare at the New Globe,* London: Routledge, 2002

Knight, G. Wilson. *The Wheel of Fire,* London: Chatto and Windus, 1930

Kott, Jan. *Shakespeare our Contemporary,* translated by Boleslaw Taborski, London: Methuen, 1965, 2nd edition 1967

Landow, George P. *Hypertext: the convergence of contemporary critical theory and technology,* Baltimore: Johns Hopkins University Press, 1992

Leader, Darian. *Stealing the Mona Lisa,* London: Faber and Faber, 2002

Levy, Deborah. *Pushing the Prince into Denmark,* in *Levy Plays 1,* London: Methuen, 2000

Loesser, Frank (Music and Lyrics). *Guys and Dolls: a musical fable of Broadway,* Book by Jo Swerling and Abe Burrows, London: Josef Weinberger, 1951

Macherey, Pierre. *A Theory of Literary Production,* translated by Geoffrey Wall, London: Routledge and Kegan Paul, 1978

Magoun, Francis P. Jr. 'The Oral-Formulaic Character of Anglo-Saxon Narrative Poetry' (1953), quoted from *An Anthology of 'Beowulf' Criticism,* edited by Lewis E. Nicholson, Notre Dame, Ind.: Notre Dame University Press, 1963

Maguire, Laurie E. *Shakespearean Suspect Texts: the 'Bad Quartos' and their contexts,* Cambridge: Cambridge University Press, 1996

Maguire, Laurie E. 'Shakespeare and the Death of the Author', in *The Renaissance Text: theory, editing, textuality,* edited by Andrew Murphy, Manchester: Manchester University Press, 2000

Mallarme, Stephane. 'Hamlet et Fortinbras', quoted in Martin Scofield, *The Ghosts of 'Hamlet': the play and modern writers,* Cambridge: Cambridge University Press, 1980

Man, Paul de. *Blindness and Insight: essays in the rhetoric of contemporary criticism,* Minneapolis: University of Minnesota Press, 1983

Manguel, Alberto. *A History of Reading,* London: Harper Collins, 1996

Marcus, Leah. *Puzzling Shakespeare: local reading and its discontents,* Berkeley: University of California Press, 1992

Marcus, Leah. 'Confessions of a Reformed Uneditor' in *The Renaissance Text: theory, editing, textuality,* edited by Andrew Murphy, Manchester: Manchester University Press, 2000

Marowitz, Charles. *The Marowitz 'Hamlet',* London: Allen Lane, 1968

Martin, Henri-Jean. *The History and Power of Writing,* translated by Lydia G. Cochrane, Chicago: University of Chicago Press, 1994

Masefield, John. *A 'Macbeth' Production,* London: Heinemann, 1945

McGann, Jerome. *The Textual Condition,* Princeton, N.J.: Princeton University Press, 1991

McGann, Jerome. *Radiant Textualities: Literary Studies After the World Wide Web,* London: Palgrave, 2001

McKenzie, D.F. *Bibliography and the Sociology of Texts,* London: British Library, 1986

McKenzie, D.F. *Making Meaning: 'Printers of the Mind' and Other Essays,* edited by Peter D. McDonald and Michael F. Suarez, S.J., Massachusetts: Massachusetts University Press, 2002

McKerrow, R.B. *Prolegomena for the Oxford Shakespeare: A study in editorial method,* Oxford: Clarendon Press, 1939

McLaverty, James. 'The Mode of Existence of Literary Works of Art: the case of *The Dunciad* Variorum', *Studies in Bibliography* 37, 1984

McLeod, Randall. 'From Tranceformations in the Text of *Orlando Fvrioso',* *Library Chronicle of the University of Texas at Austin* 20:1–2, 1990

McMillin, Scott. *The Elizabethan Theatre and 'The Book of Sir Thomas More',* Ithaca: Cornell University Press, 1987

Mills, Howard. *Working with Shakespeare,* Hemel Hempstead: Harvester Wheatsheaf, 1992

Mitchell, William J. *City of Bits: space, place and the Infobahn,* Cambridge, Mass.: MIT Press, 1995

Mowatt, Barbara. 'The Problem of Shakespeare's Texts', in *Textual Formations and Reformations,* edited by Laurie E. Maguire and Thomas L. Berger, London: Associated University Presses, 1998

Muir, Kenneth (ed.). *King Lear,* London: Methuen, 1952, 1989

Murphy, Andrew (ed.). *The Tragoedie of Othello, The Moore of Venice,* Hemel Hempstead: Prentice-Hall, 1995

Murphy, Andrew. '"Came errour here by mysse of man": editing and the metaphysics of presence', *Yearbook of English Studies* 29, 1999

Nosworthy, J.M. '*Macbeth* at the Globe', *The Library* 5th series, vol. 2, 1948

Nuttall, A.D. '*Hamlet*: conversations with the dead', in *The Stoic in Love: selected essays on literature and ideas,* Brighton: Harvester Wheatsheaf, 1989

Orgel, Stephen. 'The Authentic Shakespeare', *Representations* 21, 1988

Orgel, Stephen. *The Authentic Shakespeare,* London: Routledge, 2002

Osborne, Laurie (ed.). *Twelfe Night, or, What You Will,* Hemel Hempstead: Prentice-Hall, 1995

Parker, Brian. 'Bowers of Bliss: deconflation in the Shakespeare canon', in *New Theatre Quarterly* 24, 1990

Parker, Patricia. 'Murder in Guyana', *Shakespeare Studies* 28, 2000

Patterson, Annabel. *Shakespeare and the Popular Voice,* Oxford: Blackwell, 1989

Patterson, Annabel (ed.). *The Most Excellent Historie of The Merchant of Venice,* Hemel Hempstead: Prentice-Hall, 1995

Peters, Julie Stone. *Theatre of the Book, 1480–1880: print, text and performance,* Oxford: Oxford University Press, 2000

Pfeiffer, Rudolph. *History of Classical Scholarship from the Beginnings to the End of the Hellenistic Age,* Oxford: Oxford University Press, 1968

Pinter, Harold. *The Homecoming,* London: Methuen, 1966

Pollard, A.W. *Shakespeare Folios and Quartos,* London: Methuen, 1909

Pollard, A.W. *Shakespeare's Fight with the Pirates,* Cambridge: Cambridge University Press, 2nd edition 1920

Posener, Alan. 'Materialism, Dialectics and Editing Shakespeare', *New Theatre Quarterly* 39, 1994

Pusey, E.B. (trans.). *The Confessions of St Augustine*, London: Dent, 1907, 1946

Ragg, Edward. 'The Oxford Shakespeare Revisited: an interview with Professor Stanley Wells', *Analytical and Enumerative Bibliography*, N.S. 12:2, 2001

Reiman, Donald H. and Sharon P. Bowers (eds.). *Shelley's Poetry and Prose*, New York: Norton, 1977

Rigney, James (ed.). *The Tragedie of Macbeth*, Hemel Hempstead: Harvester Wheatsheaf, 1996

Rowe, Nicholas (ed.). *The Works of Mr. William Shakespeare*, London: J. Tonson, 1709

Rowse, A.L. *Simon Forman: Sex and Society in Shakespeare's Age*, London: Weidenfeld and Nicolson, 1974

Rowse, A.L. (ed.). *The Poems of Shakespeare's Dark Lady: 'Salve Deus Rex Judaeorum', by Emilia Lanyer*, London: Jonathan Cape, 1978

Runyon, Damon. 'The Melancholy Dane', in *Runyon a la Carte*, London: Constable, 1946

Ryan, Kiernan (ed.). *'King Lear': contemporary critical essays*, London: Palgrave, 1993

Sams, Eric. *The Real Shakespeare*, New Haven: Yale University Press, 1995

Sanders, Norman (ed.). *Othello*, Cambridge: Cambridge University Press, 1984

Sandys, J.E.W. *A History of Classical Scholarship*, Cambridge: Cambridge University Press, 1906–8, New York: Hafner, 2nd edition 1964

Sawday, Jonathan. 'Beam me up too, Scotty!', *London Quarterly* 8, 1995

Schoenbaum, Samuel. *William Shakespeare: Records and Images*, London: Scolar Press, 1969

Scofield, Martin. *The Ghosts of Hamlet: the play and modern writers*, Cambridge: Cambridge University Press, 1980

Scott, Michael. *Shakespeare and the Modern Dramatist*, London: Macmillan, 1989

Shakespeare, William, *Macbeth (1673)*, Cornmarket Shakespeare Series, London: Cornmarket Press, 1969

Shaughnessy, Robert (ed.). *Shakespeare on Film*, London: Macmillan 1998

Shepherd, Simon. 'Shakespeare's Private Drawer: Shakespeare and Homosexuality', in *The Shakespeare Myth*, edited by Graham Holderness, Manchester: Manchester University Press, 1988

Sinfield, Alan. 'Making Space: appropriation and confrontation in recent British plays' in *The Shakespeare Myth,* edited by Graham Holderness, Manchester: Manchester University Press, 1988

Smith, J.C. and E. De Selincourt (eds.). *The Poetical Works of Edmund Spenser,* Oxford: Oxford University Press, 1912

Somerset, Anne. *Unnatural Murder: poison at the court of James I,* London: Weidenfeld and Nicolson, 1997

Somogyi, Nick de (ed.). *The Shakespeare Folios: Hamlet,* London: Nick Hern Books, 2000

Spencer, Christopher. *Davenant's 'Macbeth' from the Yale Manuscript: an edition, with a discussion of the relation of Davenant's text to Shakespeare's,* New Haven: Yale University Press, 1961

Spong, Andrew. 'Bad Habits, "Bad Quartos" and Myths of Origin in the Editing of Shakespeare', *New Theatre Quarterly* 45, 1995

Stallybrass, Peter. '"Well grubbed, old mole": Marx, *Hamlet,* and the (un)fixing of representation', in *Marxist Shakespeares,* edited by Jean E. Howard and Scott Cutler Shershow, London: Routledge, 2001

Stoddard, Roger. 'Morphology and the Book from an American Perspective', *Printing History* 17, 1987

Stoppard, Tom. *Rosencrantz and Guildenstern are Dead,* London: Faber and Faber, 1968

Stoppard, Tom. *Dogg's Hamlet, Cahoot's Macbeth,* London: Faber and Faber, 1980

Stoppard, Tom. *The Invention of Love,* London: Faber and Faber, 1997

Swan, Mary, and Elaine M. Treharne (eds.). *Rewriting Old English in the Twelfth Century,* Cambridge: Cambridge University Press, 2000

Tanselle, G. Thomas. *A Rationale of Textual Criticism,* Philadelphia: University of Pennsylvania Press, 1989

Tate, Nahum. *The History of King Lear,* edited by James Black, Lincoln: University of Nebraska Press, 1975, London: Edward Arnold, 1976

Taylor, Gary (ed.). *Henry V,* Oxford: Oxford University Press, 1984

Taylor, Gary. 'Introduction' to Stanley Wells and Gary Taylor with John Jowett and William Montgomery, *William Shakespeare: A Textual Companion,* Oxford: Clarendon Press, 1987

Taylor, Gary. 'The Renaissance and the End of Editing', in *Palimpsest: editorial theory in the humanities,* edited by George Bornstein and Ralph G. Williams, Ann Arbor: University of Michigan Press, 1993

Taylor, Gary. *Cultural Selection,* New York: Basic Books, 1996

Taylor, John Russell. *The Second Wave: British drama for the 70s,* London: Methuen, 1971

Thomas, Dylan. *Collected Poems 1934–1953,* edited by Walford Davies and Ralph Maude, London: Dent, 1988

Thomas, R.S. *Collected Poems 1945–1990,* London: Dent, 1993, London: Phoenix, 1996, 1999

Thompson, Ann. 'Editing Shakespeare for the Next Millennium', *The European English Messenger* 8:2, 1999

Tiffany, Grace. 'Calling a Spadeful a Spadeful', *Shakespeare Newsletter,* Fall 1995

Tobin, J.J.M. and G. Blakemore Evans (eds.). *The Riverside Shakespeare,* Boston, Mass.: Houghton Mifflin, 2nd edition 1997

Traister, Barbara. *The Notorious Astrological Physician of London: Works and Days of Simon Forman,* Chicago: University of Chicago Press, 2001

Treadwell, T. O. (ed.). *A Midsommer Nights Dreame,* Hemel Hempstead: Prentice-Hall, 1996

Treharne, Elaine (ed.). *Old and Middle English: an anthology,* Oxford: Blackwell, 2000

Turner, John (ed.). *The Tragedie of Anthonie, and Cleopatra,* Hemel Hempstead: Prentice-Hall, 1995

Turner, John. *Macbeth,* Milton Keynes: Open University Press, 1992

Tyndale, William (trans.). *The New Testament* (Worms, 1526), edited by W.R. Cooper, London: British Library, 2000

Updike, John. *Gertrude and Claudius,* New York: Alfred A. Knopf, 2000, London: Penguin Books, 2001

Urkowitz, Steven. *Shakespeare's Revision of 'King Lear',* Princeton: Princeton University Press, 1980

Urkowitz, Steven. 'Good News about "Bad" Quartos', in *Shakespeare Study Today: the Horace Howard Furness Memorial Lectures,* edited by Georgianna Ziegler, New York: AMS Press, 1986

Urkowitz, Steven. 'Back to basics: thinking about the *Hamlet* First Quarto' in *The 'Hamlet' First Published: origins, form, intertextualities,* edited by Thomas Clayton, Newark: University of Delaware Press, 1992

Valery, Paul. 'La Crise de l'esprit' in *Oeuvres,* vol. 1, Paris: Gallimard, 1957

Vickers, Brian. '*Hamlet* by Dogberry: a perverse reading of the Bad Quarto', *Times Literary Supplement*, 24 December 1993.

Walker, Alice. *Textual Problems of the First Folio,* Cambridge: Cambridge University Press, 1953

Wallace, Jennifer. 'Tragedy grapples with gap between human meaningfulness and despair', *Times Higher Education Supplement,* 6 September 2002.

Walsh, Marcus. 'Bentley Our Contemporary: or, editors, ancient and modern', in *The Theory and Practice of Text-editing,* edited by Ian Small and Marcus Walsh, Cambridge: Cambridge University Press, 1991

Walsh, Marcus. *Shakespeare, Milton and Eighteenth Century Literary Editing,* Cambridge: Cambridge University Press, 1997

Walter, J.H. *King Henry V,* London Methuen, 1954

Ward, Graham. 'The Displaced Body of Jesus Christ', in *Radical Orthodoxy,* edited by John Milbank, Catherine Pickstock and Graham Ward, London: Routledge, 1999

Ward, Graham. *Theology and Contemporary Critical Theory,* London: Macmillan, 1996, 2nd edition 2000

Warren, Michael. 'Quarto and Folio *King Lear:* the interpretation of Albany and Edgar', in *Shakespeare: Pattern of Excelling Nature,* edited by David Bevington and Jay L. Halio, Newark: University of Delaware Press, 1978

Warren, Michael (ed.). *The Complete 'King Lear' 1608–1623,* Berkeley: University of California Press, 1989

Watts, Cedric (ed.). *An Excellent Conceited Tragedie of Romeo and Juliet,* Hemel Hempstead: Prentice-Hall, 1995

Waugh, Evelyn. *Brideshead Revisited, 1945,* London: Heinemann/Secker and Warburg, 1977

Weis, René (ed.). '*King Lear': A Parallel-Text Edition,* London: Longman, 1993

Wells, Stanley, and Gary Taylor with John Jowett and William Montgomery (eds.), *William Shakespeare: the Complete Works,* Oxford: Oxford University Press, 1988

Wells, Stanley, 'Theatricalizing Shakespeare's Text'. in *New Theatre Quarterly,* 26 May 1991

Wells, Stanley. 'Multiple Texts and the Oxford Shakespeare', *Textus* 9, 1996

Wells, Stanley (ed.). *The History of King Lear,* Oxford: Clarendon Press, 2000

Welsh, Alexander. *Hamlet in his Modern Guises,* Princeton: Princeton University Press, 2001

Werstine, Paul. 'Narratives about Printed Shakespearean Texts: "Foul Papers" and "Bad" Quartos', *Shakespeare Quarterly* 41, 1990

Werstine, Paul. 'Plays in Manuscript', in *A New History of Early English Drama,* edited by John D. Cox and David Scott Kastan, New York: Columbia University Press, 1997

Wilde, Oscar. *De Profundis,* London: Methuen, 1905

Willett, John. *The Theatre of Bertolt Brecht,* London: Eyre Methuen, 1960, 3rd edition 1967

Willett, John (ed.). *Brecht on Theatre,* London: Methuen, 1964, 2nd edition 1974

Williams, Rowan. *Writing in the Dust: reflections on 11 September and its aftermath,* London: Hodder and Stoughton, 2002

Wilson, Ian. *Black Jenny,* London: Paladin, 1992

Wood, Nigel, and Peter Smith (eds.). *Theory in Practice: Hamlet,* Milton Keynes: Open University Press, 1996

Woods, Susanne. *Lanyer: a Renaissance Woman Poet,* Oxford: Oxford University Press, 1999

Wordsworth, William. *The Prelude 1799, 1805, 1850,* edited by J. Wordsworth, M.H. Abrams and S. Gill, New York: Norton, 1979

Wordsworth, William. *The Prelude: a Parallel Text,* edited by J.C. Maxwell, London: Penguin, 1971